A Revealing Look Inside TV's Top Quiz Show

Contestants and Question Selection Process Unveiled

A Revealing Look Inside TV's Top Quiz Show

Contestants and Question Selection Process Unveiled

Harry Eisenberg
Emmy-winning Editorial Associate Producer

LIFETIME BOOKS, INC.
2131 Hollywood Blvd., Suite 305
Hollywood, FL 33020

Manufactured in the United States of America
1 2 3 4 5 6 7 8 9 0

Library of Congress Cataloging-in-Publication Data

Eisenberg, Harry, 1947–
    Jeopardy! behind the scenes at TV's top quiz show / Harry Eisenberg.
        p.   cm.
    ISBN 0-8119-0806-2
    1. Jeopardy (Television program).   I. Title.
PN1992.77.J363E38   1995
791.45'72—dc20   95-2283
                                                                          CIP

INTRODUCTION

Time magazine, the leading authority on top-ten lists (along with David Letterman and USA Today), featured (in January, 1990) a select group of TV programs as being the best of the eighties. Only one non-network, syndicated show was named. That same show was also the only game show listed in *Time*'s best ten of the decade. That show happened to be Jeopardy!

Of Jeopardy *Time* wrote: "TV's most challenging game show was too smart for the '70s: NBC cancelled it in 1975 after a decade on the air. But it reappeared triumphantly in a new syndicated version in the '80s. Who says TV is getting dumber?"

In a similar vein, the fortieth anniversary (April 17,1993) issue of *TV Guide* presented its picks for the best TV shows of all time. Beating out "Password," "What's My Line?" and "Wheel of Fortune," *TV Guide*'s selection for the all-time best game show was Jeopardy. The *TV Guide* reviewer wrote: "We admire the contestants for their striking abilities to accumulate knowledge" and said of Jeopardy, "It's not just a game show; it's a challenge, a goal."

With some 16 million people in its metropolitan area, New York is the biggest plum—or apple—in the TV ratings battle. A good rating in New York will count heavily towards overall success nationwide. While the air times of the networks' national evening news shows vary somewhat from city to city, in New York all three had long been on opposite each other at 7:00 P.M. And in the ratings race between the three networks' newscasts, ABC news had long been the third-place finisher.

Perhaps feeling they had less to lose, in 1986 the programming and scheduling brass at ABC decided that their national news should break away from the pack and come on the air a half-hour earlier than the others, at 6:30. And it worked. ABC's "World News Tonight" with Peter Jennings became the ratings leader in the lucrative New York market.

Did ABC News cop the Big Apple simply because New Yorkers, who are famous for keeping *late* hours, simply felt like watching the news half an hour *earlier*? Hardly.

ABC needed a show to lure viewers away from the competition's news while at the same time giving those viewers a news option at another time. And so New Yorkers, in droves, broke with what had been a 30-year tradition of watching the national evening news at 7:00 P.M. in order to watch . . . Jeopardy.

The fact that Jeopardy helped propel ABC news into the top-rated position in the nation's premier market came as quite a surprise to many, but it shouldn't have. Since its return to television in the fall of 1984 with Alex Trebek as host, Jeopardy has enjoyed exceptionally good ratings. With a daily audience ranging between 17 and 22 million people, Jeopardy from 1985 on has pretty much had a lock on second place among all U.S. syndicated TV shows. It is second only to "Wheel of Fortune," a sister show, both productions of Merv Griffin Enterprises and distributed by King World.

Jeopardy has been called "the game show without the cleavage." It's been described as the "Mount Everest for people who get tired of winning at Trivial Pursuit." *TV Guide* has called it "the only real quiz show on TV" and "one of the most literate game shows ever." As such, it competes for the same audience of intelligent, educated, aware people as the evening news, attracting viewers to ABC's national news in New York, while drawing viewers away from the competition. (To remain competitive in the New York market, the other networks eventually moved their evening news back to 6:30 as well.)

Host Alex Trebek has made it a point to say that Jeopardy is a quiz show, not a game show. While acknowledging that the show's primary purpose is to entertain the audience, he says, "It's making people more aware of the value of education and knowledge. If watching Jeopardy arouses a certain amount of curiosity about a particular subject, maybe they'll pick up a book and read about it. Our message, if you can call it that, is it's OK to be bright. We've heard that many teachers are using the Jeopardy format as a learning tool. All of a sudden kids get interested. If it helps teachers teach and kids learn, that's fantastic. . . ."

I was with Jeopardy for seven years, first as a writer and judge on the show and for the last three years as editorial associate producer. I managed the writing and research staffs and was responsible for providing all those categories full of answers and questions. I was there from the beginning, in June 1984, when we faced the distinct possibility we'd all be out of a job six months later, until May of 1991.

The next year was spent, in part, agonizing over whether to write a tell-all book about the show.

It's hard not to like Jeopardy. It is a wholesome quiz show promoting knowledge and education that can be enjoyed by the entire family. No violence, no sarcasm, no illicit sex, no put-downs, no subtle political messages. Just an intellectual competition of answers and questions.

But what has really been great about Jeopardy has been its success! As the second highest rated series in the history of U.S. syndicated television programs, Jeopardy helps put the lie to the widely held notion that sex and violence are necessary to succeed in the TV ratings wars.

After ten years of the current, syndicated version of the program, Jeopardy has become a household word and is a popular part of American culture. The hero of Operation Desert Storm, General Norman Schwarzkopf, calls it his favorite program. At baseball games, the Final Jeopardy "think music" is sometimes played while the manager contemplates making a pitching change. Radio promotional contests are often based on the Jeopardy answer–question format. And Jeopardy host Alex Trebek has become a well-known, much appreciated celebrity figure.

I remember sitting in my office as Jeopardy editorial associate producer in 1988 and receiving a call from Kroloff, Marshall and Associates, a Washington, DC advertising agency that was representing the National Geographic Society. The Society was sponsoring Geography Awareness Week in November and was wondering if Jeopardy could help promote it. Geography Awareness Week just happened to coincide with our annual Tournament of Champions, sort of the Jeopardy equivalent of the World Series or the Super Bowl. I very much liked the idea and took it to my boss, producer George Vosburgh. He and his superiors Bob Murphy and Merv Griffin agreed and Geography Awareness Week has been promoted on Jeopardy ever since. Not long after we began the relationship with the National Geographic Society, I was asked if there was any chance Alex might be willing to host the finals of the National Geography Bee in Washington. Now Alex had been doing a considerable amount of charitable work for years but when he heard about this, he was happy to add it to his annual calendar. Promoting education is a noble cause to which Jeopardy, in its own way, has made a contribution.

Similarly, in the summer of 1990, former Chief Justice Warren Burger sent us a letter reminding us that 1991 would mark the bicentennial of the Bill of Rights. He requested that we include a Bill of

Rights category to coincide with that event. Chief Justice Burger then added the following note at the bottom of the typed letter, in his own hand: "P.S. Jeopardy is the only quiz show allowed in our home. It is truly a fine educational piece. Long ago Mrs. Burger and I were teachers." The former Chief Justice included some information on the Bill of Rights. I passed that along to writer Steve Tamerius, who had previously written categories on the Constitution. He came up with a fine one on the Bill of Rights which we were more than happy to include on the show.

In television, seven years is a fairly long time to work on one program. Most shows never get beyond the pilot stage. Many others last only a single season. Furthermore, the Jeopardy staff is quite small—no more than 25 full-time employees. Working seven years in a small office you get to know your co-workers and they get to know you. Everyone's weaknesses eventually come to the surface and, sometimes in spite of that, friendships are formed. Many of the Jeopardy staff attended my wedding. As you get to know people, in most cases you get to like them. You rejoice in their successes and look forward to seeing them fulfill their hopes and dreams.

However, some aspects of this book are controversial. Despite that, I have concluded it is better to write the book and bring it all to light. Millions who watch the show every day would like to know about the show's inner workings and how it's all put together. A great deal more goes on than first meets the eye.

For those who have never been there, the behind-the-scenes world of television can be quite fascinating. This book represents a first-time attempt to tell it like it is, as seen in terms of Jeopardy. Some of it I hope the reader will find interesting and entertaining, some humorous, some perhaps poignant and some rather surprising.

ACKNOWLEDGMENTS

I wish to thank those whose encouragement and/or information they provided helped make this book a reality:

- My dear California friends, Ron and Judy Mills, Jim and Jeanette Lea and Ron Beideck, who always make me feel at home when I'm out there
- Franz Lidz, Cliff Pine, Richard Manzo, the readers' services departments of *The National Enquirer* and *The Advocate,* and the numerous individuals who worked for Merv Griffin Enterprises and Jeopardy at one time or another and graciously provided needed facts
- My son Dan for his invaluable expertise on the computer
- My wife Debby, without whose unflagging support, encouragement and editorial assistance this project would not have been completed

CONTENTS

To the memory of Louis Eisenberg, who
lived an honest life
and expected his children
to do the same

PUBLISHER'S STATEMENT

JEOPARDY! entertains 20 million viewers and is the second highest-rated syndicated television program of all-time. Lifetime Books is proud to have Harry Eisenberg, an Emmy-winning Editorial Associate Producer of JEOPARDY!, present an entertaining, informative and accurate account of what goes on at the set of America's favorite quiz show.

We are pleased to include a special chapter featuring unique facts about the show and expanded biographies of the two people instrumental behind its success: host Alex Trebek and creator Merv Griffin. With the permission of JEOPARDY!, we are providing hundreds of challenging answers and questions, just as they appeared on the premier episode in 1984 and subsequent shows.

We thank the staff of JEOPARDY! for their assistance in producing this account of JEOPARDY! However, by licensing material to Lifetime Books, JEOPARDY! is not responsible for the accuracy or editorial content of this book and is not to be considered as a co-author.

Of special note, Mr. Eisenberg reveals how you will obtain information on how the answers and questions are researched, written and selected and how contestants are recruited and chosen for the show. Whether you are a fan of JEOPARDY! or quiz shows, you are sure to delight in the revealing information about the world of television and Hollywood.

Let's play JEOPARDY!

Good reading,

Donald L. Lessne
Publisher

CHAPTER 1

FINDING MYSELF IN JEOPARDY!

THE BEGINNING

In June 1984, Los Angeles was awash in Olympic fever. For only the third time, the Summer Games would be held in the United States and this time, as in 1932, the Los Angeles Memorial Coliseum would be the main venue. (The 1904 games had been held in St. Louis.) For many, a chief topic of conversation was how to avoid the monumental traffic jams, which were anticipated for the upcoming games but never materialized.

Hollywood is about ten miles northwest of the Coliseum. The steep hills above Hollywood contain not only the famous HOLLYWOOD sign, but districts of expensive homes mixed in with more modest ones. In the 1980s they were all appreciating markedly in value. The Hollywood of the TV and movie studios is the level area south of the hills, running four or five miles east to west and about two miles north to south. Containing numerous homes and apartments interspersed with small ethnic groceries, it was undoubtedly a desirable area in the 1920s and '30s. But that era is long gone and much of present day Hollywood has a rather shabby appearance. Drug-dealing is not uncommon and the crime rate is above average, even for Los Angeles.

Head writer Jules Minton had called me and said that the Jeopardy writers should park in a small lot on Sunset Blvd., across from the Channel 11 studios, and then meet him at the corner of Sunset and Van Ness at 9:30 A.M. He would then escort us to the Jeopardy offices on the Channel 11 lot.

I had never been to the KTTV Channel 11 lot before. The other writers and I had briefly met Jules and Alex Trebek, who was Jeopardy producer as well as host, in a building on Vine Street belonging to Merv Griffin. The building was known as TAV, which stood for Trans American Video, a company Merv Griffin owned and whose purpose was to edit, duplicate and distribute videotapes. The building had a marquee proclaiming its TAV Celebrity Theater, which was then the home of "The Merv Griffin Show." From time to time one saw people lining up for tickets or waiting to be allowed in to see the show.

I had come to Los Angeles with my two children, Dan, age 11, and Rachelle, age 9, some five months earlier with a screenplay in hand. I soon learned that half the people in L.A. have written screenplays. I decided to set out to find a job.

An ad in the *Los Angeles Times* announced a one-day seminar on "Deal-Making for Television Productions," sponsored by UCLA. The cost was $125, which struck me as quite high for just one day's worth of learning. Nevertheless, a considerable number of TV producers would be participating in various panel discussions and it looked like a good opportunity to meet a great many people who counted in the industry.

The seminar consisted of some six panels dealing with different subjects, each running about 45 minutes. The moderator was Hollywood attorney Raymond Asher. Between panels I would dash up to the front, introduce myself and ask who in their organization might be contacted about job openings. One of the panel members was Rick Rosner, whose company had produced the popular "CHiPs" series. When I spoke with him, he suggested I contact his assistant, Rickie Gaffney. I called her and then submitted a half-baked idea for a game show. In response, she was kind enough to write me a long letter explaining why she couldn't use the idea. More significantly, in the course of her letter she pointed out Jeopardy was coming back into production.

Like many of my baby boomer generation, I was familiar with the old Art Fleming version of Jeopardy that had been produced in New York and enjoyed a highly successful daytime run on NBC from 1964–74. It might have lasted even longer had NBC not yanked it out of its accustomed lunchtime spot, exiling it to 10:30 in the morning (thereby cutting it off from much of its working and student audience who watched it while enjoying their lunch break).

Knowing Jeopardy was a Merv Griffin Production, I called the Merv Griffin offices and expressed interest in writing for the show. I was told they weren't hiring just yet but would keep my name and number on file. That was in March 1984. About three weeks later the phone call came. It was Alex Trebek inviting me to a meeting for those interested in writing for Jeopardy.

In all, some 15 people showed up at the meeting in mid-April. Indicating he would be producing as well as hosting the show, Alex spoke briefly and then introduced head writer Jules Minton. He pointed out that Jules had written both pilots for the show, one of which we later viewed.

The reason there were two pilots is interesting. The original Jeopardy was a Merv Griffin production done in cooperation with and for NBC. After a 1978 revival of the show failed, the network was no longer interested in Jeopardy. In the meantime, Merv had created "Wheel of Fortune," which first aired in daytime on NBC in the mid-70s and enjoyed moderate success.

KING WORLD

Shortly afterwards, and quite by accident, Murray Schwartz, at one time Merv's agent and at that time President of Merv Griffin Enterprises, met Bob King, who was then running King World. It was at the bar of New York's St. Regis Hotel that Murray overheard Bob telling a friend how much he'd like to be out syndicating "Wheel of Fortune." Murray introduced himself and later sold Bob the rights to a syndicated version of "Wheel" for $100,000.

The history of King World is the phenomenal success story of a family business. Founding father Charlie King was a natural-born salesman. During radio's golden era he sold programs to stations. He also produced radio programs for which he sold advertising spots. An energetic, driven man, Charlie, his wife, Lucille, and their six children were living the good life in New Jersey. Then, in 1952, conditions changed drastically.

Television had come on the scene and advertisers were deserting radio in droves. King's radio programs were forced off the air, driving him close to bankruptcy. The family was forced to sell their mansion and move to a $150-a-month apartment. Charlie wasn't one to give up, however, and he took his sense of salesmanship from one business idea to the next. He sold food plans which consisted of a refrigerator/freezer that came with a year's supply of food. He tried starting a chain of "Jackpot Golf" driving ranges, which offered a brand new Cadillac to anyone shooting a hole-in-one. He sold fire alarms and tried a "Santagram" business—personalized phonograph records to kids from Santa Claus. Some of the ideas worked briefly, and others bombed from the outset. But Charlie always saw every setback as "strictly temporary."

Charlie never lost sight of the entertainment industry and from time to time would try something connected to television. While working for Official Films, he learned that the company was about to give up its rights to distribute "The Little Rascals" series. Charlie went to

Clinton Pictures, which owned the series, and offered $300,000 for the syndication rights. The company agreed, only to quickly learn Charlie had but six dollars in his wallet and little more to his name. They were about to show him the door when Charlie convinced them to let him have the rights for just 24 hours. He quickly went to WPIX, New York's Channel 11, and pitched the show. He made a deal and got a contract along with a check for $50,000 that was to serve as his down payment for "The Little Rascals." With "Rascals" as its first property for distribution, King World was born.

The company flourished for a time. King World took on the distribution of "Superheroes" cartoons and "The Joe Pyne Show." But then Pyne died and about the same time, in the late Sixties, "Rascals" became tainted with charges of racial stereotyping, causing many stations to cancel. In 1972, at age 59, Charlie died of a massive heart attack.

Roger and Michael King joined their brother Bob in an attempt to revive the family business. Roger and Michael went to work selling advertising for a couple of radio stations while Bob kept King World alive.

Roger and Michael knew how to sell and in two instances managed to turn a radio station's cash flow from negative to positive. In one case, they were promised an interest in the station and, in the other, they tried to buy the station outright. Both deals fell through. Roger and Michael eventually found themselves back at King World. There they were joined by sisters Karen and Diane.

They cleaned up "The Little Rascals" by editing out the segments containing racist overtones. By 1977 they had that series in some 180 markets and the company was enjoying a gross annual income of about two million dollars. The following year, the Kings contracted with Colbert Television Sales to become sub-distributors in markets east of the Mississippi of "The Joker's Wild" and "Tic Tac Dough," syndicated game shows produced by Jack Barry and Dan Enright. This opportunity gave them a feel for the game show market and they began to look around to acquire exclusive distribution rights to a game show of their own. They thought both "Price is Right" and "Wheel of Fortune" were good prospects to succeed in syndication. "Price" wasn't available but "Wheel" was. It wasn't long before both King World and Merv Griffin Enterprises were rolling into high gear on the strength of "Wheel."

Merv Griffin was already producing a daytime version of "Wheel" for NBC and a deal was worked out whereby a second version of "Wheel" would be produced for syndication. (Michael and Roger King would later buy out brother Bob's share of King World for one and a half million dollars.)

Whereas the network version was locked into a morning time slot, the King brothers could and did find time slots for "Wheel" in the late afternoon, early evening and even the coveted access hour (the hour before prime time officially begins). As a result, "Wheel," in its first year of syndication, was already showing signs of the phenomenal success it would shortly become—the highest rated syndicated series in U.S. television history.

The success of "Wheel" prompted Merv and the Kings to conclude it might be worth trying a syndicated version of Jeopardy as well, to be launched in the 1984–85 season. The fact that the trivia craze, brought on by the popularity of "Trivial Pursuit" and similar games, was then at its height certainly didn't hurt Jeopardy's prospects.

Merv then set out to produce a pilot show which would give King World something tangible to pitch to the various TV station programming directors. The first pilot utilized a set that very much resembled the old Jeopardy. The game board consisted of slots into which printed cards containing the clues were dropped. Each clue was covered by another card showing a dollar value for the clue. When a player selected a clue, someone behind the board would manually pull up the dollar amount card, thereby revealing the clue.

That may have worked in the Sixties but this was the Eighties and Roger King insisted it was time for a new, more modern set. With Merv either unwilling or unable to finance a second pilot, the King brothers took that on and thereby acquired a bigger share in the show for themselves. Instead of the printed cards pulled by hand, 30 electronic TV monitors would be used to display the clues.

Equally important, the King brothers felt a new host was needed as part of the show's new look. Merv had auditioned a number of individuals to host the new Jeopardy. One that he was very much considering and might even have hired was Jeff McGregor. However Michael and Roger King were adamant that Alex Trebek was the man for the job.

ALEX TREBEK

George Alexander Trebek was born July 22, 1940 in Sudbury, Ontario, which made him 43 at the time. His late father was Ukrainian and his mother is French-Canadian. His mother, Lucille, said of Alex that as a child, "He kept very much to himself. He'd sit on the steps and watch the other children play." He had a less-than-easy childhood in that his parents separated and subsequently divorced, with his mother leaving the family. Alex's father struggled to raise him and his sister, Barbara, while working to make ends meet. Alex experienced certain periods of solitude at home and later at boarding school. As a child he developed a love of reading and knowledge, along with a pensive personality.

Alex had the benefit of a fine Catholic school education, which gave him a great deal of knowledge. Apparently this experience had a significant effect in shaping and molding his character and values. He has a good deal of self-control and self-discipline. These qualities were often in evidence during his tenure as the Jeopardy producer.

Alex stands six feet tall and has a passion for chocolate. The staff once gave him a case of Snickers bars for his birthday. Rumor had it that one reason Art Fleming wasn't considered to host the revived version of Jeopardy was that he'd put on weight. Alex has made it a point to watch his weight, as he doesn't want to jeopardize either his job or his appearance.

Alex attended the University of Ottawa, a Catholic-sponsored school, where he majored in philosophy. A 12-year career with the Canadian Broadcasting Company (CBC) followed. This included stints on radio as well as television—some in French as well as English—reading the news, hosting game shows, special events, and various other shows, such as a program devoted to figure skating.

Then, in 1973, his friend and fellow-Canadian Alan Thicke was hired by NBC to develop a game show. The result was a game called "The Wizard of Odds." After others were considered for hosting the show, Thicke suggested Alex and he got the job. That show lasted a year, after which he hosted "High Rollers" with Ruta Lee from '74–'76. He then did "Double Dare" and "The $128,000 Question" before coming back for another two-year run of "High Rollers" from '78–'80. That was followed by a game called "Pitfall," which aired in Canada, and two incarnations of "Battlestars," a game similar to NBC's "Hollywood Squares."

After "Battlestars" was cancelled for the second time in the summer of 1983, Alex thought he'd had enough of game shows. Soon afterwards he received a call from Merv Griffin, asking if he'd like to be considered for Jeopardy. Alex had been interested in producing for many years and now had over 20 years of experience in television. When offered the opportunity to host Jeopardy, Alex indicated he'd take the job but only on one condition: that he be producer as well. Merv wasn't too thrilled at that but the King brothers knew who they wanted and, as the old saying goes, he who pays the piper calls the tune. And so when I first met (and was hired by) Alex, it was in his capacity as producer, rather than host, of the show.

JULES MINTON

Jules, the head writer, is originally from Southern California and a UCLA grad. He'd previously taught fifth grade before working on the game show "Dream House" for three years. He is a large man who alternated between wearing a short beard and shaving. At that point in time the beard was in. He could be quite charming in either case, but what I most remember about that first meeting was his great excitement and enthusiasm about playing a key role in bringing Jeopardy back to television. The show had enjoyed such a long, successful run in the past (although a 1978 attempt to revive it with Art Fleming was short-lived) that Jules was quite confident it would make it this time, especially with its all-new, electronic game board utilizing 30 TV monitors in place of the old printed answer cards.

To be a hit, the show would also need good writers, and Jules went on to explain what makes a good Jeopardy clue. A Jeopardy answer/question shouldn't just be factual. It should also be interesting, informative and entertaining. The ideal viewer reaction should be something like, "Wow! I didn't know that!" For example, instead of just saying "He wrote *The Communist Manifesto*," we could say "Horace Greeley hired this man to be his London correspondent after he wrote *The Communist Manifesto*." The question of course is "Who was Karl Marx?"

To say "It's the capital of New Zealand" is rather boring. To say "It's the southernmost national capital in the world" tells you something you may not have known before. This clue's intended response is "What is Wellington?" The answer "He was the only U.S. President never to marry" is fairly interesting but to phrase it "All U. S. Presidents except James Buchanan had one" may be a bit more amusing and entertaining.

So we were told to make the material as interesting as possible. Then Jules explained that each show needed a balance among the categories. For example, you wouldn't have a category dealing with Colonial America in the same show as one about the Civil War, since both were history categories. Likewise, you wouldn't have World Capitals and Bodies of Water, or Biology and Astronomy in the same program.

Jules pointed out that Jeopardy categories fall into four broad, general areas: *Academic* subjects such as science, literature, history and geography; *Lifestyle*, such as fashion, food and drink, religion, automobiles and business and industry; *Pop Culture* included movies, TV, pop music and sports; finally, *Word Play* consisting of categories like 13-Letter Words, "T" Time, Famous Quotes and Number, Please. The idea was to have an interesting and varied mixture of categories—something for everybody, so to speak. The bulk of the categories should be the weightier academic subjects, but that should be rounded out with material from the other, lighter groups. The aim was to maintain the show's integrity as a tough quiz program while balancing it with elements of humor and fun.

We were also told how the electronic TV monitors would work. The printed cards for the old Jeopardy allowed for a clue no longer than four lines, and numerous standard abbreviations had to be utilized and many new ones invented. The TV monitors for the new Jeopardy allowed for seven lines of material with each line consisting of 15 spaces. Since we were given more room, abbreviations would not be allowed unless absolutely necessary. However to give us a bit more additional space, "&" would always be used in place of the word "and." We were also told to always put commas outside quote marks for consistency as well as to make the words in quotes stand out better.

Finally, Jules told us the dollar values of the individual clues had been raised considerably. The old Jeopardy first round clues ranged from $10 to $50, with Double Jeopardy clues worth twice that. On the new version, Jeopardy round clues would run from $50 to $250; Double Jeopardy clues would range from $100 to $500.

TRYOUTS

Four writers' positions were to be filled and there were about 15 applicants in the room. In addition, two other groups of 15 or so would be coming in that afternoon. To be considered, we each had to write one complete Jeopardy game board—six categories with five clues in each, each clue progressively more difficult. Every clue would have to fit into the allotted space. We were to turn in our material at the front desk of the TAV building within 48 hours. I immediately went to the public library and got to work.

I found books on various subjects—American history, proverbs, sports—and culled some material out of them, but mostly I was writing off the top of my head. Being something of a trivia buff and having majored in history, I had a fairly good store of otherwise useless facts floating around in my head. After writing the clues, I would check the facts in the encyclopedias to make sure I hadn't made any mistakes and that my spelling, dates and other facts were fully accurate. I was writing the material in longhand and it didn't take me long to realize I was enjoying it. I kept at it and by the time I stopped I noticed I had written more than I needed for a single game board. There were so many interesting facts to write about!

Then it hit me. Why waste any of the work I had already done? Why not do *two* game boards? So I returned to the library the next morning to finish up. The afternoon was spent in my apartment typing up the material and pasting two 8 and 1/2 by 11 sheets together to make up each game board. The following morning I ran it down to the front desk at TAV, arriving some two hours before the deadline. I couldn't wait to hear what Alex and Jules would say.

Here's the actual material I submitted for consideration for a writing position on Jeopardy. Keep in mind these sample clues were written back in 1984:

JEOPARDY! SAMPLE #1

The American Revolution
$50   It was actually fought on Breed's Hill.
$100   He wrote, "These are the times that try men's souls."
$150   Ethan Allen captured it "in the name of the great Jehovah and the Continental Congress."
$200   This Polish patriot unsuccessfully fought for his country's freedom after helping us.
$250   Killed in the 1770 Boston Massacre, he's considered the first American casualty.

Proverbs
$50   It makes you healthy, wealthy and wise.
$100   It's better than to have never loved at all.
$150   According to Lord Acton, it tends to corrupt.*
$200   According to Harry Truman, it's what those who can't stand the heat should do.
$250   What he that troubles his own house will inherit.*

Horsin' Around
$50   The Lone Ranger rides him.
$100   TV's talking horse.
$150   Ulysses thought of it to help the Greeks win the war.
$200   On Roy Rogers' show, Dale Evans rode this horse.
$250   Racing's last Triple Crown winner.

The Bible

$50   He fought the battle of Jericho.
$100   Kinds of food Jesus gave the 5,000.*
$150   Paul's companion at the miraculous jail break at Philippi.
$200   Old Testament prophet whose name now refers to predictors of doom.
$250   Disciples whom Jesus called "sons of thunder."

Dry Up!

$50   A dried plum.
$100   Type of battery used in a flashlight.
$150   Its dried form is Jerky or biltong.
$200   George Jefferson's occupation.*
$250   It consists only of solid CO_2 and contains no water.*

Comedians

$50   She's no longer married to Fang.
$100   He was Freddie the Freeloader and Klem Kadiddlehopper.
$150   This clown had more pies thrown at him than anyone else on TV.*
$200   Baseball comic who now calls play-by-play for the Milwaukee Brewers.
$250   Rocky Graziano was her "Goomba."

JEOPARDY! SAMPLE #2

The Fifties

$50   Former Illinois governor and two-time presidential candidate.
$100   In the '50s it was advertised as "the pause that refreshes."
$150   Country whose forces were defeated at Dienbienphu.
$200   His show was originally called "The Toast of the Town."
$250   President Eisenhower's last Secretary of State.

Famous Quotes

$50   Leo Durocher's reply when asked why wasn't he a nice guy.
$100   What Gen. MacArthur promised the Filipinos.
$150   She said, "Come up an' see me some time."
$200   It's what President Ford's "WIN" button stood for.
$250   Shakespearean character who said, "Let me have about me men that are fat."

Silly Songs

$50   His advice was, "Ooh, eee, ooh, ah, ah, ting, tang, wahly, wahly, bing bang.*
$100   Brian Hyland's 1960 hit about a girl in a swimsuit.*

$150   Famous English king or the name of a song by Herman's Hermits.*
$200   Ahab the Arab's camel.
$250   Hollywood Argyles' song about a cave man.*

U. S. Cities
$50   Tennessee city on the Mississippi named for Ancient Egyptian city on the Nile.
$100   Anciently the home of Ulysses, now the home of Cornell University.*
$150   New Mexico city named for radio—later TV—game show.
$200   Ohio River port whose name derives from an ancient Roman patriot.
$250   Large U. S. city named for the brother of King Charles II.

Sports Stadiums
$50   Only stadium to host two modern Olympiads.*
$100   The house that Ruth built.
$150   Only major league ballpark without lights for night games.
$200   A housing development sits on the site of this old home of the Brooklyn Dodgers.
$250   Located in North London, it's England's largest.

The Comics
$50   This red-headed teenager is now over 40 years old.*
$100   Their names were Hans and Fritz.
$150   Dagwood Bumstead works for him.
$200   He originally said, "I have seen the enemy and he is us."*
$250   In the '60s he drew Joanie Phoanie and Students Wildly Indignant about Nearly Everything (S.W.I.N.E.).*

For those of you who have been playing along, here are the correct responses:

JEOPARDY! SAMPLE #1

The American Revolution
$50   What was the Battle of Bunker Hill?
$100   Who was Thomas Paine?
$150   What is Fort Ticonderoga?
$200   Who was Thaddeus Kosciusko?
$250   Who was Crispus Attucks?

Proverbs
$50   What is early to bed and early to rise?
$100   What is to have loved and lost?

$150   What is power?
$200   What is get out of the kitchen?
$250   What is the wind?

Horsin' Around
$50   Who is Silver?
$100   Who was Mr. Ed?
$150   What was the Trojan Horse?
$200   Who was Buttermilk?
$250   Who was Affirmed? (1978)

The Bible
$50   Who was Joshua?
$100   What were loaves and fishes?
$150   Who was Silas?
$200   Who was Jeremiah?
$250   Who were James and John?

Dry Up!
$50   What is a prune?
$100   What is a dry cell?
$150   What is beef or meat?
$200   What is dry cleaning?
$250   What is dry ice?

Comedians
$50   Who is Phyllis Diller?
$100   Who is Red Skelton?
$150   Who is Soupy Sales?
$200   Who is Bob Uecker?
$250   Who is Martha Raye?

JEOPARDY! SAMPLE #2

The Fifties
$50   Who was Adlai Stevenson?
$100   What is Coca-Cola?
$150   What is France?
$200   Who was Ed Sullivan?
$250   Who was Christian Herter?

Famous Quotes
$50   What is "Nice guys finish last?"
$100   What is "I shall return?"

$150   Who is Mae West?
$200   What is "Whip Inflation Now."
$250   Who was Julius Caesar?

Silly Songs
$50   Who was the witch doctor?
$100   What was "Itsy Bitsy Teeny Weeny Yellow Polka-Dot Bikini?"
$150   Who was Henry the Eighth?
$200   Who was Clyde?
$250   What was "Alley-Oop?"

U. S. Cities
$50   What is Memphis?
$100   What is Ithaca?
$150   What is Truth or Consequences?
$200   What is Cincinnati?
$250   What is New York?

Sports Stadiums
$50   What is the Los Angeles (Memorial) Coliseum?
$100   What is Yankee Stadium?
$150   What is Wrigley Field?
$200   What was Ebbets Field?
$250   What is Wembly Stadium?

The Comics
$50   Who is Archie (Andrews)?
$100   Who were the Katzenjammer Kids?
$150   Who is Mr. Dithers?
$200   Who was Pogo?
$250   Who was Al Capp?

About two weeks later Jules called. Had I made it? Well, sort of. I had made the cut. We were each judged by the number of clues we wrote that Alex and Jules really liked. The ones they liked are shown with an asterisk (*) above. Since I'd submitted twice as many to begin with I suppose I had more that they liked than most of the other applicants. I probably had more that they hated as well, but fortunately those didn't count.

But I didn't have the job yet. They had narrowed the field from about 45 applicants for the four writing positions down to eight. I now had at least a 50–50 chance. Those of us still being considered were asked to write two more categories and turn those in within 24 hours. I asked when a final decision would be made, and Jules wasn't sure. He did indicate they needed to start working the first week in June, as taping would begin the first week of August.

And so it was another quick trip back to the library where I came across an interesting book dealing with words that came from people's names. I also prepared a category of former occupations of people who had become famous for other reasons and checked out the facts in various reference books. Here are the two categories I turned in. Once again I've marked the ones Jules and Alex liked with an asterisk (*).

Former Occupations

$50   Former New York lawyer who stated his case on Monday Night Football for 13 years.

$100   Church altar boy and seminarian who became infamous Soviet dictator.*

$150   Former Kansas City haberdasher, he was our last president without a bachelor's degree.*

$200   Caribbean ruler once considered a U.S. Major League pitching prospect.

$250   While observing "God and Man at Yale", this conservative spokesman taught Spanish there.

Word Origins

$50   Stuffed toy named for President Theodore Roosevelt.*

$100   From the father of psychoanalysis, it's an unintentional slip of the tongue.

$150   GM car named for the Indian chief who tried to take Fort Detroit.

$200   Slang for prostitute, from Civil War General who believed they raised troops' morale.*

$250   Begun in Harlem, this jitterbug dance was named for a 1920s aviator hero.

Now for the correct responses:

Former Occupations

$50   Who is Howard Cosell?

$100   Who was Josef Stalin?

$150   Who was Harry Truman?

$200   Who is Fidel Castro? (He was scouted by the old Washington Senators of the American League—now the Minnesota Twins.)

$250   Who is William F. Buckley?

Word Origins

$50   What is a teddy bear?
$100   What is a Freudian slip?
$150   What is a Pontiac?
$200   What is a hooker? (from Union General Joseph "Fighting Joe" Hooker)
$250   What is the lindy? (from Charles "Lucky Lindy" Lindbergh)

I was not sure why, but I felt confident about being selected. Perhaps it was because I'd enjoyed doing the work so much. But when I had not heard anything by May 15, I decided to call Alex myself. I'd been a successful salesman of photocopiers in the past and thought it was now time to try to sell myself. One thing commonly taught in sales training is, when dealing with a potential buyer, always assume you've got the sale. I then called Alex, exchanged pleasantries and simply asked, "When do we start"?

I'M HIRED!

"Monday, June 4th at the KTTV lot on Sunset," he replied. Jules would call me with the details. I thanked Alex and told him I looked forward to working with him. I could not have been more pleased.

I later learned that of those final two categories I'd submitted, it was the "hooker" question that got me the job.

Two days later Jules called, apparently unaware I'd spoken to Alex.

He told me I was one of the writers selected and indicated the salary would be $450 a week. I wasn't too thrilled at the amount, but figured the show was just starting out and that Merv Griffin was risking a considerable amount of money in launching the show. In fact, I had no idea how incredibly low this salary was by TV standards, even for a new show. As for the risk factor, there actually wasn't much of one, since King World had sold the show for 39 weeks in most markets. While some stations could cancel early if the ratings were low, it was quite unlikely that most would do so.

I knew it was going to be hard to support myself and two children on $450 a week. But working for Jeopardy was something I wanted to do, and I trusted that the salary would go up if the show did well. If the show bombed, I'd be out looking for work in a fairly short time anyway. I told Jules I accepted the job and he gave me the details as to the starting date and time. Two researchers had been hired, and on June 4th they would be setting up a small library for us to use. The writers would therefore start on June 5th and Jules would meet us at 9:30 in the morning on the corner of Sunset and Van Ness.

Jules walked us onto the lot of KTTV, Channel 11. The portion of the lot overlooking the freeway has a building with a strange sculpture on the roof. It looks like a three-dimensional ladder built from an erector set. It leans over as if it is about to fall onto the freeway. People familiar with the Hollywood Freeway all know it. The lot contained various studio and office buildings. Besides producing its own local news broadcasts and televising whatever road games the L.A. Dodgers wished to make freely available to their fans, Channel 11 did not carry a great deal of original programming. Most of the studio space was rented out to producers of syndicated shows. "The People's Court" was on the lot, as was a game show called "Anything for Money." Our immediate neighbors were the staff and cast of "Rituals," a new attempt at a syndicated soap opera.

THE STAFF

The three other new writers were Steven Dorfman, Gary Lee and Michelle Johnson.

Michelle was about my age, 37. She was married and had two sons. Between taking care of the boys, she had worked on some game shows in the past. Her husband, Gary, had written for "Hollywood Squares" for 10 years. In 1974 he and the other "Hollywood Squares" writers had won Emmys for "Best Writing for a Game Show." It was the only year that Emmys were awarded in that category. In June 1984 Gary was head writer for "Sale of the Century," a Q & A game show that NBC was carrying in the mornings. Michelle and Gary are originally from Nebraska.

Like Jules, Gary Lee had also been a teacher in L.A. Originally from Illinois, he grew up in Southern California and had gone to high school with Jules. Gary and Jules had worked together in trying to develop and market game shows of their own. Gary was 39 at the time.

The youngest in the group, Steven Dorfman, was about 29. He had come out to L.A. after graduating from Detroit's Wayne State University with a degree in communications. Steven had spent the last seven years working in the credit department of J.C. Penney and, most recently, as a cashier for Hamburger Hamlet, a restaurant chain. All the while he was knocking on doors all over Hollywood seeking a job in television. Finally, he had one. Steven had passed the contestant tryouts for the 1978 version of Jeopardy but the show was cancelled before they had a chance to use him.

Jules brought us into the Jeopardy offices and reintroduced us to Alex. We also met Alex's secretary, Anne Burgeson, and Julie Ruthenbeck, who was the receptionist. Anne was an attractive blonde and very Scandinavian in appearance. She seemed a bit on the quiet side. Julie is a tall young lady who seemed pleasant and jovial all of the time. During my seven years at Jeopardy, Julie worked her way up in the entertainment industry and went on to become a vice president at Walt Disney Productions.

The show's runner, or "gofer," was Nicky Trebek. Nicky is the daughter of Alex's former wife, Elaine, and her first husband. Though Alex and Elaine were no longer married by the time we started at Jeopardy, he still considered Nicky his stepdaughter, or, as he put it, his "daughter by osmosis," and seemed to take a fatherly interest in her. Nicky struck you as someone who liked people and seemed to make friends quickly.

Also on staff was Tony Griffin, Merv Griffin's only son. Tony is friendly and outgoing. The year he worked for Jeopardy he would pop in and out from time to time.

Tony's mother and Merv's ex-wife, Julann Griffin, was, by the way, the one who had actually thought up Jeopardy. Originally a big band singer, Merv had done some acting and had gone on to host some game shows before making it big as a talk show host. Aware of the great profit potential of game shows, he had become interested in producing one of his own. (Game shows are potentially more profitable than just about any other type of TV program because they have the smallest staffs and lowest production costs.)

QUIZ SHOWS

On a coast-to-coast flight during the early sixties, Merv and Julann were discussing the game show scene and what they might possibly do. When Julann suggested they produce a question and answer quiz show, Merv pointed out that those were no longer "in," mainly because their credibility had been destroyed by the quiz show scandals of the late fifties.

Q & A shows had their heyday in the fifties. The most popular ones were carried by the networks in prime time and were on only once a week, just like sitcoms, westerns and dramas. And they did just as well as those other shows in the ratings. In fact, the highest rated show for the entire '55–'56 season was "The $64,000 Question."

But then the scandal broke. It turned out the producers were feeding the correct answers to the contestants they wanted to win. Some losers were also paid off, but a disgruntled one went public. An uproar resulted that made front-page headlines all over the country, and a Congressional investigation ensued.

Quiz show contestants had been winning $60,000, $100,000 and eventually over $200,000. In 1957, $200,000 was really big bucks, the equivalent of $1,250,000 or more today. The big winners were fast becoming national celebrities. In 1957 Charles Van Doren, the first to win over $100,000, was probably as well known as Mickey Mantle, who had won baseball's triple crown the year before. Tens of millions had seen Van Doren. Mantle could only hope for those kind of ratings if his team made the World Series.

In some ways the quiz shows resembled sporting events—contests of brain rather than brawn. But the bubble burst when the public came to realize the sport the quiz shows most resembled was professional wrestling. The quiz show producers claimed their programs were more like TV dramas. To them, providing answers was no different than writing a script, deciding beforehand who would be the killer and who the victim.

But Congress and the public weren't buying. The quiz shows were run off the air. Co-producers Dan Enright and Jack Barry—the latter hosted as well as co-produced "Twenty-One" (the show that featured Charles Van Doren)—were blacklisted from working in television for about ten years.

With the quiz shows gone, what remained were game shows, and those were carefully monitored by the networks' Compliance and Practices departments to make sure that everything was on the up and up and all contestants were treated equally and fairly. The game shows now featured contestant stunts, guesswork and luck, and occasionally memory skills and hunches—anything but hard questions and answers.

When Merv pointed out that quiz shows were no longer believable because winning contestants had been fed the correct answers on the sly, Julann had an idea. Why not feed *all* the contestants the correct answers *in front of everybody?* Merv didn't see how that could work. Julann came up with an example: "Supposing we told everyone the answer is 5,280 feet."

"A mile," Merv responded. Although he didn't say, "What is a mile?," it was the first Jeopardy answer and question ever, and Julann credited him with a correct response.

Merv took the concept and worked on it. Money values were assigned to the clues which increased as the material became harder. In most question and answer games, you win the value of the clue if you respond correctly but are not penalized for a wrong response. Merv decided to deduct the value of any answer if a contestant answered it incorrectly. That is why the game is called Jeopardy.

DEVELOPING JEOPARDY

The second round, Double Jeopardy, was played with harder material for twice as much money as the first. Daily Doubles, for which a player could bet as much money as he had, or less if he wanted, were added to make it more interesting. The original Jeopardy, which debuted on NBC in 1964, had only five categories per game board. A sixth category was added to each game board when it was realized it would fit within the allotted time. The monetary values of the clues in the Jeopardy round ran from $10 to $50 and from $20 to $100 in Double Jeopardy. Unlike the current version, all players got to keep whatever money they had at the end of Final Jeopardy.

For a time, Merv thought the emphasis should be on humor, with the Jeopardy material resembling the answers and questions of the comedy routine made famous by Johnny Carson as "Carnac the Magnificent," formerly done by Bill Dana on the "Steve Allen Show." But producer Bob Rubin pointed out they'd soon run out of funny material and altered the format to hard-core Q & A, which it has been ever since.

Jules proceeded to take us down to the writing and research area. Its focal point was a small, central room in the basement that had been turned into a library. The library consisted almost entirely of books that had belonged to the old Jeopardy. Included was a copy of Grolier's *Encyclopedia International,* which had at one time been the show's "source authority" and was given to departing contestants as a consolation prize (along with Rice-a-Roni). There were also a few books someone had forgotten to return to the New York Public Library.

We were now introduced to the show's two researchers, Suzanne Stone and Barbara Heller, who had set up the library the day before. Suzanne, from the San Fernando Valley, was in her late twenties. She has a Bachelor's Degree in Art and had previously met Jules while working as a freelance writer.

Barbara looked to be in her mid-thirties. A one-time Spanish teacher with a Master's in Spanish Literature from the University of Cincinnati, she was married and was a friend of both Elaine and Alex Trebek. She'd gotten to know them through her husband, Stan, who was from Toronto and had known fellow-Canadian Alex from the time Alex had worked in that city.

Both Barbara and Suzanne were quite outgoing and easy to get to know. We writers felt like the upper class when we learned they were earning only $350 a week. Fortunately, Suzanne, who was single, was living with her parents and Barbara's husband, who appeared to be a professional deal maker, seemed to be doing quite well, as they lived in Beverly Hills.

There were a few tiny offices off the main room. Figuring Michelle and I would have something in common as the only two parents in the group, Jules assigned one office to the two of us. Steven and Gary became office mates as well, while Barbara and Suzanne had their desks out in the main room. Jules had a room for himself, and the last and smallest room was being saved for a secretary/typist who was yet to be hired.

One thing Jules made sure to do that first day was to play for us the popular video "I Lost on Jeopardy!" by "Weird Al" Yankovic. The video featured Art Fleming and the old set of Jeopardy. I would recommend it for light-hearted laughs. We later invited Weird Al to the wrap party we had at the end of that first season, and he proved to be as nice and friendly as his songs were fun.

I was surprised "I Lost on Jeopardy!" was so popular. It got ample air play even though the show hadn't been on in years. Maybe it was an omen of good things to come.

CHAPTER 2

LAUNCHING A TV PROGRAM

The next day, June 6, happened to be my 37th birthday, but after just one day on the job, I didn't feel I knew my co-workers all that well, so I just kept it to myself. In future years Suzanne, Barbara or Ruth Deutsch (a later hire) would always bake me a cake.

Alex and Jules called a meeting with the six of us: four writers and two researchers. They went over the game boards we had submitted in applying for the job and pointed out which clues they liked and why. Surprisingly, they did not like many, but we apparently had more good ones than the other applicants. Shortly thereafter, Alex admonished us to do "great works" and then excused himself.

Jules disclosed that one of the reasons we were selected was that our individual interests seemed to complement each other. I have a master's in history and had taught American history at a community college. My strengths and interests include history, government and politics, geography, Bible and religion, business and industry. Gary, who had taught elementary school, was good in history but was also strong in movies and television. Both of us could handle sports. Steven was the uncrowned king of word-play. He was always trying to add humor to the show. Sometimes it would work and sometimes he would get on Alex's nerves, but he was always appreciated. All three of us could occasionally contribute a science category. Michelle was quite strong in literature and anything having to do with children, such as fairy tales, toys and games, etc. Michelle and Steven tended to write easier clues, Gary and I the harder ones. It seemed to balance out as well.

CATEGORY SELECTION; Q&A VERIFICATION

Jules then explained the writing procedure. We were free to write categories on any subject we liked. Jules and Alex were assuming the diversity among the writers would result in a balance and diversity among the various categories. Each category was to consist of *six* clues. Five of them would be submitted in order of increasing difficulty. The sixth one, which should be of average difficulty, would be an extra to be placed into the actual game in case something went wrong at the taping.

Each individual clue was to be typed on a separate three-by-five card. At the top we were to type in the name of the category in capital letters. The clue was to be in all caps and had to fit entirely within the allotted space on the TV monitor—seven lines of 15 spaces each. We were then to skip a few lines and type in the response in question form. Below that we were to cite the source, including the page number. Finally you identified the card as one of your own by putting your initials somewhere in the lower right-hand corner.

Here's a sample clue:

MIDDLE NAMES
J.R. WOULD BE PLEASED TO KNOW THAT THIS 2-TIME
PRESIDENTIAL CANDIDATE'S MIDDLE NAME WAS EWING
WHO WAS ADLAI STEVENSON?
WB (World Book) 18/897   HE
Complete Directory to Prime Time TV P. 178-9 (J.R. Ewing)

The writer had to provide a source for all aspects of the clue. In the above clue the information on Adlai Stevenson's middle name came from the World Book Encyclopedia, volume 18, page 897. The information on J.R.'s last name, showing it was the same as Stevenson's middle name, came from the Complete Directory to Prime Time TV. The researcher's job was to then find a second source that confirmed every fact of the clue and response.

Some clues required an explanatory comment from Alex. If such were needed, we were instructed to add it after the sources. Here are two examples:

FAMOUS MISQUOTES
MANY MISTAKENLY THINK HE SAID "COME WITH ME TO THE
CASBAH" IN THE 1938 FILM "ALGIERS."
WHO WAS CHARLES BOYER?
Boller & George, They Never Said It, p. 9   HE
*Boyer said his press agent made up that line.

SPORTS STADIUMS
SERVICE ACADEMY THAT'S THE HOME TEAM AT
MICHIE STADIUM
<u>WHAT IS THE U.S. MILITARY ACADEMY?</u>
(Acc: WEST POINT)
1985 WORLD ALMANAC, P. 830   HE
*Named for Dennis Michie (Mi-key), class of 1892, 1st football coach & team
captain at West Point. Died in action in the Spanish-American War, 1898.

Finally, Jules urged us to keep in mind some of the categories that
were widely associated with the original version of Jeopardy. Those
included Unreal Estate, Foreign Phrases, All Numbers, Silly Songs
and, of course, Potpourri. Merv was eager to have those traditional
categories well represented in the early shows in order to demonstrate
continuity with the old Jeopardy program.

And so we went to work. I began with an American History category and then did Silly Songs. I then came up with two interesting
geography categories. One was Former Capitals, dealing with cities
that used to be, but no longer were, capitals of their respective countries. These included Rio De Janeiro, St. Petersburg (Russia), Calcutta,
Nanking, Krakow and Istanbul. The other was called "Foreign" U.S.
Cities and had to do with American cities named after cities in other
countries such as Moscow, Idaho; Syracuse, New York; Troy, Michigan; Bethlehem, Pennsylvania; Athens, Georgia; and Paris, Texas.

REVIEWING CLUES

As soon as we had completed a category we would review it with
Jules. His primary task was to edit the material. He is a talented writer
and would often come up with a way to make a clue cuter or funnier.
Sometimes he would agree with the order of difficulty in which I had
put the material, and sometimes he would re-order. His main concern
was that some of the clues were too difficult. Some clues could be
eased by rewriting. For example, instead of asking for two of the four
state capitals whose names end with the word "city," we would ask
for only one. The four, by the way, are Carson City, Nevada; Jefferson
City, Missouri; Salt Lake City, Utah and Oklahoma City. To ease up
"An ermine is a type of this animal," the clue was re-worked to read,
"When husbands 'pop' for an ermine coat, they're actually buying this
fur." The correct response is, of course, "What is weasel?" Clues that

were too difficult and could not be eased up in some way had to be replaced.

It is difficult—virtually impossible—for one person to be totally objective as to what is difficult and what is not in all the various subjects covered by Jeopardy. We were encouraged to test clues on one another and eventually concluded that if another writer could answer correctly, the likelihood was at least one of three contestants could do so as well.

It was always intended that at least one contestant question each clue correctly. The clues at the top of the board were supposed to be easy for two reasons: First to encourage the contestants to aggressively ring in and quickly get into the rhythm of the game and, secondly, to get the viewers to play along at home. The questions at the bottom of the board were supposed to be harder, but we never deliberately intended that any clue should be missed by all three players.

From the very outset, we would be turning in clues only to learn the same clue had already been turned in by another writer. Both Jules and Alex were extremely anxious that we not repeat any material. As Jeopardy went on year after year, it became more and more difficult not to repeat material. For one thing there is only so much information that is common knowledge to most people. Thus, repetition of material would generally tend to occur in the easier clues. The more you tried to come up with new material that had never been done before, the more likely that material was to be difficult.

Early in the first season of the show, it was decided to enter all the material into a computer and use the computer to print it out. Large printouts listing every clue by key word were kept so that we could look up any subject or person to see what had been done about that subject or person before. Eventually we settled on a rule of thumb: we would not knowingly repeat a clue within a period of two years.

Of course, we never deliberately repeated clues. Rather, it was usually two different writers unknowingly writing the same thing. Occasionally a writer would write something without remembering he or she had written the same clue a year or two earlier. This is understandable when you realize Jeopardy currently does 230 shows a year, 73 clues per show, including extras, for a total of 16,790 answers and questions per season. As such, it is the most material-heavy U.S. TV quiz show of all time.

Final Jeopardy clues are never repeated. In the seven years I was with the show I can recall just one slip-up. I believe we twice asked contestants in Final Jeopardy to name two of the four state capitals that are named for U.S. presidents. It was the same clue written by two different writers and, as I recall, we ran it in the second and fifth seasons of the show. Sure enough, a few viewers caught us on it. The correct response, by the way, is Jefferson City, Missouri; Madison, Wisconsin; Jackson, Mississippi and Lincoln, Nebraska.

Once Jules was satisfied with a particular category, he would number the cards in order of difficulty: 1, 2, 3, 4, 5 and E for the extra. He would then initial the top card to indicate he'd seen and approved the material. In addition, he would mark it "J," to be used in the Jeopardy round if he thought it was on the easier side, or "DJ," to be used in Double Jeopardy if it was somewhat on the more difficult side. He would then turn it over to the researchers for verification.

THE CORE AND THE FRILL

I would describe a Jeopardy clue as having two aspects, the core and the frill. The core was what we were really asking the contestants, and the frill was additional information we included in the clue to make it more interesting and entertaining to the viewers. For example, a clue read "The last time a King of this country was crowned was in 1906 in Trondheim." What we were really asking is, in what country is Trondheim? That's the core. The correct response is "What is Norway?" Now, if a writer put "What is Sweden?" on the card, the researcher would have to catch it and correct it, or we'd have to throw the entire clue out. On the other hand, if there was a problem with the frill, such as the last year being 1908 instead of 1906, we need only change it or come up with a new frill.

Another example: "He became viceroy of Ireland 17 years after he surrendered at Yorktown." The core here is "Who surrendered at Yorktown?" We absolutely had to be correct about that. If the frill about his becoming viceroy of Ireland was inaccurate, we could correct or replace it. (The correct response here: "Who was Lord Cornwallis?")

It was the researcher's responsibility to double-source all aspects of a clue, both core and frill. The writer had to show a first source for everything he wrote. In the early days of the show we were somewhat loosy-goosy about this. For a question about a TV show, a writer could have put down "I saw the show" as his source. For a clue about a landmark he could have said, "I've been there." This was tolerated in part because we were under tremendous time pressure to launch the show.

The 1984–85 season was to consist of 39 weeks or 195 new shows, to be followed by 13 weeks of re-runs. Taping was to begin the first week in August and was to be completed before Christmas. Since time

had to be allowed for the material to be entered into the Chyron computer system, which made the clues appear in the 30 TV monitors on
stage, and for the material to be proofread, we had less than six
months to write the games.

BOB MURPHY VISITS

But at least we'd made a start, or so we thought. At the end of the
week, Bob Murphy came to see Alex and to talk to us. Bob is about
Merv Griffin's age, and the two of them were childhood friends in the
San Francisco Bay area. Bob had worked for Merv for years, going
back to the old Jeopardy in New York. In 1984 he was the third-rank-
ing executive in Merv Griffin Enterprises, behind Merv and Murray
Schwartz. Bob had been married for years. His nephew Rob heads up
PIC TV, a promotions organization which obtains prizes for "Wheel
of Fortune" as well as the second- and third-place prizes for the new
version of Jeopardy. Bob's brother Ed works there as well, while his
daughter Katie is the travel agent who handles all travel arrangements
for Merv Griffin Enterprises.

Bob's task, as I understood it, was to see to it that Merv made as
much money as possible. He had the proverbial charm of the Irish and
reminded me of the old saying, "Only an Irishman can tell you to go
to hell in such a way that you're actually looking forward to getting
there."

Bob had been going over all the material we had submitted and
had been showing it to Merv as well. After meeting with Alex and
discussing our work with him, Bob came to see us. He claimed the
material was still much too difficult and had to be eased up or replaced. The worst thing that can possibly happen on a game show is
when all three contestants just stand and stare after hearing a clue,
with no one able to come up with a response. Many contestants are
nervous on stage under the hot TV lights and are sometimes too jit-
tery to ring in, even when they know the correct response. A Jeopardy game has 60 answers and questions prior to Final Jeopardy. If
we define a missed clue as one where Alex would have to give the
correct response because the contestants either answered incorrectly
or did not ring in at all, then, said Bob, a good show should have no
more than five to seven missed clues at most.

Bob was concerned the contestants might not be able to handle
the material we had written. The old Jeopardy, which had been produced in New York for 11 years, had a reputation for tough clues.
However, the short-lived 1978 version of the show was produced in
L.A. and had not done very well. Conventional thinking seemed to be

that more bright, well-educated contestants could be found on the East Coast than in Southern California. My experiences both as a student growing up in New York and as a parent in California tended to confirm that. Educational standards seemed higher in the East. While Southern California may have some good colleges and universities, the prevalent atmosphere seemed rather anti-intellectual. The elementary and secondary schools seemed to put a lot more emphasis on sports, extracurricular activities and self-esteem than on plain old reading, writing and 'rithmetic.

In any case, Bob was quite worried that the contestants might not be able to handle the material, and we had to make the clues easier.

MARK RICHARDS

The contestant coordinator was Mark Richards. He had previously been married to the daughter of famed Cleveland DJ Alan Freed, who, it is said, coined the term "rock 'n' roll." Freed had passed on his record collection to Mark, who would tell us he could always come up with some rare golden oldie should we ever need it for an Audio Daily Double. Mark had formerly been a radio DJ, as had a number of TV game show hosts, while some, such as Wink Martindale and Jim Lange, were at that time working both TV game shows and spinning discs on the radio. Mark, too, had hopes of becoming a game show emcee and would "host" what we called "the run-through," a rehearsal game prior to tapings.

A sample game would be inserted into the Chyron computer system and played live on stage. This enabled the director, cameramen, sound and lighting people, as well as announcer Johnny Gilbert, to all practice what they had to do. The 12 or 13 contestants for that day would take turns, with each playing part of the rehearsal game on stage. This enabled them to handle the ring-in button, properly distance themselves from the microphone and generally get a feel for what it was like on stage.

In 1985, Mark was replaced by Greg Muntean, who was brought over from the Contestant Department of "Wheel." Greg was very much a gentleman all the way around. Combining the qualities of enthusiasm and professionalism, Greg did a superb job for us in his three years with the show. He subsequently served as contestant coordinator for the Dick Clark Q&A show, "The Challengers."

During that first season, Mark Richards didn't have anyone formally assigned to assist him, and so various people took turns. One of those who helped out and actually oversaw his work was Dave Williger. Dave's formal title was Production Executive. A friendly, jovial sort, Dave had been with Merv Griffin Enterprises for most of his working life, having started out as a page on the Merv Griffin Show some 12 years earlier. He was assigned to Jeopardy primarily to assist Alex, since it was assumed Alex would have his hands full as both producer and host of the show. Alex was quite the workaholic in those days and left little for Dave to do. Consequently, Dave spent much of his time overseeing the contestant side of things.

CONTESTANT APPLICANT PROCESS

Contestant applicants were given a 50-question test and had to get 35 of them correct in order to pass. Jules came up with the original contestant tests in 1984. Subsequently, the writers would work with Jules in putting together new tests. Originally two new tests would be compiled every year and used on an alternating basis to prevent cheating. Later, new tests would be created every six months because some people were returning to take the test more frequently. Still later, a special, easier test oriented towards young people would be drawn up each year to be used in finding contestants for the Teen and College Tournaments.

The test was intended to accurately reflect the program and weed out people who would not make strong contestants. In those early years, the tests followed a pattern of 15 academic questions, 10 lifestyle, 15 pop culture and 10 word play. Beginning in 1987, when Alex was no longer producer, the 15 pop culture questions were reduced to five and the 10 word play to just two, as the thrust of the program was changed.

Individuals who passed the written test were then invited to play practice rounds against other would-be contestants, using bells to ring in. The idea was to see how quickly they could respond, how well they could stand the heat of competition and to get an idea of their personalities. Most game shows look for lively, ebullient, bubbly, boisterous personality types. Men and women in uniform and those with regional dialects are especially welcome, as are people with any other traits that might add color to the program. Over the years we had country lawyers from North Carolina, Frank Rizzo types from Philadelphia, hillbillies from the Ozarks, nuns and clergy of various denominations, househusbands, professional gamblers, starving writers, budding actresses, people from the various medical professions, tax collectors and political hopefuls. The occupations most represented on the show, however, seemed to be teaching and law—two professions associated with the ability to speak well in front of others.

Unlike other game shows, however, at Jeopardy personality clearly took a back seat to game-playing ability. Contestant coordinators who were used to picking the attractive, outgoing types for other shows seemed to look down on us for selecting players who were more average in looks and personality. I believe that is one of Jeopardy's secret strengths. Over the years our viewers have come to see Jeopardy contestants as ordinary, everyday people—brighter than average, perhaps, but people with whom they could personally identify.

It is the contestant coordinator's job to separate the good game players from the wanna-be's. Some of the finest players we ever had were people who were not outstanding on the written test. Occasionally, however, people with very high scores on the written test did horribly on the program, finishing in a negative situation at the end of the show. I recall one case in which a man had passed the written test, but Greg concluded his performance against other players was totally inadequate. The would-be contestant called Alex to complain, arguing that inasmuch as he had passed the written test he ought to have a chance to be on the show. He claimed that Greg had exercised poor judgment. Alex, being a merciful sort, let him come on the program. He ended the Double Jeopardy round with a score of minus $3400.

In the first few years of the show it was not hard to find contestants. Jeopardy had had a wide following since the days of Art Fleming, and many who had watched that show as high school and college students were now eager to try out and see how far they could get. In those early years of '84 and '85 it was not uncommon for people to fly out to L.A. at their own expense, just to take the Jeopardy test. They were that confident of making it onto the show, and many of them did.

By the time we completed two or three seasons of shows, most of those people who felt confident enough to try out at their own expense had already done so. Since the Los Angeles area has only so many potentially good Jeopardy players, and we wanted a mix of people from around the country and even around the world, it was decided early on to send the contestant coordinators out on contestant searches. Jeopardy was one of the first game shows to do this, once Merv Griffin found a system whereby it wouldn't cost him anything.

Jeopardy is a syndicated program. That is, it is sold separately and individually in every market. In one city it might be on an ABC affiliate, in another on a CBS or NBC affiliate, in yet another on FOX or on an entirely independent station. Generally, King World will sell the show to whichever station will pay the highest price. Once a station buys the program it must sell the commercial spots it has available so as to cover what it paid for the show and, ideally, realize a profit as well. (King World retains a few commercial spots, which it sells for itself on a national basis.)

How much a station can realize from the sale of those commercial spots depends on just one thing: the show's ratings in that particular local market. So stations are generally eager to do all they can to promote the show in order to boost its ratings. One of the things many stations have done to promote Jeopardy locally is to sponsor contestant searches in their areas. They announce the Jeopardy staff is coming to town and invite their viewers to try out for the show. They play it up locally as much as they can, often interviewing the contestant coordinators and some of the would-be contestants on local news or talk shows. The best promotion is when the celebrity of the show, Alex, comes along on the contestant search. This is something Alex has done over the years as much as he could, whenever his schedule permitted. When Alex comes to town, a station can play up the promotion for all it's worth. Obviously, it will draw more attention.

In order to sponsor a contestant search, a local station must pay all of the expenses of the Jeopardy staff. These include accommodations, meals and a place to administer the test. Transportation is paid for by the local station or acquired from an airline in exchange for a mention on the show. Contestant searches last two to four days in a single area, depending on what the station wants to provide and how many people want to take the test. In New York City, the nation's largest TV market, whenever WABC would sponsor a contestant search, there would be so many applicants that only those lucky enough to have their postcards drawn would be allowed to take the test. For our first contestant search there, out of 22,000 postcards sent in, only 400 were selected at random.

Whether or not the Jeopardy contestant department comes to your local area has nothing to do with whether or not they like the area, have an uncle nearby or want to see your town's top tourist attraction. It's strictly a matter of whether or not your local station wants to fork out the money to sponsor the event. Usually when a contestant would come to the show as a result of one of these contestant searches, Alex would give the local station a plug on the air. It should be noted that even if you passed all the hurdles at a local contestant search, you still had to come to L.A. at your own expense in order to go on the show. The only exceptions to that rule were the players in the four annual tournaments: the Tournament of Champions, the Teen Tournament, the College Tournament and the Seniors Tournament.

Dave Williger had accompanied Mark Richards and Alex on a

number of these contestant searches before quitting the show in 1985. As Dave was leaving the Jeopardy offices, his last words to me were, "Don't do what I did. Don't give this company 13 years of your life." Dave went on to work for Ralph Edwards, who produced "The People's Court." After that he wrote for the sitcom "Cheers." He then got his first crack at a producer's job with "Fun House," an after-school kids' show, but left that to join his friend Paul Gilbert who was to be producer of "The Pat Sajak Show." Dave and Paul had worked together in the Griffin organization for a number of years. Paul had most recently been producer of "Dance Fever," another Griffin production. Dave took the position of Associate Producer on the Sajak show and stayed with it for its entire year-and-a-half run. Since then he has been working on developing and producing game shows of his own.

Back at Jeopardy in June 1984, we were continually rewriting our material to make it easier. In the meantime, Jules and Alex were looking to hire a typist.

After the researchers had worked a category, they would go over it with Jules, who would make any needed changes. Any clues proven to be untrue would have to be replaced by the original writer, re-approved by Jules and re-researched. When the category finally passed muster, a typist would be needed to transfer it to a long strip of the same color: blue for academic, green for lifestyle, pink for pop culture and yellow for word play. Once Jules had enough strips of varying colors, he could paste them on large sheets resembling Jeopardy game boards. Using strips of different colors would help him make sure there was a good balance between different types of categories in each game.

Alex and Jules ran an ad for a typist in *The Hollywood Reporter.* They soon hired a young lady named JulieAnn Davis (now Hartman). JulieAnn was only 22 at the time. She has always been outspoken, to say the least. She let everyone know she was a grandniece of Lucky Luciano, the famous (or infamous) mobster. She was quite proud of the maternal, Italian side of her family. When she told me her mother's family used to live in Brooklyn, I guessed correctly that they lived in Bay Ridge, considered by many the borough's best neighborhood and the one often favored by reputed mobsters.

We soon noticed that JulieAnn seldom ate anything. She had just quit smoking, partly in order to take the job at Jeopardy. Alex is an athletically inclined non-smoker who strives to keep in good shape and he was running a non-smoking office. People who quit smoking seem to have a tendency to put on weight, and so JulieAnn was eating as little as possible.

I found this out because one day, shortly after JulieAnn began with us, Bob Murphy arranged for the Jeopardy staff to have lunch at Hollywood's Brown Derby restaurant. It was the first and last time in my seven years at Jeopardy that we were ever taken as a group to lunch at the company's expense. JulieAnn came along but ate nothing other than perhaps a carrot stick. Her ambition was to be an actress and she had obtained small parts in *Bachelor Party* (in which she played a hooker) and some other films. She later played a major role in one episode of the TV series "Superior Court."

With JulieAnn typing away, Jules was able to amass sufficient category strips in order to assemble some games. It was now July and there were less than four weeks to go until the start of taping. Having to ease up the material more and more had left us way behind schedule. Jules had hoped to have at least 50 shows' worth of material prepared in advance because, once we started taping, we would be using up more material than we could produce. Now way behind, Jules was scrambling for any usable material he could get his hands on. The writers were expected to turn out five categories a day, 25 a week. Researchers Barbara and Suzanne were co-opted onto the writing staff and research was temporarily suspended. The writers were told they had to get it right the first time.

Barbara continued as a writer for the rest of her career at Jeopardy. Suzanne later went back to doing research, which she seemed to enjoy more. Steven, Michelle and I seemed to have no problem meeting the five-category-a-day quota. Gary and Barbara were slower. Barbara always contended that she could have written more but would not because they continued to pay her less than the other writers. Jules tried to get her salary increased but to no avail. Jules and Barbara then reached an agreement that her quota would be lower as long as her salary was.

That first season I would estimate that no more than 25 percent of the answers and questions were researched, almost all of them by Suzanne. Apparently Alex did not have the authority to go out and hire more researchers, as his operating budget was nearly frozen. Management never seemed to particularly value research. On the old New York version of Jeopardy they did not research clues, and the show managed to keep going for 11 years. However, there were some slip-ups, and contestants occasionally had to be brought back for a second appearance when they had been disadvantaged in a game due to an error, either on the part of the Jeopardy staff or in whatever source the writer may have been using.

Just about all the question-and-answer game shows that were being produced in Hollywood used researchers to double-check the material, and Jeopardy management eventually came around to recognizing the need. Alex certainly campaigned for it. He is very much a perfectionist and would like the show as factually perfect as is humanly possible. On the other hand, he realized the pressure we were under, particularly when we didn't have researchers to back us up, and was quick to forgive our few mistakes in the material.

Considering that so little of our material was researched, we didn't do too badly that first season. Over 400 contestants appeared on the show and only three had to be brought back.

In one instance a contestant answered incorrectly and Alex forgot to give the other players a chance to ring in. Another time the correct response was "Who were the Puritans?" A contestant said, "Who were the Roundheads?" and was ruled wrong, as Alex and Jules (who was also the show's judge) didn't realize or didn't remember that in 17th-century England "Roundhead" was synonymous with Puritan.

The third instance had to do with a Final Jeopardy clue. The answer read "The oldest university in the western hemisphere is in this city." The response we were going for was "What is Mexico City?" I was using as my source the edition of *Encyclopedia Britannica* that was most recent at that time (1983). In an article under "Mexico, National Autonomous University of," they claimed the university in Mexico City, founded in 1551, was the oldest in the hemisphere.

In the game, one contestant responded "What is Lima?" She was ruled incorrect. She later protested. When we checked it out we found that Lima's National University of San Marcos was also founded in 1551, and it wasn't clear which university was older. However, we also found that the University of Santo Domingo had been founded in 1538, which should have been the correct response. We brought the contestant back and gave her another chance on the program. *Britannica* corrected that fact in their later editions.

We made some other small *faux pas* that first season, but only brought back a contestant if our mistake in some way might have affected the outcome of the game. In any case, the viewers have always been quick to correct any mistake we make, no matter how small, via phone calls and letters. If we said something inaccurate about the Pony Express, we would invariably get a letter from someone who said his great-grandfather had been a Pony Express rider.

Most of the letters, however, did not point out mistakes on our part, but represented misconceptions on the part of the viewers. Sometimes people misheard or misread a clue. Then again, there are some inaccuracies that people simply cling to. Many New Yorkers, for example, when speaking of "Long Island" mean the suburban and rural parts of Nassau and Suffolk Counties. Geographically speaking, Brooklyn certainly is on Long Island. Nevertheless when we said so, some New Yorkers took issue with us. To them, Long Island means the suburbs and Brooklyn is part of the city. Case closed.

Then there was my dispute with some members of the Church of Jesus Christ of Latter Day Saints, commonly known as the Mormon Church. Religion is a very sensitive personal matter, and at Jeopardy we would try to say the same things about religious denominations that the denominations say about themselves. We certainly didn't want to get into disputes about any denomination's particular doctrines; we were glad to take each denomination at its own word. For example, if there was a question about the Catholic Church, we usually checked it with Father Battaglia, who was the media spokesman for the Archdiocese of Los Angeles. One time a writer misread something and called Archbishop Mahoney of Los Angeles a cardinal (which was a mistake at the time but was probably a good omen, as he was elevated to cardinal a year or two later). Another thing we used to do with questions on religion was to check with individuals on staff who belonged to that particular denomination. Catholicism, Judaism and mainstream Protestantism were all represented on staff. For questions on Islam we would usually check with L.A.'s Islamic Center. From time to time we would call Buddhist and Sikh temples and houses of worship of other eastern religions, all of whom are well represented in Los Angeles.

Prior to my dispute with the Mormons. I had borrowed a book from the library that was a publication of the Church of Jesus Christ of Latter Day Saints. It appeared to be a textbook that was used to teach the religion to children. The book stated that the Church believes American Indians to have descended from some of the Lost Ten Tribes of Israel. I took the book at face value, and wrote a clue about it because it seemed like an interesting fact. The clue read something like "According to Mormon teaching, American Indians are descended from them." The correct response: "Who were the Lost Ten Tribes of Israel?"

A number of Mormons wrote in to protest that simply was not the case, that the Church did not teach that Indians descend from the ancient Israelites. I re-checked my sources and confirmed that the book was indeed a publication of the Mormon Church and it said precisely what I had read it to say. I also found another Mormon textbook on the Church's teachings that said the same thing. Then I noticed that both books dated back to the 1940s. I called the Mormon Temple in Los Angeles, who indicated to me that the Church no longer teaches that Indians descend from the Israelites, although, as they put it, the Church *may* have taught that in the past. I resolved to be sure to keep up to date when it came to matters of religion.

One of our more complicated snafus involved a clue I wrote in a Newspapers category that was used in our first Tournament of Champions. The clue and its response read as follows: "What the *New York World-Telegram & Sun, St. Louis Globe-Democrat* and *Washington Star* currently have in common." "What is they're no longer being published?"

We taped the program containing that clue, but I don't remember whether a player came up with the response or if Alex had to give it. Either way, we were surprised a few weeks later, when the show aired, to get a barrage of phone calls and letters. "What do you mean the *Globe-Democrat* is no longer being published? I have today's edition right in front of me." I was shocked to say the least. I was even more shocked when a letter came from the newspaper itself threatening legal action.

People often ask where we get our clues. The answer is: anywhere and everywhere, but one thing is for certain: We don't make them up. And the *Globe-Democrat* clue was no exception. The *New York World-Telegram & Sun* was killed by a newspaper strike back in 1966. The *Washington Star* went belly up in 1981. As for the *Globe-Democrat*, my source was the November 21, 1983 edition of *Time,* which indicated the paper would cease publication on the following December 31st, which it did.

What neither I nor anyone else on the Jeopardy staff knew was that the paper had found a new publisher and had been revived in February 1984. The paper's city editor, Mike Montgomery, sent me a note with the admonition "May you never again make a mistake again." Along with that he included a tear sheet of pages one and two of the Nov. 22, 1985 issue of the *Globe-Democrat*. A headline on page two read, "Wrong answer, Jeopardy!" with a sub-head "TV quiz show goofs on closing of newspaper." The article went on to point out the paper had received hundreds of phone calls, while many more were directed to KSDK, the St. Louis affiliate that carried the show. Throughout the article, Alex is referred to as "Alex Threbek," which proved we were not the only ones to make mistakes.

Nonetheless, I was quite embarrassed at what had happened. In order to make amends, we promised the *Globe-Democrat* that we would write a new clue telling all the world the paper is alive and well in St. Louis. And so I wrote that clue as well, and the show that included it was taped. But by the time that one aired, the St. Louis *Globe-Democrat* had once again bitten the dust—this time for good. And of course the letter-writers lost no time in pointing out the error. But you could hardly blame us for trying.

Then there was the time I managed to offend an entire city. Kansas City, Missouri has about three times as many people as Kansas City, Kansas, and a couple of books we had described the latter as a suburb of the former. When I did the same in a clue, we got a phone call from The Honorable Joseph E. Steineger, Jr., Mayor of Kansas City, Kansas. He complained, "This city has sat in the shadows long enough. The people that live in this town are so tired of being put down by anybody or anything. Kansas City, Kansas is a city. It's not a suburb of anything." There's no legal definition of "suburb." What actually constitutes a suburb is largely a judgment call. Nevertheless, we were sorry to have offended, and later devoted an entire category to Kansas City, Kansas.

The most important answer/questions used on the show are usually the Final Jeopardy clues, since, more often than not, the outcome of the game hinges on them. Jules and the writers were under such pressure to provide enough categories of material to meet the taping schedule that the Finals were treated almost as an afterthought that first season.

Final Jeopardies differ from regular clues in that the contestants have a full 30 seconds to come up with a response. The Final clues should therefore require a little extra thought in order to figure out the correct response. There should be more than one possible, plausible response. It should not be the type of clue in which you can immediately tell whether or not you know the right response.

Ever so often Jules would come to us and say, "I want everyone to write Finals for the next two hours." We would then spend that time trying to crank out clues that would require extra thought. Some of them would turn out to be good regular clues, but not really ones suited for Final Jeopardy. At times, Jules would come across a clue in a regular category that he thought would make a good Final. He would pull it out of the category to save for a Final, and the writer would have to come up with a new clue to replace it.

Final Jeopardies were always typed on large blue five by eight index cards. Here's an example of what one looked like:

FINAL JEOPARDY
CATEGORY: AMERICAN INDIANS
HE TOLD ANNIE OAKLEY, "THE WHITE MAN KNOWS HOW TO MAKE
EVERYTHING, BUT HE DOESN'T KNOW HOW TO DISTRIBUTE IT"
WHO WAS SITTING BULL?
Conlin, Morrow Book of Quotations in American History, p. 267.   HE

The quote isn't all that well-known. What we are really asking for is the name of the famous Indian who knew Annie Oakley. If you remember Annie Oakley toured with Buffalo Bill's Wild West Show and that Sitting Bull was also with the show, you can make the connection.

That first season we were in such a hurry to come up with suitable Final Jeopardies that none of them were double-sourced.

Here are a few of my favorite finals that I'd written over the years:

1. Category: First Ladies
Of all of our living former first ladies, she is the youngest.
(Note: This was written in 1985.)

2. Category: Astronomy
Since it can be seen with the naked eye, it was the farthest planet away from the sun known to the ancients.

3. Category: 1968
On Christmas Eve and Christmas Day, 1968, Frank Borman, William A. Anders & James A. Lovell, Jr. did this 10 times.

4. Category: Gay '90s
By 1897 as many as half of Seattle's police and firemen had left the city to go there.

5. Category: Fruits & Vegetables
According to the Guinness Book of Records, the heaviest fruit or vegetable ever grown is one of these.

6. Category: The Supreme Court
This 20th C. president was the only one in history to serve a full term but appoint no Supreme Court justice.

7. Category: American History
McLean House in Virginia was the site of this event.

8. Category: The Calendar
It's the latest date on which Labor Day can occur.

9. Category: Languages
The language spoken by the most people in South America.

10. Category: Animals
With a young one valued at $1.4 million, Guinness calls them the most costly zoo animals.

11. Category: Historic Names
Slave trader, land swindler & knife wielding brawler known as a hero of the Alamo.

12. Category: The Bible
This book opens with God telling Moses to take a census of the Israelites.

Now for the correct responses:

1. Who is Jacqueline Kennedy (Onassis)? (Rosalyn Carter is next.) (This was back in 1985.)
2. What is Saturn?
3. What is orbit the moon?
4. What is the Klondike? (Accept: The Yukon, Alaska) Even the mayor left.
5. What is a pumpkin? (816 lbs. 8 oz.)
6. Who is Jimmy Carter?
7. What is Lee's surrender (to Grant)? The surrender did not occur at a court house. Appomattox Court House is the name of the *village* where the surrender occurred.
8. What is September 7? Labor day is the first Monday in September.
9. What is Portuguese? Brazil has more people than all the other South American countries combined.
10. What are (giant) pandas?
11. Who was Jim Bowie?
12. What is Numbers?

Interviewed in the November 7, 1987 issue of *TV Guide*, five-time champion John Podhoretz said what a contestant needs is "associative memory," which he described as "the ability to rapidly grasp and piece together seemingly unrelated bits of information—using a flexible search pattern made up on the spot." Podhoretz, at the time a 26-year-old contributing editor with *U.S. News and World Report* and now a television columnist for the *New York Post*, went on to give an example:

For instance, my finest moment was solving one of the "Final Jeopardy" answers. It was: "On September 30, 1960, 'Goodbye, kids' became the first and last words this character ever spoke." At first I was in despair. What do I remember of 1960? But then I thought: if he said

"Goodbye, kids," it must be a kids' show. What kids' show was big in 1960? *Captain Kangaroo*? Yeah, but why would they be saying goodbye in 1960? Was it *Howdy Doody* then? Yeah, that sounded right. It's been off a long time. But which character said that? The character that would usually be mute. The clown! It was. . . Clarabelle the clown!

THE FIRST SEASON DRAWS NEAR

As July moved precipitously closer to August and the start of taping, the pressure we were under was also being felt by the show's Production Department. The Production Department was responsible for all technical aspects of the program, from the set and props down to getting the final tapes "in the can."

Heading up the Production Department that first season was Sue Shelley, a pleasant, petite young lady originally from Chicago. She had come up through the ranks in the Griffin organization and at Jeopardy had attained the title of Associate Producer. She was assisted by Production Coordinator Linda Smith, a tall, attractive blonde from Yazoo City, Mississippi. Linda had come out to L. A. right out of college and had previously been Murray Schwartz's secretary. In addition, the Production Department employed two or three all-around helpers known as Production Assistants, or P.A.s for short. One of them that first season, Michelle Grasso, later became Joan Rivers' personal assistant.

The production people were responsible for getting the game material entered into the Chyron computer system which would enable the clues to be seen on those 30 TV monitors which made up the Jeopardy game board. To help with that and to make sure the material was being entered accurately, Jules hired Tina Levine to serve as Jeopardy proofreader. Tina is a bright, petite young lady originally from New York who likes to write. Her job as proofreader had two aspects: first to make sure the game sheets, consisting of the category strips Jules had pasted on them, were correct in terms of spelling, grammar, usage and punctuation; and second, to proofread the Chyron to make sure the material was being accurately entered. This latter aspect was particularly demanding since you could only look at one clue at a time. Tina always did a good job for us during her two-year stay at Jeopardy but was quite unhappy about her salary, as it was hard to live on $300 a week in Los Angeles circa 1984.

The Chyron operator was Patrice Long, a clever, outspoken lady with good business sense from Charlotte, NC. Patrice wasn't a regular employee but an independent contractor who was called upon as needed. Since there seemed to be a shortage of trained Chyron operators in Hollywood, particularly those who could work flexible hours, Patrice was able to command a high hourly rate for her services.

In those earliest days of the show both Merv and Bob Murphy, as well as Alex, had to approve the contents of each game. It was only after the changes they required had been made could Jules pass the games on to Sue in order for them to be entered in the Chyron. In many ways the month of June had been a classic case of Parkinson's Law: A job will expand to fill the time allotted for it. There seemed to be time to spare and so we played around, easing up the material. As taping drew closer we all realized we had to get it down the way management wanted it the first time.

The Production Department was "downstream" from the writing/research staff. They couldn't get the material until we were finished with it. As a result they were under even greater pressure than we were to meet the schedule. They often had to work until midnight and on weekends. Sue was always after Jules to get her the material as quickly as possible, but Jules couldn't do so until the material was satisfactory to Bob and Alex. Sue and Jules never seemed to get along and Sue left the show after the first season to become Associate Producer of "Headline Chasers," a short-lived Griffin production.

Sometime that summer of 1984, Bob Boden threw a "JEO-party" at UCLA to celebrate the return of Jeopardy to the TV screen. Everyone who works in game shows in L. A., or is interested in working in game shows, should know Bob. He's made a career in TV game shows and is probably the number one fan of Jeopardy to boot. Over the years he's worked on numerous game shows and in various network development departments. He's currently working for Sony's Game Show Channel, which became a functioning cable network in the fall of 1994. Bob knows a good game show when he sees one and I've come to consider him one of the best sources around to find out what's going on in the game show business.

Bob came by one day to introduce himself and invite the staff to the "JEO-party". I made sure to attend and had a nice time playing home game versions of various successful and not-so-successful TV game shows.

The highlight of the evening was getting to meet Julann Griffin, who had actually thought up Jeopardy. She proved to be a charming and delightful person which was not all that surprising when I learned she'd formerly been a comedienne.

PRIZE MONEY DOUBLES

The dog days of August came and taping was just a few days off. On the weekend just before we went to taping, Alex convinced top management to make a major change. The pilot of the show called for dollar values for the clues in the Jeopardy round to range from $50 to $250 and twice that in Double Jeopardy. Bob Boden and Jules had been discussing the dollar values of the clues when Jules told Alex he felt they should be *doubled*. Alex thought so, too, and somehow, at the last minute, convinced Merv and Bob Murphy it was a good idea. Jeopardy round clues would now be worth from $100 to $500, Double Jeopardy clues from $200 to $1000. Per Jules' and Alex's suggestion, the $50 figures were eliminated and only multiples of 100 were used.

Merv and Bob wanted the show to move as rapidly and smoothly as possible. They were aware that on the old Art Fleming version viewers preferred to have all the clues in the game uncovered. This could only happen if everything moved quickly. By making the change, the extra syllables "and fifty" were eliminated 12 times from each show. Eliminating the fifties would also tend to make the wagering on Daily Doubles simpler and that would save time for the show as well. It should also be pointed out that Alex had considerably less time to complete the games than did Art Fleming on the old show. For one thing, the new syndicated version had seven minutes of commercials— eating up considerably more game time than did the old NBC show. In addition, the second and third place contestants would not be keeping the money they accrued as was the case on the old show, but would have to settle for prizes that would have to be announced and described on the show.

Alex had pulled off the impossible and had just gotten Merv and Bob to double the prize budget for the show. It was a decision that was to cost Merv about $800,000 extra as contestant winnings averaged about $8,000 per show that first season. I understand, however, that the show's profits that first year were considerable and so it was an expense he could live with.

I believe it was a smart decision, which had it not been made then, would have had to be taken eventually anyway, just to keep up with inflation. It made the show look more exciting and classier from the start and Merv Griffin is hardly the poorer for it.

One decision which evoked a lot of controversy was not to allow the second- and third-place contestants to keep the cash they had accumulated in the game. This had not been the case previously and many fans of the old Jeopardy felt this was how Merv was able to up the dollar amounts of the clues—by not paying the losing contestants anything.

When the first pilot, using the old printed card system, was produced in the fall of 1983, plans still called for all three players to keep their winnings. For that pilot, however, the dollar values of the clues ranged from just $25 to $125 in the first round, $50 to $250 in Double Jeopardy. Under that system an average champion's one-day winnings would be about $2,000 to $2,500. Generally speaking, the combined total for the second- and third-place players is about equal to that of the champion and so the prize budget would have been about $4-5,000 per game. When numerous individuals connected with the show pointed out those amounts were just too low for the 1980s and needed to be substantially increased, Merv seemed hesitant at first to change.

He finally agreed to do so on condition that only the winning player kept his accumulated cash. And so for the second pilot, the dollar amounts were doubled, but the winner-only-keeps-the-cash rule was instituted. That way dollar amounts on the game board could be doubled without giving away any more prize money.

Merv and Bob Murphy believed that paying only the winner in cash was a good idea in that it would force all three contestants to bet as much as they had to in Final Jeopardy in order to win the game. Under the old system, if a player felt weak in the Final Jeopardy category he might bet little or nothing, being content to keep the money he had accumulated thus far. In other words, Merv and Bob thought it would make the outcome of Final Jeopardy more exciting by forcing the contestants to make more competitive bets.

Actually, what they have done by making a player's money of no value unless he wins is to make the game *less* interesting. On the old show, where all players kept their cash scores, the viewer had much less of an idea as to what each player would bet, since they could either go for the championship or elect to more or less keep what they had. Or the contestant could take a middle course. Bet enough to beat his opponents if they were wrong but still leave himself a nice amount of money to take home if he was wrong. The old Jeopardy was interesting because the players were betting with what had become *their* money. On the new show the bets are almost always predictable. The Final Jeopardy category is of little significance, as in nearly every case each player simply bets as much as is needed to win the championship regardless of how he feels about the category.

On both the old and new versions of Jeopardy some shows are what we call runaways. That occurs when one player has accumulated more than twice as much as his nearest opponent prior to Final Jeopardy. On the old show, Final Jeopardy in a runaway game was still interesting because even though the champion had already been determined, it was still fascinating to see how much of his own money each player was willing to risk on his knowledge of a particular category. On the current show, Final Jeopardy in a runaway is a meaningless exercise for the players, unless there is some great competition for the second place prize, and is of interest to the viewers only to the degree that the Final Jeopardy clue is interesting.

Nevertheless, by not paying the second- and third-place players, the show has, over the years, saved millions. I would estimate savings of about two-and-a-half million a year in cash that would otherwise have been an expenditure. As for those second- and third-place prizes, they generally don't cost a thing as they are promotional considerations, given in exchange for having the product or service promoted on TV. In some cases, where the promotional value is said to exceed the prize, the show may even be paid money in addition to the free prize.

FIRST DAY OF TAPING

The first day of taping had finally arrived. I believe it was Tuesday, August 14. We were all nervous to some extent. The show absolutely had to work well or we would all be out of a job by Christmas. No one was more nervous than Alex. Bright and talented though he was, he'd been out of work for about a year prior to Jeopardy. As both host and producer, he had far more to gain if the show made it and far more to lose if it didn't than any of us.

That day we met director Dick Schneider for the first time. Dick has and continues to enjoy an illustrious career as a TV director, mostly for NBC. A native of the tiny town of Cazadero, California, Dick served in the Navy in World War II. After that, he started out as a page at NBC in New York and worked his way up from there. Eventually he directed Kate Smith's TV show, followed by "Big Story" and "The Today Show" with Dave Garroway, all in the '50s. He went on to direct numerous game shows including "Who, What and Where?". From the '70s and well into the '90s, Dick served as both producer and director of Macy's Thanksgiving Day Parade. He worked the year round organizing that very special event and still lives and works in New York. He would fly back and forth some 20 times a year in order to do Jeopardy in L. A. A class guy, Dick is mild mannered and very professional in his style of working and is clearly one of the best directors in the business.

The stage manager was Keith Richmond, who was also serving in that capacity on "Entertainment Tonight." While the director sits in the control booth where he can see everything the cameras are picking up, the stage manager is his right arm on the floor. He is in constant touch with the director via headphones and is physically present on stage to see that the director's wishes are carried out. Keith enjoyed his job and liked to kid around. He is a dark-haired guy with a closely cropped black beard. One day Keith came up to me and innocently asked, "Do you know who Mephistopheles is?" Jeopardy writers are supposed to be knowledgeable about things like that.

"Why do you want to know?" I inquired.

"Well," he said, "a woman in the audience came up to me and told me I reminded her of Mephistopheles."

"I hate to tell you this," I said, "but Mephistopheles is another name for the Devil." I called him Mephistopheles from then on, but he didn't mind. Later, when I got engaged he offered to videotape the wedding.

That day we also met announcer Johnny Gilbert. Originally from Newport News, VA, Johnny is the consummate Southern gentleman. A TV veteran, Johnny is, at the time of this writing, in his fifth decade of announcing game shows. He had done quite a few prior to Jeopardy, including a long stint back in the '50s in New York with the original "Price Is Right," then hosted by the late Bill Cullen. He had even emceed a few game shows himself, including "Music Bingo," which had a year's run on ABC in 1959 and the shorter-lived "Beat the Odds" and "Fast Draw."

Incidentally, the announcer on the original Jeopardy was Don Pardo, whom Johnny liked to refer to as "my father." Don stayed in New York and has for years been the announcer on NBC's "Saturday Night Live."

Besides actually announcing the show, one of the duties of nearly all game show announcers is to warm up the studio audience. That entails telling a few jokes while at the same time explaining how and when to applaud, not to make noise or get up at the wrong time and, in the case of a quiz show like Jeopardy, not to say the correct response such as "It's the President's dog" out loud. That was and probably still is one of Johnny's favorite lines. We heard it so often that the following season, Jules had one of the new researchers, Carlo Panno, write a category titled "The President's Dog." Sorry, Millie wasn't in it, since Mr. Bush was still Vice President at the time.

Jeopardy was taped the way most game shows in Hollywood are done—five shows a day, two days a week. Since we were taping ten shows a week, we could occasionally skip a week, but we weren't slated to skip very many, as the schedule called for taping to be completed by Christmas. The first studio audience would come in about 2:10 in the afternoon, right after we'd done the run-through with the contestants. Taping was to start at 2:30 and that audience would stay for three shows. If all went well, that would be over at 4:30. We would then take a one-hour dinner break. The two additional shows would be taped afterwards.

The contestants who had not yet been on the show, as well as the returning champion, had to be fed. Sending them out to local restaurants could be a problem, since there was no guarantee they'd get back in time. So Merv Griffin Enterprises arranged for a caterer to come to the studio to feed them. Naturally, people from the Contestant Department had to keep them company, and so Merv allowed all those employed by the show, even the writers and researchers, to have dinner as well, if they so desired.

Of course we couldn't sit with the contestants. The meals cost $10 a head and, in all, about 40 people were fed each time. You could even occasionally bring guests, but that was later limited to one guest per staffer per season. The studio crew was not invited, since they were employed by the studio and not by Merv Griffin Enterprises.

After dinner, a new audience was brought in to see the final two programs and Johnny went through his warm-up routine a second time. You really had to hand it to Johnny. He's done that Jeopardy warm-up well over three thousand times now and yet, every time you hear it, he sounds as excited and enthusiastic about what's he's doing as ever.

Between shows, Alex would come out to talk to the audience as well. Often there would be some good-natured banter back and forth between Johnny and Alex. By the time he'd completed the fourth show, especially on the second tape day, Alex would be pretty tired, but he always came out to give the audience a little extra, to show his appreciation of their coming out to see us.

If all went well, we'd be finished between 7 and 7:30 in the evening. (Later the entire schedule was moved up an hour earlier.) Not that it always went well. Murphy's Law is very much a factor in the world of television. If you want to see whatever can go wrong actually go wrong, by all means come to a TV show's very first taping. Be sure you have lots of time to kill. People are not yet used to working together and there are a great many technical kinks to be worked out. The first tapings of Jeopardy were no exception: we were in the studio until after 11 at night.

Speaking of Murphy's Law, Bob Murphy had come over to make sure the show got off to an OK start. I thought Merv Griffin would come too, since he obviously had a great deal riding on the show, but that was not to be the case. In the seven years I was with the show Merv came to the tapings once or twice at most and as far as I know never so much as set foot in the Jeopardy offices. Ironically, Hollywood employees of the late Mark Goodson, the famous game show producer who lived in New York, got to see far more of him then we ever saw of Merv. The same could be said for the Hollywood staff of Reg Grundy, a major Australian TV producer who lives in the Sydney area but also produces some shows in this country. Merv's office was only five blocks from ours.

The writers very much looked forward to see how our material would play that first tape day. We even made a small bet among ourselves as to whose answer/question would be the very first one chosen. The first clue picked by a contestant in the current version of Jeopardy was in the category "Animals" for $100. It read, "These rodents first got to America by stowing away on ships." The response, "What are rats?" (We would have also accepted mice.) Even though I didn't have much material in the Jeopardy round of that first game, I did write that one and won the bet.

That very first Jeopardy program of the current series aired on September 17, 1984. For those who find such matters to be of historic significance, here is the material we prepared for that program in its entirety:

JEOPARDY ROUND

Lakes & Rivers
$100 - River mentioned most often in the Bible.
$200 - Scottish word for lake.
$300 - AUDIO DAILY DOUBLE   River in this famous song: (Play "Song of the Volga Boatmen.")
$400 - American river only 33 miles shorter than the Mississippi.
$500 - World's largest lake, nearly five times as big as Superior.

Inventions
$100 -   Marconi's wonderful wireless.
$200 -   In 1869 an American minister created this "oriental" transportation.
$300 -   A 1920s hunting trip to Canada inspired Birdseye's food preserving method.
$400 -   This fastener gets its name from a brand of galoshes it was used on.
$500 -   Designed over 100 years before airplanes to save people who jumped from burning buildings.

Animals

$100 - These rodents first got to America by stowing away on ships.
$200 - There are about 40,000 muscles and tendons in this partof an elephant's body.
$300 - When husbands "pop" for an ermine coat, they're actually buying this fur.
$400 - Close relative of the pig, though its name means "river horse."
$500 - If this species of hybrid's parents were reversed, you'd get a himmy.

Foreign Cuisine

$100 - The "coq" in coq au vin.
$200 - A British variety is called "bangers," a Mexican variety, "chorizo."
$300 - Jewish crepe filled with cheese.
$400 - French for a toothsome cut of beef served to a twosome.
$500 - A stew of various meats or a Jeopardy category.

Actors & Roles

$100 - Video in which Michael Jackson plays a werewolf and a zombie.
$200 - 2 "Saturday Night" alumni who tried "Trading Places."
$300 - He may "Never Say Never Again" when asked to be Bond.
$400 - The blonde preferred in the film "Gentlemen Prefer Blondes."
$500 - Sam Shepard played this barrier breaker in "The Right Stuff."

Number, Please

$100 - Not company, but a crowd.
$200 - Number of people blowing their own horn in a brass quintet.
$300 - Roman numeral D.
$400 - Number on telephone dial corresponding to "WXY."
$500 - You can't get to first base without going this far.

DOUBLE JEOPARDY

The Bible

$200 - When "Joshua fit the battle of Jericho," these took a tumble.
$400 - His price was 30 pieces of silver.
$600 - According to the Bible, it wasn't necessarily an apple.
$800 - Though it means "city of peace," it's seen 30 wars, the last in 1967.
$1000 - According to First Timothy, it is the "root of all evil."

'50s TV

$200 - Occupation of Richard Diamond, Peter Gunn & Mike Hammer.
$400 - She was "Our Miss Brooks."

$600 - Amount Michael Anthony gave out each week on behalf of John Beresford Tipton.

$800 - His card read, "Have gun, will travel."

$1000 - Name under which experimenter Don Herbert taught viewers all about science.

National Landmarks

$200 - She came from France to harbor America's freedom.

$400 - When he was home, George Washington slept here.

$600 - The cornerstone of Massachusetts, it bears the date 1620.

$800 - Site where John Hancock signed his "John Hancock."

$1000 - D.C. building shaken by November 1983 bomb blast.

Weights and Measures

$200 - Jules Verne title which coverts to "60,000 miles submerged."

$400 - Unit measuring intensity of sound named for inventor of the phone.

$600 - This measure is 40 gallons for "proof spirits," 42 gallons for oil.

$800 - DAILY DOUBLE   Found by multiplying the diameter of a circle by 3.1415.

$1000 - In "Law of 1866," only weight system ever sanctioned by Congress.

Notorious

$200 - It was probably a lyre, not a fiddle, if he played it while Rome burned.

$400 - His book, translated as "My Struggle," outlined plans to conquer Europe.

$600 - Lenin called him ruthless, and his purges proved he was.

$800 - He was both an American and British General in the Revolutionary War.

$1000 - After the deed, he leaped to the stage shouting "sic semper tyrannis."

4-Letter Words

$200 - Pulled the trigger or what's in a jigger.

$400 - Basketball defense or Serling's twilight area.

$600 - Little girls do it with a rope, Van Halen does it in a song.

$800 - DAILY DOUBLE   It's the first 4-letter word in "The Star-Spangled Banner."

$1000 - The President takes one before stepping into office.

FINAL JEOPARDY

Category: Holidays

The third Monday of January starting in 1986.

Now for the correct responses:

Lakes & Rivers

$100 - What is the Jordan?
$200 - What is loch?
$300 - What is the Volga?
$400 - What is the Missouri River?
$500 - What is the Caspian Sea?

Inventions

$100 - What is the radio?
$200 - What is a rickshaw?
$300 - What is freezing?
$400 - What is a zipper?
$500 - What is the parachute?

Animals

$100 - What are rats (or mice)?
$200 - What is the trunk?
$300 - What is weasel?
$400 - What is a hippopotamus?
$500 - What is a mule?

Foreign Cuisine

$100 - What is chicken?
$200 - What is sausage?
$300 - What is a blintz?
$400 - What is chateaubriand?
$500 - What is potpourri?

Actors & Roles

$100 - What is "Thriller"?
$200 - Who are Dan Aykroyd & Eddie Murphy?
$300 - Who is Sean Connery?
$400 - Who was Marilyn Monroe?
$500 - Who is Chuck Yeager?

The Bible

$200 - What are the walls?
$400 - Who was Judas?
$600 - What was the forbidden fruit? (Accept: Fruit of the Tree of Knowledge.)

$800 - What is Jerusalem?
$1000 - What is the love of money?

'50s TV
$200 - What is private detective?
$400 - Who is Eve Arden?
$600 - What is one million dollars?
$800 - Who was Paladin? (Accept: Richard Boone.)
$1000 - What is "Mr. Wizard"?

National Landmarks
$200 - What is the Statue of Liberty?
$400 - What is Mt. Vernon?
$600 - What is Plymouth Rock?
$800 - What is Independence Hall?
$1000 - What is the Capitol?

Weights & Measures
$200 - What is "20,000 Leagues Under the Sea"?
$400 - What is the bel? (Accept: decibel.)
$600 - What is a barrel?
$800 - What is the circumference?
$1000 - What is the Metric System?

Notorious
$200 - Who was Nero?
$400 - Who was Hitler?
$600 - Who was Stalin?
$800 - Who was Benedict Arnold?
$1000 - Who was John Wilkes Booth?

4-Letter Words
$200 - What is "Shot"?
$400 - What is "zone"?
$600 - What is "jump"?
$800 - What is "what"?
$1000 - What is an "oath"?

FINAL JEOPARDY

What is Martin Luther King Day?

Written hurriedly many years ago, this game probably seems somewhat primitive compared to Jeopardy games of later seasons. The articles "a" and "the" and words such as "it's" which help clarify what we're going for are often missing. That's because Jules and the rest of us assumed we were to write in the style of the old Jeopardy where those words were often left out to conserve the limited space they had on the printed cards. On the whole, the game seems rather easy, which it was supposed to be, although the "rickshaw" clue seems tough for the $200 position. In later seasons, we would not have had a reference to the Bible, such as in the Lakes & Rivers clue about the Jordan, in a game that also had a Bible category.

Something unusual happened during the second program. Jules had written the Final Jeopardy for that show. The category was The Calendar and the clue read, "Calendar date on which the 20th century began." All three contestants responded "What was January 1, 1900?" All three contestants were incorrect. All three had bet all the money they had in the game and all three therefore ended up with no money. As a result no one was the champion for that program and we had to start the third show with three brand new players.

That was the first and only time in my seven years with Jeopardy that all three contestants ended up at zero. Subsequently the contestant coordinators would warn the players of that possibility, which is why you often see contestants betting everything they have save one dollar.

By the way the correct response to that Final Jeopardy clue is "What was January 1, 1901?" This is something many people have difficulty understanding. A new century always begins in a year ending with the number one, not zero. The Twenty-first Century will begin on January 1, 2001, not 2000. The reason for this is simple. A century consists of 100 years, not 99. Historically speaking, there was no year zero. The First Century AD therefore ran from the year One through the year 100. The Second Century began with the year 101 AD and so on.

For the next five years, towards the beginning of each new season, we did a variation on when a century begins as a Final Jeopardy. For example, "The first U.S. presidential election of the Twenty-first Century will be held in this year" or "It will be the first leap year of the Twenty-first Century." In those subsequent times we always had a player who knew the correct response but we always had some who didn't and we always got letters from viewers who didn't quite understand why the year 2000 will not be the start of the Twenty-first Century.

Also in that second show we had a category we called Homonyms. Some of the clues read: "It stops a car or ends a fast." What is a break (brake)? "Orville, Wilbur, or Mr." What is Wright (right)? "Wheaties or 'The Edge of Night' " What is a cereal (serial)? "Spelled one way it's to burn to the ground; the other, to lift to the sky." What is raze (raise)?

After that show aired we got some letters from viewers complaining those weren't homonyms at all but homophones. Homonyms, they claimed, are words which sound alike *and are spelled alike* but have different meanings, such as "bore," meaning to make a hole and "bore," meaning to tire with dullness. Words which sound alike *but are spelled differently* are not homonyms, they said, but *homophones*. We checked the dictionary definitions and found that homonyms are not necessarily spelled alike, but to satisfy these viewers we from then on always referred to words which sound alike but are spelled differently as homophones.

We had plenty of time to think about how the material was playing that first tape day, as the equipment kept breaking down. Fortunately the Channel 11 studios were fairly modern and the air conditioning worked well. By the time we finished, around 11 P.M., there were only about eight people left in the audience. They had the staff members fill in seats for the final "head shot," which shows the backs of the heads of about 15 or so people in the audience while they are running the show's credits. Applause was of course dubbed in. To encourage people to come and be in the studio audience, Jeopardy gives away two or three door prizes in a drawing at the end of each taping session. That first night those eight remaining audience members had pretty good odds.

On the whole, the material had played rather easy that day. The contestants missed relatively few clues, and Bob was pleased about that. Alex was quite nervous, however, though you could hardly blame him, and I'm sure he would be the first to admit his performance on those first few shows was rather stiff. It didn't take him long to loosen up. By the second week of tapings he was the smooth, suave and glib Alex millions have come to admire.

Like Alex, we too were nervous, but of course nobody saw us. The TV ratings wars are sort of like sports competition in that you want very much to win. But unlike sports where the last place finishers can come back the next season to try again, if you don't do well in the ratings game, you don't come back at all. In other words, Jeopardy had to do well or we would all spend the next Christmas holiday period in the ranks of the unemployed. It may have been hard to support a family on $450 a week in Los Angeles but unemployment insurance paid a lot less. I believe it was about $175 a week (maximum) back then.

The first Jeopardy programs featuring Alex aired in September, 1984. There was a great deal of ballyhoo in the press about the return of one of the most popular game shows of all time, and the newspapers and wire services were quick to seek out Art Fleming for his reaction. Art was living in St. Louis at the time and doing a radio talk show.

According to some accounts, Art was angry at not having been invited back to do the new version of Jeopardy. He pointed out that in the 11 years he'd done the show, he never missed a taping for illness or any other reason. Some claimed that Merv hadn't invited Art back because he was now older and had put on some weight. In any case, Art told his interviewers that the new show was too easy and therefore not to be compared with the old Jeopardy, which had long set the standard for an intellectually challenging TV quiz show.

PR spokespeople for Jeopardy and King World denied that the show had gotten easier. It was just that those fans who remembered the old show were now that much older and had therefore acquired more knowledge over the years, which made the current show look easier. Or, to put it another way, they were younger when they watched the Art Fleming version and didn't know as much, which made that version of the show seem harder.

In fact the new show, when it debuted in 1984, had deliberately been made easier. However, as the weeks went on and it became clear the contestants had no difficulty in handling the material, we were allowed to make the clues tougher.

People who have watched the show over the years can probably tell it has gone through a number of cycles of harder and easier material. When top management wanted us to ease up the material, we always did, and when they wanted us to toughen it, we did that as well.

We didn't want the contestants to miss more than five to seven clues, at most, in a game. On the other hand, we didn't want the material so easy that the entire game was reduced to nothing more than a contest to see who was fastest to ring in. One time that Merv wanted us to toughen up the material came in the fall of 1989, after New York City Transit Authority policeman Frank Spangenberg became the first Jeopardy contestant to win over $100,000 in regular competition (that is, prior to the Tournament of Champions). I don't want to take away anything from what Officer Spangenberg accomplished, because he was an excellent player and he certainly beat the competition. He did happen, however, to be on during an easier cycle, and that didn't hurt. His employment as a New York subway cop, where you have to be alert constantly, probably didn't hurt his finger reflexes for ringing in on the clues.

In September 1984, although the critics thought the show was on the easy side compared to the old version, they were nonetheless quite pleased to see it back on the air. Eased up or not, it was still the toughest game show around, and in that sense it was in a league by itself. Reviews on Alex were mixed. Some claimed he lacked the warmth of Art Fleming. However, with time he won over just about everyone. Eventually he became so popular that in the '90–'91 season he became the first person to simultaneously host three ongoing, five-day-a-week game shows. Besides Jeopardy, he was at that time already doing "Classic Concentration" for NBC when he took on the emcee role on "To Tell The Truth," which was also carried by NBC.

THE RATINGS GAME

Despite the general critical approval, in those early days of the show our ratings situation was very much touch and go. New York is important because it is the largest media market in the country. In New York we were on the NBC-owned-and-operated Channel 4. Story had it that King World had gone to them first because they had carried the old Jeopardy nationwide. Still, they had so much confidence in this new version of the show that they put us on at two o'clock in the morning. Fortunately we were already in the era of the VCR and those die-hard Jeopardy fans who had to go to work the next day could set their VCRs and watch us later.

In Los Angeles, the nation's number two market, things weren't much better. There we were on Channel 2, a CBS owned-and-operated station, at 3:30 or 4 or in the afternoon, when most people are either still at work, on their way home from work or starting to prepare dinner. After two months they cancelled the show altogether. At that point it really felt strange working on a show you could neither watch nor tape at home. And so we found ourselves going into the November sweeps, a key ratings period that determines the value of advertising on the show for the next few months, almost nowhere in the nation's top market and literally nowhere in the second market.

The November sweeps turned out to be a pleasant surprise despite New York and L. A. We did especially well in Cleveland and Detroit, two major markets in which King World managed to get the show on in the access hour. The access hour is the hour Monday through Saturday prior to when the networks start the prime time programming. In the Eastern and Pacific time zones it is seven to eight PM and one hour earlier in the Central and Mountain zones. A few years back, the Federal Communications Commission (FCC), which has always encouraged local programming, concluded there was a need for more shows of local interest and therefore created the access hour, forbidding the networks to offer their affiliates national programming after the evening news and prior to eight PM (seven Central and Mountain time).

The FCC thought that would encourage more local programming, which it did to a degree. But many local network affiliates were either unwilling, unable, or both to produce that new local programming. Instead, they simply opted to buy syndicated programming. It was that loophole in the law that made Merv Griffin one of the richest men in America. While some stations decided to buy syndicated reruns, many preferred first-run syndicated programming such as "Wheel of Fortune" and Jeopardy, both of which were owned and produced by Merv.

Both "Wheel" and Jeopardy did particularly well in that access hour, finally demonstrating once and for all that game shows weren't only for people who stayed at home during the day. In New York King World was able to move Jeopardy to ABC, which had it on briefly in daytime before embarking on a bold move. In the Big Apple, all three networks' evening news broadcasts had traditionally been on opposite one another, at 7 P.M. ABC broke with that by moving Peter Jennings up to 6:30 and putting Jeopardy on opposite Dan Rather and Tom Brokaw. As a result ABC's "World News Tonight" took a jump in the ratings while Jeopardy clobbered "The CBS Evening News" and "NBC Nightly News." Both Jeopardy and the national news tend to appeal to the more intelligent, educated viewer and ABC was able to line up the two programs in such a way they supported one another. Needless to say, Jeopardy was very popular with the people at ABC News in New York, and they later had reporter Bob Brown come out to do a nice "20/20" segment on us.

Management was sufficiently pleased with the ratings that we were each given a $50-a-week raise. It was the first and last time in my seven years at Jeopardy that I ever got a raise at any time other than at the start of a new season. Still, it was a pleasant surprise.

Jeopardy's success that first year in Cleveland and Detroit enabled King World to sell it in the access hour in more and more markets, to where the show is now on at that time almost everywhere. The fact that we were on right before or after lottery drawings in Cleveland and Detroit didn't hurt either. In any case it wasn't too long before "Wheel" and Jeopardy became the two highest-rated U.S. syndicated series of all time.

CHAPTER 3

WRITERS AND RESEARCHERS

Writing for Jeopardy was considerably harder than writing for any other game show. First you had to transpose your question and answer into the backwards answer/question format. Then you had to make sure it would fit within the allotted space. Finally you had to be sure your spelling and punctuation were correct since Jeopardy clues, unlike the questions used on most game shows, appear on screen.

The fact that Jeopardy clues appear on screen is, by the way, one of the show's hidden strengths. Merv Griffin may have been the first to come up with that concept and if so, he certainly deserves credit for it. What it does is enable the information we are conveying to reach the viewer's mind via the eye as well as the ear. In this way the show has a greater impact on the viewer and he is more likely to be drawn in to play along, than if the clues were only read aloud.

That first season we were under a tremendous amount of stress. Jules needed the material as quickly as he could get his hands on it and sometimes lost his temper if it wasn't sufficiently to his liking. All the while we had to work like madmen trying to keep up with the tight schedule. Those of us who had the ability had to produce extra material to make up for those who were producing less. The problem was that we had started taping that year with a rather small backlog of games already written. Jules vowed that for next season we would begin the August tapings with no less than 100 games ready to be used.

In the meantime, I felt as if we were literally throwing material at the Chyron computer system, which had become an insatiable monster whose appetite for more and more material could never be fully satisfied. No sooner would we have a category written than we would run it in to Jules for his approval. Jules had reached the point where he was looking for material from anywhere he could find it. He asked Bob Boden if he'd like to contribute some categories on a freelance basis and Bob was pleased to do that. Lots of people wanted to work for Jeopardy, many just so they could say "I wrote for Jeopardy." But the glamour does wear off eventually. The stress of having to work evenings and weekends in a desperate attempt to keep up does do that to you. Then once taping began, numerous additional tasks would arise that had to be done.

On many shows, Alex didn't have enough time to clear the game board. Most often this was due to situations recurring in which a contestant didn't answer a clue correctly and others would ring in. That meant additional time being used up *on the same clue*. The more that happens, the less likely Alex is to clear a board.

Many wonder what happens to those clues that are left over. If a whole category is left on the board untouched, it is kept intact and simply re-used in a later game. I recall Sailing and Honduras categories that took at least three games to dispose of, since the contestants kept shying away from them. Remaining clues that constituted part of a category are returned to the writer who wrote them. These include not only the clues on the board that went unused but also all the unused "extras" the viewers never see and don't know about. If a writer gets back three American History clues, the logical thing is to write three more and he'll have a complete category to turn in. If a writer has an assortment of leftover clues from different categories, he can combine them in a category we called Leftovers.

It was important to get all the unused clues back to the writers so they could be recycled as quickly as possible. Since no one else wanted the job, I took it. The day after tapings, I would go through all the clue cards of the ten games that had just been used. I would pull out the ones that hadn't played and return them to their writers. I needed to retrieve my unused clues to help meet my quota and the other writers needed theirs as well. Some were good clues I really looked forward to seeing in games. Others were weak, less interesting clues that had been designated as extras, which was where many borderline clues tended to end up. They were good enough to be extras but not really good enough to be in the regular game. As Barbara Heller used to say, "Always a bridesmaid, never a bride." Over the years I've seen some clues serve as extras in ten or more games.

We were a few weeks into the taping season when Steven asked if he could write an entire show by himself. Jules needed material any way he could get it and had no objection. Alex agreed to the idea as well. We referred to shows written entirely by one person as signature games. Shortly after Steven did his I wrote the following game which first aired on January 11, 1985:

JEOPARDY ROUND

Famous Quotes

$100 - Nixon's Secretary of State who said, "Power is the ultimate aphrodisiac."

$200 - Country that's been called "a nation of shopkeepers."

$300 - J. Paul Getty supposedly said, "The meek shall inherit the earth but not" these rights.

$400 - Hamlet's "vocational" advice to Ophelia.

$500 - He wrote "All animals are created equal, but some are more equal than others."

Hungary

$100 - Probably Hungary's most famous citizen, thanks to his cube.

$200 - This famed magician apparently pulled off the trick of being born in both Budapest and Wisconsin.

$300 - "A man in love is incomplete until he marries; then he's finished," said this Hungarian actress.

$400 - AUDIO DAILY DOUBLE Though not a Hungarian, he's the composer of "Hungarian Dance No. 5." (Play "Hungarian Dance No. 5.")

$500 - To promote family ties, it's banned on Mondays in Hungary; on Thursdays in Iceland.

Trivia

$100 - He used to sing under the name Dino Martini.

$200 - Actor who entered a Charlie Chaplain look-alike contest and came in third.

$300 - The first heir to the British throne to have earned a university degree.

$400 - Canadian P.M.'s ex who reportedly said, "Castro is the sexiest man I've ever met."

$500 - British Prime Minister known for "Peace in our time."

Gambling

$100 - The expressionless visage of an expert 5-card draw player.

$200 - Theoretically, you can beat this game by card counting.

$300 - Illegal daily lottery common in poor areas of large cities.

$400 - Card game in which the desired total value is 9.

$500 - Number that's missing on European roulette wheels.

Business & Industry

$100 - "I wish I was" one of this family that's America's biggest hot dog maker.

$200 - Pillsbury broils its hamburgers under this name.

$300 - Country that's home to the Nestle Corporation.

$400 - This company's President, Victor Kiam, asks, "What have you got to lose except your whiskers?"

$500 - Pilot of Staten Island Ferry, he became 19th Century shipping and railroad tycoon.

Wild About Harry

$100 - Clint Eastwood has played this tough guy in 4 films.

$200 - Only President born In Missouri.

$300 - Revolutionary War hero and father of Robert E. Lee

$400 - The only blonde in "Blondie."

$500 - Big band era trumpeter who married Betty Grable.

DOUBLE JEOPARDY

Geology

$200 - It's a fault's fault that these occur.

$400 - Many a fool has taken iron pyrites for this.

$600 - Weak chemical bonds cause it to occur in crystals; low-cut dresses show it on women.

$800 - DAILY DOUBLE Rising 30,000 ft. from the ocean floor, this world's largest active volcano is in Hawaii.

$1000 - Lou Henry, first U.S. woman geology grad, was married to this mining engineer President.

Music on the Map

$200 - "Start spreading the news, I'm leaving" for there.

$400 - To John Denver it's "almost heaven."

$600 - Where Linda Ronstadt is "glad to be livin'."

$800 - Harry Belafonte's "Mathilda" took his money and ran there.

$1000 - Roy Acuff's Indiana express.

Wars

$200 - Though illiterate, she was the military genius who defeated the English at Orleans.

$400 - Sales of this drug set off 19th Century was between Britain and China.

$600 - Picasso's "guernica" protests bombing carried out in this war.

$800 - In 1986 this East African country defeated Italy.

$1000 - DAILY DOUBLE Side George Washington was on in French & Indian war.

Laws and Principles

$200 - The Bible says this "is more blessed that to receive."
$400 - Law discovered by Newton while under an apple tree.
$600 - Columnist Walter Morrow's "Economics in 8 Words" says, "There's no such thing as" this.
$800 - According to George Bernard Shaw. "Those who can, do; while those who can't," do this.
$1000 - Parkinson's 2nd law says expenditures rise to meet this.

Presidents

$200 - His grandfather was mayor of Boston.
$400 - '70s President who, as a model, once appeared on Look Magazine.
$600 - He considered his greatest honor becoming Supreme Court Justice.
$800 - Said he could either run the country or control daughter Alice "but not both."
$1000 - After his term ended in 1829, he served 17 years in the house as a foe of slavery.

Starts With "X"

$200 - Company which urges people not to use its name as synonym for photocopy.
$400 - Once an L.A. Times cartoonist, this bandleader was married to Abbe Lane & Charo.
$600 - Fear of foreigners.
$800 - King Ahasuerus of Biblical Book of Esther was probably this powerful Persian King.
$1000 - Mexican city famed for its floating gardens.

FINAL JEOPARDY

Category: Food
By weight of total catch, the world's leading fishing nation.

Now for the correct responses:

Famous Quotes

$100 - Who is Henry Kissinger?
$200 - What is England?
$300 - What are the mineral rights?
$400 - What is "Get thee to a nunnery?"
$500 - Who was George Orwell?

Hungary
$100 - Who is (Erno) Rubik?
$200 - Who was Harry Houdini? (Accept: Erich Weiss)
$300 - Who is Zsa Zsa Gabor?
$400 - Who was (Johannes) Brahms?
$500 - What is television?

Trivia
$100 - Who is Dean Martin?
$200 - Who was Charlie Chaplin?
$300 - Who is Prince Charles?
$400 - Who is Margaret Trudeau?
$500 - Who was Neville Chamberlain?

Gambling
$100 - What is a poker face?
$200 - What is blackjack (or 21)?
$300 - What are the numbers?
$400 - What is baccarat? (Accept: Chemin de fer)
$500 - What is double zero?

Business & Industry
$100 - Who is Oscar Mayer?
$200 - What is Burger King?
$300 - What is Switzerland?
$400 - What is Remington?
$500 - Who was Cornelius Vanderbilt?

Wild About Harry
$100 - Who is Dirty Harry?
$200 - Who was Harry S. Truman?
$300 - Who was "Light Horse Harry" Lee?
$400 - Who is Deborah (Debbie) Harry?
$500 - Who was Harry James?

Geology
$200 - What are earthquakes.
$400 - What is gold?
$600 - What is cleavage?
$800 - What is Mauna Loa?
$1000 - Who was Herbert Hoover?

Music on the Map
$200 - What is New York, NY?
$400 - What is West Virginia?
$600 - What is (in) the U.S.A.?
$800 - What is Venezuela?
$1000 - What is the Wabash Cannonball?

Wars
$200 - Who was Joan of Arc?
$400 - What is opium?
$600 - What was the Spanish Civil War?
$800 - What is Ethiopia?
$1000 - What was the British side?

Laws and Principles
$200 - What is to give?
$400 - What is gravity?
$600 - What is a free lunch?
$800 - What is teach?
$1000 - What is income?

Presidents
$200 - Who was John F. Kennedy?
$400 - Who is Gerald Ford?
$600 - Who was William Howard Taft?
$800 - Who was Teddy Roosevelt?
$1000 - Who was John Quincy Adams?

Starts with "X"
$200 - What is Xerox?
$400 - Who is Xavier Cugat?
$600 - What is Xenophobia?
$800 - Who was Xerxes?
$1000 - What is Xochimilco?

FINAL JEOPARDY

What Is Japan?

As was the case with the first show, we were still writing the games quite hurriedly and with a minimum of research. "Wild About Harry" for $400 would have been clearer had we said "the rock group

'Blondie' " Also, once we became more sophisticated we wouldn't have had a clue about Herbert Hoover on the same board as an entire "Presidents" category. Likewise, the Final Jeopardy clue was as much about Business and Industry as about Food, while the overall writing style still resembled that of the old Jeopardy.

"Trivia" was a common category in those early years of the show until Merv let it be known he hated the term. Which is not to say we ever stopped writing the stuff. Trivia may not be profound but it's fun and entertaining. For example: "All bearded U.S Presidents belonged to this political party. What is the Republican Party." Not of earth-shattering significance, but interesting nevertheless. All the Democrats, by the way, were clean-shaven, except for Grover Cleveland, who sported a walrus mustache. Needless to say, Jeopardy has never stopped running trivia categories. But since Merv prefers the illusion of *significa*, we ran the categories under headings like Potpourri, Pot Luck, Hodgepodge, Odds and Ends, or Leftovers, with an occasional Mishmash or Goulash thrown in. Later the word "trivia" started creeping back into our category titles.

APPOINTED AS A JUDGE

We started that first season of Jeopardy pretty much on a trial and error basis. As producer, Alex wanted the best show possible and each time a weakness or error in the show was found, he did his utmost to correct it. Alex concluded it would be good to have an additional judge besides Jules, as two heads are better than one. With my academic background, particularly in history, I was selected to fill that slot.

That of course meant from then on I would have to be present at all tapings. Up to that time Jules had also been operating a switch which activated the contestants' signalling buttons. That first season Jules would immediately flip the switch as soon as the clue was revealed on the board, which is how it was done on the old Jeopardy. When I started going to the tapings to assist with the judging, Jules asked me to take over the switch so he could better concentrate on the material, and I did.

Tape days would begin with Jules calling or being called by someone from the network Compliance and Practices Department. At first it was NBC but it soon became ABC when the show was moved to the ABC-owned- and-operated flagship station in New York. All game shows, even syndicated ones, are overseen by a Compliance and Practices department in order to make sure that the games are fair and totally on the up and up. This was an outgrowth of the quiz show scandals of the late fifties. A Compliance and Practices representative is therefore present at each taping and makes sure that all contestants are treated fairly and equally. If a contestant feels he was in some way dealt with unjustly, he has the right to appeal to Compliance and Practices and they will thoroughly investigate the complaint.

In those days we did everything humanly possible to be scrupulously fair and to avoid even the appearance of any possible wrongdoing. Any person related to or even just acquainted with anyone on the Jeopardy staff or other employees of Merv Griffin Enterprises was automatically disqualified from being a contestant. The contestant coordinators could not have access to the material and we on the writing and research staffs did not know in advance when any particular contestant would play. In fact, the contestants themselves were not told in which particular game they would be playing until just before that game was to be taped.

Prior to a tape day we didn't even know which games were to be used that day. The purpose of the phone call in the morning was to have the Compliance and Practices person pick out the five games to be used that day at random, by game number. Originally we gave them a pool of ten from which to pick. Later, as it became harder to keep up with the taping schedule and we were running low on material, they allowed us to reduce the pool to eight.

After the C & P rep made the pick, it was my job to obtain three sets of copies of the games selected from production coordinator Linda Smith. I gave Jules his set of copies and saved one for myself. The third set was for Alex but before I gave it to him, I had one more thing to do. Suzanne Stone had gathered up all the game cards for the games we would be using—the ones the writers had originally typed their material onto. She then separated the cards that had asterisks on them. Those contained the clues for which the writers had added some point of explanation or comment for Alex. Suzanne then gave me the cards and I reviewed the ones with asterisks. Any of the comments I thought Alex might want to use, I wrote onto his copy in red. On average I would say he used maybe 25% of the comments we gave him—more if he felt he had the time to spare, less if he felt he was running out of time.

I then gave Alex his copies and the three of us, Alex, Jules and I, individually went over the games, primarily to re-familiarize ourselves with the material that would play that day, but also to spot any last minute changes that might be necessary to make. Alex and Jules also went over the music for Audio Daily Doubles, deciding which part of a recording was best to use to fit the clue. In those days, Audio Daily Doubles were very much a part of the show, a brief musical interlude to provide a change of pace. They had been popular on the old Jeopardy and that first season we had one in just about every program.

After we went over the games, Alex, Jules and I met to discuss them and point out any changes any of us felt were necessary. At this point in time we wanted to keep changes to an absolute minimum. Generally the only changes we made at the last minute were to correct grammar and spelling errors that had slipped through or clues that had become incorrect due to changes in the news that had taken place since the original clue had been written. Jules also made it a point to apprise Alex of any category that needed to be introduced in a unique way or required a special explanation of some sort.

It was then my job to inform the Production Department of the changes, so they would have them for their copies, which they used to follow the game in the control booth. After that, I went to the Chyron booth in the studio, where I had Chyron operator Doris Diaz (now Montes) make the changes. Doris is a pleasant lady from Brooklyn who married a marine and is now a mother. She always came in on tape days to operate the Chyron. Since the tapings were done according to schedule, they did not require last minute calls and so the pay was a little less than the other Chyron work. Patrice therefore didn't want the job but recommended Doris. Doris had been with the show from the outset and even drove in from Las Vegas when she lived there for a time.

Finally, I had to inform the Compliance and Practices representative of the changes and she would be sure to enter them on her copy. At first I had to explain the reason for each and every change. With time, the C & P people saw we were making every effort to run an honest and above board show and a relationship of trust developed to where I no longer had to explain the changes.

I was quite busy on tape days, putting in a 10-hour work day. Having to activate the switch at precisely the right moment, time and time again, really took it out of you. Dan and Rachelle got used to Dad coming home late on those nights and I would generally crash as soon as I could, especially on the second night of tapings.

Then there was my category quota to keep up with. Since I could no longer write on tape days, I found myself writing eight categories a day on non-tape days. I suppose I could have done less, but I liked the work, even though it was tiring. Rather than ask for a smaller quota because of my additional tape-day duties, I asked Alex for a raise. He couldn't disagree with the justice of my request, but said management would allow no further expansion of his budget. He promised I would be paid more than the other writers come next season.

MORE CORRECT ANSWERS

In the meantime, there was still this season to deal with. From time to time we were having problems at the tapings with contestants coming up with unexpected responses. I remember one short clue under the category "Starts with 'A.' " The clue read simply "A bird's abode." The response we were looking for was "What is an aviary?" A contestant rang in and said, "What is an aerie?" It didn't sound right and so we ruled against the contestant. At the commercial break we looked up "aerie" in our dictionaries. It's defined as "the nest of an eagle or other predatory bird built on a crag or other high place." As such, it did fit the clue and we therefore reversed ourselves and credited the contestant.

On most game shows they would have stopped the tape and looked it up as soon as the contestant said it. They would have then resumed the game and the viewers would never notice a problem. However, Alex hated to stop tape as it broke his rhythm and he was always rushing to get as much material in as possible before time ran out.

To try to avoid this problem of alternate correct responses, Alex requested that the writers as a group go over the material after the various category strips had been organized into games. We called it "roundtabling" the game. Jules or one of the writers would read the clues as the rest of us tried to come up with the correct response. If we found an alternate answer that worked, we could add it in as an additional acceptable response. For example, under U.S. Presidents, if the clue read, "This President was a graduate of West Point," both Eisenhower and Grant would be acceptable responses. If the category were just "Presidents" someone would have also been correct had he said, "Jefferson Davis." If a clue had too many possible responses, it would be considered "unpinned" and would have to be replaced. A clue under U.S. States that reads "This state was once an independent country" is unpinned. Too many states fit. They include Vermont, Texas, Hawaii, and California. Some might even say Tennessee, arguing that eastern Tennessee was an independent country under John Sevier, when it was known as the state of Franklin. And there might be other possibilities as well, such as South Carolina when it first seceded from the Union. On the other hand, if we said "This state was once an independent monarchy," that would be pinned. In that case, the only possible correct response would be "What is Hawaii?"

On another occasion we had this clue: "Humans can catch psittacosis, a feverish disease, from these birds." Psittacosis also is known as parrot fever and the intended response was "What are parrots?" At the roundtable session the question was raised as to whether parrots are the only birds that carry parrot fever. When we pursued the matter we learned there are a number of other birds that sometimes carry the disease. It was simply too much trouble to try and put together a list of all the other birds in which the disease occurs and so that particular clue was dropped.

In going over the games in these roundtabling sessions, we sometimes found other problems. France might be mentioned in a clue under Literature, only to be the correct response to another clue in a World Geography category. Obviously one or the other would have to be replaced. Generally, the writer of whichever clue came second (and third, which sometimes happened as well) would have to replace their clue with a new one, but could get back the old one to use later.

Finally, the roundtable would consider the order of difficulty of the clues. If we found a higher-valued clue easier than a lower-valued one, we would suggest the clues be reversed. Sometimes Jules agreed with us, sometimes not.

Jules was under so much pressure to keep putting out additional games that he concluded he could be going over material with one writer while the rest of us roundtabled the games. And so he put me in charge of roundtabling the games as well.

Everything seemed to evolve that first season. Just as we could have two mentions of France in the same game, we might have three mentions of Indonesia in a group of five games to be taped the same day.

We found we could program the computer to run printouts of the game material with all clues listed by key words. We could cue in the particular game numbers in a certain pool to be offered to Compliance and Practices and get a printout by key words for just those games.

Let me explain how key words work. We had a clue in a Food category which read "Jewish crepe filled with cheese." The response: "What is a blintz?" Jewish, crepe, cheese and blintz are all key words here, since any one of them could possibly be the correct response to another clue. And so that clue would be entered under all four key words.

This clue, under Islands has only two key word listings: "New York's largest, it has more people than 41 of our 50 states. What is Long Island?" The key words here are New York and Long Island.

Jules and I would run these printouts and go over the key words. If the same key word turned up in two or more responses, one would have to be replaced. Sometimes we could use the extra clue for this purpose if it didn't conflict. If it did, we had to get a new clue from the writer. If a key word occurred once in a clue and once in a response, it would depend on the order in which the games played. If the one in which the key word was in the correct response played first, no problem. If the one in which the key word was in the clue played first, it could tip off the correct answer for the one in which it was in the response.

Compliance and Practices allowed us to set the order of the games once they made a pick. What we would therefore do in the instance described above would be to make a list indicating if so-and-so game were picked, it should play before so-and-so game, so the correct response wouldn't be given away in an earlier game taped the same day and seen by the same group of contestants.

Jules and I would do this a day or two before taping. After we went over the material, I would type up a summary of the changes to be made and turn it over to the Production Department. They would enter those changes on all copies of the games while I would meet with Patrice in the Chyron room to enter those changes in the Chyron.

Jules had originally assigned a Final Jeopardy clue to each game when he assembled the game, but we soon found there could be conflicts between the Finals and material in the earlier parts of the game. We concluded it would be best to assign Finals to the games at this point, when we had the key word printout with which to compare them. I then gave copies of the selected Final Jeopardies to Production and had them entered in the Chyron.

Another change we would make had to do with the categories of clues. We wanted to make the games as interesting and diverse as possible. Often a Presidents or Civil War category might occur two or even more times in a pool and both would be among those picked by Compliance and Practices. To make sure the viewers knew they were seeing a new, different category, we came up with alternate titles for many of the categories. Though we usually called it Presidents or U.S. Presidents, we sometimes called it Hail to the Chief. The Civil War was sometimes changed to The Blue and the Grey. Birds became Feathered Friends while Potent Potables became Bottoms Up. Business and Industry could become Business Biggies or Corporate America, provided the clues fit those latter categories. Of course there were some category titles such as Foreign Phrases and Opera for which we had no alternate titles.

The repetition of some categories was annoying Alex and towards the end of the season, he decided to try something different. Our weekly taping pool consisted of 13 games. Compliance and Practices would pick five out of eight to be used the first tape day and five out

of the remaining eight the second day. Alex decided to plan a pool of
13 games by selecting the categories for each game in advance. No
category would occur twice in the pool. The categories were then assigned to the individual writers to create the material.

That seemed to work okay and so Jules designed a set of 13 templates. Each represented a single game of 12 categories. Each tem-
plate called for a variety of categories: One might call for a U.S. History, a World Geography, a Literature, Movies, two Word Plays etc.
Within those guidelines the writer could select which specific categories he would like to do. For example, The American Revolution would
qualify under U.S. History; World Capitals under World Geography,
etc. Jules would keep track of all 13 templates to make sure no category would be repeated within the pool. This worked fine—up to a
point.

Each week we would tape ten games out of a pool of 13. But the
three games that were left over would have to be used eventually. Later
on, we would have pools consisting entirely of games that had been
left over from other pools and there were a great many category conflicts within those. And so we were back to changing the names of
categories for the sake of variety. I didn't think that was so bad. After
all, the material in each category was quite different and we had a
balanced assortment of categories in each game.

Later on we dropped the idea of templates for the pools of games.
In subsequent years we were able to go into taping season with between 80 and 100 games written in advance. One of my jobs was to
create pools well in advance, when there were lots of games to choose
from, in order to keep repetition of categories to a minimum. I got
Steven to help me with that. He also assisted in going over the key
word printouts and doing the game-change memo when Jules put me
in charge of those the second season.

SALE OF THE CENTURY

I had been sharing an office with Michelle Johnson. As the mother of
two children, she was sympathetic to my plight as a single parent.
Her husband, Gary, worked for Reg Grundy Productions where, until
recently he'd been head writer for "Sale of the Century," a daytime Q
& A show on NBC. He was then named producer of "Scrabble," a
new game show Grundy was doing for NBC based on the famous word
game. Michelle heard there was an opening for a writer on "Sale" and
told me about it. All of Reg Grundy's writers were Guild members
and that meant a salary of at least $585 a week which was $85 more
than I was getting at Jeopardy. In addition, there was the pension plan

as well as the promise of steady work, while at Jeopardy there were rumors of an impending temporary layoff at the end of the season.

I decided to apply for the job at "Sale." I called the show's producer, George Vosburgh. He told me to come up with a sample of 25 questions and answers. That wouldn't take long to do, I figured, so I made an appointment to meet with him as well.

The Reg Grundy offices are on the west side of Los Angeles, about five miles from Hollywood. I went over there and submitted my material to George. George Vosburgh had originally been a dancer on the "Your Hit Parade" TV show in the 1950s and on Broadway. He somehow got in with Merv and had worked on the old Jeopardy in New York. He went on to become producer of the short-lived 1978 version of Jeopardy in Hollywood.

While we were going over the material I met Burt Wheeler, who had become the show's head writer after Gary left to produce "Scrabble." Burt had been named for and is the grandson of the late, famous U.S. senator from Montana, Burton K. Wheeler.

After a brief chat with Burt, George called me back to his office. He liked my material and wanted to know when I could start. I told him I would give Jeopardy the customary two weeks' notice, after which I was all his. George indicated he needed somebody right away. It was a tough decision but I turned down George's offer. I told him I didn't have the heart to just walk away, without any advance notice, from Jeopardy in the middle of their taping season when they were under such pressure for material.

I did feel a sense of loyalty to Alex and Jules. After all, they had hired me and trained me. I knew I was working hard and was underpaid for what I was doing. Still, I considered Alex a straight shooter and wanted to do the right thing by him. Two weeks' notice, which is rather standard in the business world would be fair, I figured. But George had to have someone right away and so that was the end of that. There is something in the nature of television that just about everything, it seems, gets done at the last minute. I told Michelle what had happened but didn't mention it to anyone else at the time. It's hard to say whether or not I'd have been better off going to "Sale," since that show was eventually cancelled in 1989.

Back at Jeopardy we were coming precariously close to running out of material. We got a break when some tape dates had to be cancelled because they conflicted with director Dick Schneider's obligations to the Macy's Thanksgiving Day parade in New York.

Since no one wanted to work at Christmas, the taping schedule had to be pushed forward into January. That was no problem as far as the air dates went since we were dealing with shows that would be airing in late April and May, but it pretty much forced management to give us some time off at Christmas. They had been hoping to have the tapings completed by then, at which point we would have gotten laid off without pay. Instead they let us have up to two weeks off at Christmas, since some people had made plans to go home to spend the holidays with their families. The first week was given to us as paid vacation while the second week was optional; those who wanted to take off could do so without pay.

Just as we were starting to come into the holiday season, I got a lucky break myself. Steven Dorfman is very much into radio contests. You might call it a hobby, but it may be even more than that, as it virtually provides him with a second income. Now radio contest prizes tend to match the size of the particular station's market. Small markets. Small prizes. Big Markets. Big Prizes. Over the years Steven has literally won thousands of dollars in cash and other prizes.

It was Wednesday afternoon, about 4:30 PM, the day before Thanksgiving. Most people had already left work in order to keep their holiday plans. I was working away when suddenly Steven told me to grab a book on rock 'n' roll and look up "The Night Tripper." A local radio station, KMET, was asking what is the Night Tripper's real name and was giving away $1000 to the first person to call in with the correct answer.

The book said Malcolm John "Mac" Rebbenack. I called the station and told them "Malcolm John 'Mac' Rebbenack." The person on the phone said I was incorrect. Someone then called up and said "Mac Rebbenack." That person was ruled correct and told he'd won the $1000.

Steven and I felt a sense of outrage. Since the KMET studio was located on the same lot as Jeopardy we simply walked right over there, book in hand. It turned out the person who was answering the phone for the contest was a college student who was working there part-time as an intern. She was given "Mac Rebbenack" as the answer and assumed what I said was wrong. We spoke to the DJ and he told us to come back next Monday and speak with their director of promotions.

When we came back Monday the director of promotions agreed we were right. A few days later we got a check for $1000, which we divided between us. I used most of the money to buy a refrigerator, since the one in my apartment was on the blink.

Steven used to play radio contests all the time. One time a radio station offered a Sony Walkman to the first person who would bring them a small appliance. Since Steven had already won something from them that month he wasn't eligible. But the station wasn't very far away and it just so happened someone had a popcorn popper in the office. And so Steven sent Michelle over with the popcorn popper, making her the winner of the Walkman radio—and making her day a bit more interesting.

KFOX is a small station in Redondo Beach. Every afternoon they would have "Trivia Time" for a half hour. You would phone in for the opportunity to answer up to three questions. For each correct answer you got a prize. One wrong answer and your game was over. First you had to get through on the phone but that wasn't hard to do because the station had a limited range. You could just barely pick it up in Hollywood. You then selected a category from among Movies, TV, Music or Sports.

Steven had it set up that someone else from Jeopardy played just about every day. He advised them to select the TV category since he could then help them with the answers and if he didn't know, he could quickly look it up in a book, usually either *Total Television* or *The Complete Directory to Prime Time Network TV Shows*. At first he advised us not to say we were from Jeopardy, as he thought it would be embarrassing. We weren't doing anything against the rules: The rules didn't allow a person to win more than once in 30 days, but there was no rule about people helping one another or calling from the same office.

After a while someone inadvertently let the KFOX people know we were all from Jeopardy. It seemed rather embarrassing to me. But when they found out, they didn't seem to mind in the least. One of the first things they wanted to know was if there were any openings for writers on the show. Alex didn't particularly care for Steven playing contests from work, but he was a very prolific writer and always did more than his share of the work. And just about everyone else felt the radio games represented a nice break from the regular grind and thereby served as a morale booster.

Just before Christmas both Alex and Jules gave us gifts. Rather than give everyone the same thing, Alex would try to pick out each gift individually with the recipient in mind. That first year, he gave me a pair of his and her wine glasses. In my thank you note I told him I hoped they might portend romance in my future.

In Hollywood, TV shows customarily provide their staffs with warm-up jackets with the show's logo on the back and the person's name on the front. Since our management was not about to pop for something like that, Alex decided to pay half the cost out of his own pocket for anyone who wanted one. That meant we still had to pay $30, but everyone appreciated Alex's offer and just about everyone got one.

Everyone on staff was invited to Merv's Christmas party, which he put on each year for his employees. People had heard it wasn't anything too great, so few from Jeopardy showed up. I was curious, so I went anyway. The party was held in a large tent that was pitched in the parking lot of Merv's TAV building. It was a cold, damp night, and so there were heaters on inside. A band played and hors d'oeuvres were served. The highlight of the evening was when they gave away some door prizes which had been left over from "Wheel of Fortune." None of the handful of Jeopardy staffers present won. I recall walking up to Merv, introducing myself, and asking him how he liked what we were doing on Jeopardy. He said he was quite pleased.

Steven and I kept writing away that second holiday week while some of the others were gone. After New Year's it was back to working some evenings and weekends to keep cranking out the material. We had enough games for the first week of taping in 1985 but still had two more weeks to go. We managed to crank out enough material for the second week of tapings but the third looked really tight. We then got another reprieve but not in a way we would have liked.

ON HIATUS

We were all set to do that second week of tapings when Alex came down with kidney stones. We were sorry to hear that but knew it was a fairly routine surgical procedure. At first we didn't know if the tapings would be cancelled or not and there were rumors they might bring in Pat Sajak to take Alex's place. Alex had substituted for Pat on "Wheel" but Merv and Bob Murphy decided not to have Pat reciprocate. The host of Jeopardy needs to fly through the material at lightning speed in order to use up all, or nearly all, of it in the allotted time. It would be next to impossible for an inexperienced newcomer to do it. Perhaps they would fly in Art Fleming, some joked, but as much as Merv hated to lose the money due to the cancelled tapings (he had to pay for the studio crew and the use of the studio regardless), there was no way he would do that.

They now have a procedure by which they can dissolve kidney stones using lasers, so Alex's surgery went well and his recovery was speedy. He was back within two weeks and did the final programs of the first season without a hitch. The extra time enabled us to finish writing all the necessary game material. When the season ended we should have had reasons to rejoice.

Ratings-wise the show had been a resounding success, as it was in the top five of all syndicated programs. The show had proven exceptionally profitable for both Merv Griffin and King World and plans were afoot to sell the show in the access period in as many markets as possible. We were informed the show was officially going on "hiatus" for about two and a half months. Everything would be shut down for that length of time.

This was clearly going to be a problem for me. I had virtually no savings at the time and I didn't see how the three of us could live on $175 a week. I told Alex I was going to go out and look for another job. If I didn't find one, I would be happy to come back for another season of Jeopardy but if I did find another job I would simply stay there.

I guess Alex didn't want to lose me, as he got an OK from Bob Murphy for me to work at home through the hiatus. We had just come through a season where we'd been desperately short of material most of the time. Alex therefore convinced Bob it would be a good idea for me to spend the nine or ten weeks writing new material for the second season. Jules thought it was a good idea, too. Plans were afoot to augment the staff with additional researchers for the second season and this way there would be a supply of material available for them to work on right from the start.

Alex had hardly finished making those arrangements for me when he informed everyone he wasn't going to be coming back next season. At first I thought top management didn't want to retain him and couldn't understand why. I wrote a memo to Bob Murphy urging that Alex be brought back for next season saying "if it ain't broke, why fix it?"

In fact, it wasn't that they didn't want to keep Alex but like most of the rest of us, he thought his salary ridiculously small for what he was doing and wanted changes for next season. Unlike us, he at least enjoyed the benefit of being able to negotiate through an agent. Nevertheless, it did not look as if he was coming back. We all said our farewells and the hiatus was on.

Alex had arranged for me to pack up the office. We were definitely moving to another location, but it was not yet certain where. After having done that, I spent the rest of the hiatus working at home and in the library. It was a pleasure to be able to crank out my categories apart from the pressures of taping, roundtabling, the game change memo and the Chyron booth. My paycheck came in the mail and the days went by quietly and uneventfully.

The other writers were slated to return to work the second week of April. Jules called me the week before. He told me the Jeopardy studio and offices for the next season would be on the lot of KTLA,

Channel 5, which is right next to the KTTV lot on Sunset Blvd. This year, we would have a dedicated stage, meaning the Jeopardy set could remain in place week after week. In '84 it had to be taken down and re-assembled week after week. That meant that we almost always had technical problems on the first day of taping. The second day would be much better—but then we would have to start all over again. At Channel 11 each studio had its own control booth, whereas at Channel 5 two studios shared a control booth. That way Jeopardy wouldn't have to tie up and pay for a control booth they would be using only two days a week.

The studios on the Channel 5 lot were, however, much older and less attractive than those at KTTV. In fact, the KTLA lot was the oldest in Hollywood. It was originally the home of Warner Brothers' studios and the place where they filmed the movies' first talkie, *The Jazz Singer*. Later, on that same lot, the bad guys would challenge Marshall Dillon on the main street of Dodge City. Other former denizens of the lot included Bugs Bunny, Porky Pig, Daffy Duck and the other Looney Tunes characters. What had originally been movie sound stages were converted into television studios. The buildings, of course, maintained their large, cavernous and rickety appearance.

When I phoned Jules to arrange to turn in the material I had written over the hiatus, I asked if he had heard about Alex.

"Oh yes," Jules told me, "Alex is back."

Jules then asked me to bring my material in and meet him in the third floor conference room of the TAV building. My going over material with Jules a few days before the others returned would help him get a jump on the next season.

As I was walking through the TAV building I ran into Alex. I told him I was glad he was back and asked if he'd gotten what he wanted.

"Most of it," he replied.

CHAPTER 4

JEOPARDY! COMES INTO ITS OWN

At Jeopardy the 1985–86 season (which for us ended in December '85 though the shows continued to air through the following June) was a turning point in the history of the show. That second season proved to be the one in which the program in many ways took on its present-day configuration. For one thing we moved to the KTLA lot in Hollywood which would remain the site of Jeopardy tapings for the next six years. But there were far more important changes in the show itself.

It was Alex who instituted some major modifications in the show's format with the approval of Merv and Bob, of course. To begin with, he changed the point at which the contestants could be able to ring in. Hitherto, and on the old Jeopardy, the contestants could ring in as soon as the clue was revealed on screen, which was the same point at which Alex *began* to read it. Eager to have first crack at a clue, contestants would often ring in, particularly in the case of the easier clues towards the top of the game board, with absolutely no idea as to what the clue was all about. In such cases they'd often ring in only to offer no response at all. The player would lose the value of the clue and precious time would be lost from the game. Occasionally you'd get a player with good reflexes who was adept at ringing in this way and could handle the easier material fairly well. But all that would do is frustrate the other players who would then try it with harder clues to which they could not respond correctly. As a result we had a considerable number of players the first season end up in a minus situation and in one or two cases we had games in which two players ended the Double Jeopardy round in the red so to speak and the champion got to play Final Jeopardy all alone.

Alex's idea was from now on he would read the clue when it was revealed, but the contestants would not be able to ring in *until he was finished.* In other words, I was not to activate their signalling buttons until Alex had gotten to the last syllable of the last word of the clue.

A thin fluorescent tube running all around the game board was attached to it and automatically lit up when I activated the signalling buttons, showing the players they were now free to ring in.

This was a change for the better in many ways. For one thing, the games became more competitive and we had far fewer runaways. In the first season, nearly half the games had been runaways, making the outcome of the game a foregone conclusion. You will rarely, if ever, see a player that far ahead wager so much in Final Jeopardy that were he to miss the final and one of his opponents get it, he would lose the game. I seem to recall a player named John Ryan who did it once or twice and still won the games but he is the only one I can think of that I ever saw take such chances. As a result of Alex's change, only about 20% of the games in the second season were runaways.

In addition, fewer players were ending the Double Jeopardy round with a negative score and the champions were winning more money. In the first season the average champion's take was $8,000 per game. In the second season it was about $10,000 a game. That cost the show around $400,000 that it hadn't anticipated spending, but then Jeopardy profits that second season soared.

That second season I was given a second switch to operate at the tapings, besides the one for the players' signalling buttons. This one was for the electronic pens the players use to write out their Final Jeopardy responses. In the first season, it had been something of a problem to get certain contestants to put down their pens once the 30 seconds allotted for Final Jeopardy were up. You then had a difficult judgment situation if a contestant had gone overtime and his response was correct. Should he be counted correct or not. We tended *not* to rule against them for going overtime that first season but some opposing players complained and Alex was determined to eliminate the problem. With the new switch I could activate and deactivate all three electronic pens. I would turn them on as soon as Alex said "Good luck players" and turn them off on the last note of the "think" music. After that, some players might continue writing but nothing more would come out of the pens. That new system also worked well for us over the years.

The Jeopardy think music, incidentally, was written by Merv Griffin. Called "A Time for Tony," it was written by Merv in honor of his son, when Tony was just a baby. Merv still owns the rights to it and receives a royalty for each time it is played, which is eight times per show. On the old Jeopardy another tune called "Take Ten," written by Julann Griffin, was used to introduce the show, but it was never used on the current version.

That season Alex also introduced another change related to the players' signalling buttons. From time to time viewers will notice a frustrated contestant pushing down again and again on his signalling button, unable to get in. This is because the signalling buttons now contain a lockout mechanism: If a contestant pushes the button too soon, he will be locked out for about a second and cannot ring in so as to get through until that second has passed. If he pushes the button sooner he will remain locked out, having only succeeded in reactivating the lockout for an additional second.

This change would not have been made, except that towards the end of the previous season, we had a contestant, Michael Day, who kept constantly jiggling his finger up and down on the button from the time a category and dollar amount were selected, in order to be the first to ring in. It worked for him and he won five games, but Alex and most others on staff didn't care for this style of play which had the effect of largely shutting out the other players. The lockout device was introduced to eliminate this possibility. That contestant, by the way, came back to play in the Tournament of Champions the following season and looked rather surprised during the rehearsal game when he first learned his signalling button didn't work the way it had in the past.

Speaking of the Tournament of Champions, that was yet another innovation in the second season. We obviously couldn't do one the first season, since we didn't have any champions from the previous year, but we were all looking forward to it ever since Elise Beraru became our first five-game winner in 1984. There had been tournaments of champions on the old Jeopardy, but Alex put together the two-week, 15-player format we've always used on the current show and which is standard for our other tournaments as well.

Now it just so happened we had 15 undefeated five-time champions the first season. In subsequent seasons we never had as many as 15 five-game winners, so we always added those four-game winners with the highest scores until we had the requisite 15 contestants for the tournament. If a player should win four games in a season, he may or may not make the next year's tournament, depending on where the "cut" is. The more five-time champs we have, the fewer four-timers will be invited. One season we had as few as five five-game winners, but we always had enough four-game winners to round out the tournament.

Alex instituted the following tournament format: The first week would consist of five games, each with three new players. Since we tape five shows in one day, those players who had not yet played were

sequestered; that is, they could not see, and did not know the result of
the games prior to the one in which they were to participate. The winners of those five games that first week (the quarter-finals) automatically advance to the semi-finals. Since Jeopardy is played by three
players and five is not a multiple of three, those five players would
be joined by four wild card players, making a total of nine. The four
wild card players would be the four players with the highest scores at
the end of their respective games, out of the ten non-winners. That's
why the players were sequestered. If they were not, those playing in
the latter games of the first week would have an advantage, knowing
what scores they would have to beat to earn a wild card position in
the semi-finals.

The semi-finals took up the first three days of the second week of
the tournament, with three of the nine semi-finalists playing each day.
Each of the winners of the semi-finals games went into the finals,
which are always a two-game affair with each player's scores of both
games combined to determine his ultimate standing in the tournament.

Jeopardy tournaments are the only times contestants are brought
out to Los Angeles at the show's expense. In the earlier years accommodations were provided by a hotel in Universal City in exchange for
a promotional mention on the show. Now the players are housed at
Merv Griffin's Beverly Hilton hotel, located at the southeastern edge
of Beverly Hills, which Merv bought some years ago. All contestants
are guaranteed at least $1,000 in cash winnings for participating in a
tournament. Those who make it to the semi-finals get $5,000 if they
go no further. In the finals, the third place finisher gets $7,500 or the
sum total of his two-day cash total, whichever is greater and the second place player gets $10,000 or the sum total of his two-day win-
nings, whichever is greater. Jeopardy tournament finals are the only
instances on the show in which losing players can get to keep the
cash they accrued in the game. The winner of the Tournament of
Champions receives $100,000. The winners of the other tournaments,
which were introduced later, receive $25,000 or more, if their two-day
total is higher than that.

Our first Tournament of Champions was taped in October 1985
and aired the following month. Because we tape in advance, we had
to go to extra lengths to keep the identity of the winner a secret until
the shows aired. Over the years we were usually successful in this,
though once or twice the winner's name did get into the press before
the entire tournament had aired.

That first tournament we had some exceptionally strong players
including Elise Beraru, Bruce Fauman from Canada, Southern Califor-

nia mailman Steve Rogitz and North Carolina attorney Ron Black. The winner, however, was an underdog, Jerry Frankel, a musician originally from Buffalo. In the quarter-finals, Jerry was the lowest-scoring of the four wild-card players to go on to the semi-finals. In the end the entire Tournament hung on the last Final Jeopardy clue, which was in the category World Capitals. The clue read, "It is the westernmost national capital in the western hemisphere." Jerry was the only one of the three finalists to get it right. The correct response: "What is Mexico City?"

Just a year or two later, we were saddened to learn that Jerry Frankel, our first Tournament of Champions winner, had died of AIDS. *Newsweek,* in a feature story, included his picture among those of 100 prominent individuals who had succumbed to the disease.

THE SOURCE OF JEOPARDY

1985 was a year of other innovations as well. The new Jeopardy offices on the lot of KTLA were many times more spacious than what we had at KTTV. There was more than enough room to shelve the Jeopardy library, which was growing a little bit each year as the show was given a certain amount of money to spend on new books. Also, each year we got a few sets of encyclopedias from whichever encyclopedia had agreed to be the "source authority" for that season. That particular encyclopedia got a credit in the show's crawl which read, "Verification of some material provided by . . . ." In return, we got the encyclopedias gratis. The first season it had been *World Book.* In 1985 it was the *Encyclopedia Americana* which belongs to the Grolier Company. The following year it would be *Encyclopedia Britannica.* In 1987 researcher Ruth Deutsch suggested Jeopardy try to strike a deal with *Facts On File* and we did. Almost every year we switched to a new company.

Despite the addition of the new encyclopedias and the other books we obtained from time to time, the Jeopardy library remained quite limited. In 1985 it numbered less than 2,000 books, most of which went back to the old Jeopardy and were somewhat out of date. The show was not subscribing to any magazines at the time, though people brought in their own copies. Alex would bring in many of the magazines he had been getting at home and Steven would bring in his daily copy of the *Los Angeles Times.* In 1985 we started getting *USA Today* in the office. It wasn't until 1988 that Jeopardy finally began to subscribe to *Time, Newsweek, U.S. News & World Report, People* and *Us.*

Due to the lack of resources in the office, most of the writers and researchers found it necessary to spend considerable time at the library. As a result, each was assigned a "library day," one day a week when he or she could go to a library and have access to a great deal more source material. When a researcher was at the library, he would phone in a few times a day in order that the other researchers could ask him to look up things for them.

During my library day, I would usually go to the library and then work at home the rest of the day. I'd then come into the office the next day with a pile of books I'd borrowed and work out of them until my next library day. Michelle Johnson, who had written for game shows before Jeopardy, told me that she found children's books particularly valuable. For one thing, they were obviously easier and therefore useful if you were trying to keep the material from getting too difficult. In addition, they were usually written in a lively, interesting manner, with lots of fascinating facts intended to hold the kids' attention.

One of the things I came across in the children's section of the public library was the *Enchantment of America*, a series of books by Allan Carpenter. Each of these books, about 90 pages in length, deals with a different state. They are filled with unusual facts. For example, did you know Delaware's northern boundary is the arc of a perfect circle that was centered at the cupola of the old courthouse in New Castle; or that the French called Idaho's Snake River the Accursed Mad River because of its many inhospitable stretches?

I thought it would be a good idea to do a category on every state of the union and suggested it to Jules. He agreed and had me post a list of the 50 states. That way each writer could sign up for the ones he or she wanted and we wouldn't do any state a second time until they had all been done once. The writers generally wanted to do their home states: Gary, Illinois; Barbara, Ohio; Steven, Michigan; Michelle, Nebraska; and I did New York. It wasn't hard to do the big, populous states, but when it came to the less populous ones such as Wyoming, the Dakotas and Delaware, it was harder to come up with six facts to create clues easy enough for the average contestant to answer. Since I enjoyed working the Carpenter books, I did most of the states that second season. The researchers didn't always enjoy researching those clues, since some of Carpenter's facts were so interesting it was difficult to find second sources confirming them.

In later years we would also do categories on people from the various states, such as Michiganians, Bay Staters and Down Easters. (You wouldn't want to call them "Mainiacs.") The *World Almanac* includes small listings of famous people from each state, while larger ones can be found in the *Encyclopedia Americana* and the Carpenter books. Another useful book in this regard was *Who Lived Where*, published by *Facts On File*.

PERSONNEL CHANGES

The most significant change that season came in personnel. Contestant Coordinator Mark Richards was replaced by Greg Muntean. Judging from the quality of the contestants he brought us, I would have to say Greg is one of the best contestant coordinators in the business. Many of the contestants he selected were not only adept at handling the tough Jeopardy material but had outgoing, memorable personalities that made the shows more fun. They included the first really big winner on Jeopardy, Chuck Forrest.

Chuck, who was a law student at the University of Michigan at the time, won $72,800 on the five regular shows on which he went undefeated that second season. That set a record for regular season winnings, which held for four years until it was topped by both Bob Blake, an actuary from Canada, and Frank Spangenberg.

Ironically, Chuck's score on the written contestant test was mediocre. Greg, however, spotted something in him in terms of his game playing ability and winning personality. Chuck was as adept at handling the material as any player we've ever had. It seemed as if nothing we wrote could be too tough for him. I recall writing a clue in a category titled Bear Facts. It read: "Few Americans ever got to see this mascot of the 1980 Moscow Olympics." The correct response: "Who was Misha (the bear)?" Now that's about as tough as we've ever gotten on Jeopardy. When we were roundtabling the game people predicted that clue would never be gotten. I happened to be more of a sports buff than most of the people on staff and therefore thought it would be gotten. For fun, I bet some people that Misha would be gotten. I knew I was in luck when the game it was in turned up on the day Chuck was playing. Needless to say, he was the one who got it right.

I also recall two Final Jeopardies that I'd written that Chuck got (and I believe the other contestants missed). Under Business & Industry I wrote, "Over 1/2 of Fortune 500 & 43% of all N.Y. Stock Exchange companies are incorporated in this state." The correct response "What is Delaware?" And under Vice Presidents, the Final Jeopardy clue read, "It was the last year in which we went for an entire calendar year without a vice president." "What was 1964?" That was

Lyndon Johnson's first full year in office following the Kennedy as-
sassination. The Twenty-fifth Amendment to the Constitution now calls
for the president to appoint a vice president (to be confirmed by Congress) should the office of vice president fall vacant. It was ratified in
1967. Chuck later wrote a book along with Mark Lowenthal, a future
Tournament of Champions winner when both worked together at the
State Department. It is titled *Secrets of the JEOPARDY! Champions.*

Receptionist Julie Ruthenbeck moved over to the contestant department to assist Greg in that area. Julie left us shortly afterwards to
begin her career in the film industry, where she's done quite well.

Julie Ruthenbeck was replaced in the contestant department by
Ingrid Hirstin-Woodson. Reared in Southern California, Ingrid is an
attractive, capable lady whose personality is characterized by an air of
professionalism. After about five years at Jeopardy she started her own
management business, working to promote the careers of rock artists.

Associate Producer Sue Shelley did not return for a second season
at Jeopardy but moved over to take on the same responsibilities on
"Headline Chasers," a new show hosted by Wink Martindale that was
also produced by Merv Griffin Enterprises and distributed by King
World. "Headline Chasers" was a show that Wink had thought up and
convinced Merv and Bob Murphy to produce, with himself as host.
Merv added his personal touches to the idea and when it was done it
somewhat resembled "Wheel of Fortune." The difference was you had
to guess headlines from the past rather than phrases or people's names.

The previous year, when Wink was pitching the show to Bob
Murphy, a call came in to the Jeopardy office asking for volunteers to
go over and play the game in order to demonstrate it to Bob. Steven,
Suzanne and I thought it would be interesting and so one weekend
day the three of us went to the TAV building to act as Wink's contestants and play "Headline Chasers." We played the game a few times,
enabling Bob to get a feel for how it worked. No one asked our opinion, but afterwards the three of us unanimously agreed the show didn't
have those special qualities needed for a game show to make it.

A good game show draws the viewer in—it virtually compels him
or her to play along. Both "Wheel of Fortune" and Jeopardy do that,
each in its own way. The magic of Jeopardy lies in how the clues are
rapidly revealed, one after another, on that big game board. The viewer
can't help but wonder what lies behind each dollar amount and before
he knows it, he's playing along. Weak game shows, on the other hand,
leave the viewer with the impression he is just *watching others* play.
"Headline Chasers" was, unfortunately, one of the latter.

King World nonetheless succeeded in selling "Headline Chasers"
for a full 39-week season into a great many markets. The King Broth-

ers, Michael and Roger, have been described as street hustlers. They started out with the syndication rights to the old "The Little Rascals" films and built that up into a major public corporation listed on the New York Stock Exchange. By 1991 King World was boasting annual revenues of over $475 million. Besides syndicating "Wheel" and Jeopardy, they took Oprah Winfrey, who had been doing a local talk show in Chicago, and helped make her the most popular talk show host on American TV. As a result of all that, King World became the most successful syndicating company in history and has now gone on to produce its own shows, starting with "Inside Edition." In most markets, the Kings were able to sell "Headline Chasers" as part of a package, along with "Wheel" and Jeopardy. That got "Headline Chasers" incredibly good placements for a brand new syndicated show. Unfortunately the King brothers could do nothing to make "Chasers" more palatable to the viewers, and after that one season the show was history. Not long after that, Sue Shelley was injured in a bad accident when her car was hit by a truck. She made what I would call a miraculous recovery and later went to work for the Disney Channel.

Back at Jeopardy, Alex replaced Sue with Sherry Hilber. About 33 at the time, Sherry is a pleasant, tall blonde originally from the Bronx. She had spent virtually her entire working life in TV in Hollywood. She started out as a production assistant and managed to advance the old fashioned way, by hard work. All the while she was going to school part time until she completed the requirements for a bachelor's degree in Psychology at UCLA. Alex met Sherry while working on the pilot of a game show. That show had been successful on Italian TV and its producers thought they could make a go of it here. Apparently the tastes of American viewers and Italian viewers are not sufficiently alike and the show did not sell here. To welcome Sherry to Jeopardy, writer Gary Lee presented her with a bouquet of flowers, a nice gesture on his part. Gary was a close friend of Jules and was hoping, as we all were, that Jules and Sherry would get along better than Jules and Sue did.

Gary liked to do things like that and would often bring a cake to the office. Barbara, Suzanne and others would bring cakes, donuts, fruit and other things that helped keep up morale. Besides getting us into radio contests, Steven liked to go to the annual convention of the National Association of Television Programming Executives (NATPE), where the syndicators exhibit their programs for the benefit of those who do the buying. The convention is generally a four-day affair featuring lots of wining and dining and partying with a good time usually had by all.

In order to get in, Steven would get a pass from King World. He'd come back with all kinds of souvenirs of shows that would make it and those that would not, which he would distribute among the rest of the group. At the end of the season he went out and bought a microwave for the office. There wasn't much upper management would do for us, so we had to do it for ourselves. There seemed to be a certain camaraderie and *esprit de corps* that kept us going, especially in those early years.

Our numbers grew significantly, as Alex prevailed upon Bob and Merv to substantially enlarge the research staff. For his part, Alex wanted the highest degree of accuracy humanly possible. Merv Griffin has a policy, which I think is a good one, that the producer of every show is responsible for answering all letters to the show. In other words, the letters of viewers, who after all are essential if a show is to succeed, are not to go unanswered. At Jeopardy the purpose of most viewers' letters, and there were lots of them, were to point out errors in the material, both real and alleged. Alex obviously wanted to minimize the flaws, but the fact that he was answering the letters himself in those days gave him further incentive.

RESEARCH

Thus, four additional researchers, Ruth Deutsch, Carlo Panno, Carol Campbell and Sean Wright came on to help Suzanne, who for all practical purposes had been the entire research department the previous season. Since the newcomers had not done game show research before, Jules had Suzanne train them in their new jobs. Actually, all four of them were hoping to eventually write for the show and perceived the research job as a stepping stone in that direction, which Alex had told them was a distinct possibility. That being the case, Jules gave them each one "writing day" per week when they could write some categories, and they worked on research the other four. Only Suzanne elected not to take the writing day. She enjoyed being a researcher, though she had written a lot the previous year because the need had been so great.

Over time a certain degree of friction developed between some of the researchers and writers. Writing for Jeopardy is highly creative, as each writer strives to make his material cute, different, interesting, memorable, unusual, fascinating or just fun. Research is not as creative, for all a researcher is trying to find out is whether the facts, as presented in a clue, are accurate or not. Oftentimes the researchers who wanted to be writers would come up with "better" ways of presenting clues and would attempt to rewrite them. The writers did not usually appreciate their material being changed in that way.

Some clues were easy to research. If the original source for a "Word Origins" clue was a dictionary, all you had to do was go to another dictionary for confirmation. Other clues could take longer. A clue read, "At her request, she was buried next to Wild Bill Hickok in Deadwood, South Dakota." The response: "Who was Calamity Jane?" (or Martha Jane Canary, her real name.) That she was buried next to Wild Bill would not be hard to find. That it was "at her request" would probably take more time. Library trips were often needed and the researchers would pour through detailed biographies. Often phone calls would be made to museums, national parks, historical societies and the like. Needless to say, our phone bills for research were quite high. I recall a clue about Imelda Marcos and some of her excesses, which seemed to be a favorite Jeopardy topic. Researcher Sean, who was new at this, was checking it out and was about to call Manila when I suggested he try the Philippine Consulate or Embassy instead. The researchers were subsequently told to limit their calls to the U.S. and Canada.

When shopping around for a long distance phone company for my home I came upon one that seemed to offer considerably lower rates during business hours. I told Alex about it and the switch was made at Jeopardy. This must have saved the show a couple of hundred dollars a month. The researchers continued making a great many calls and got to befriend on the phone various officials of different organizations who would help them frequently. Carlo Panno came up with a category he would write once a year called "Thanks Guys" in which he would mention some of these individuals who had been particularly helpful. On the other hand, some people such as those at the library of the Baseball Hall of Fame got tired of the numerous phone calls from Jeopardy and asked the researchers to desist.

Occasionally we got to talk to celebrities. Suzanne Stone was researching a clue that said Dr. Albert Sabin was so confident of the safety of his polio vaccine that he first tried it on himself, his wife and family. Suzanne spoke to Dr. Sabin's wife and found out that was true. She later asked Beverly Sills if it was true that as a 10-year-old, Miss Sills had said "I'm 10 years old and can sing 13 arias." That was indeed true. Neil Armstrong, on the other hand, told her a quote attributed to him was inaccurate. Steven Dorfman had heard that Howdy Doody had 48 freckles on his face, one for each of the states in the union in the early '50s, when that children's show was in its heyday. He managed to track down Buffalo Bob Smith in Maine and called him for confirmation. Again, it was true. I personally recall reading somewhere that Roy Orbison was so popular in England that he was the only singer for whom the Beatles served as an opening act after they'd become famous. One day I heard Roy was on our lot taping a show in one of the studios. I went by to see him and asked if that were true. Roy told me they actually had co-billing. Not long afterwards, Roy died of a failed heart. I was sorry to hear that, as he was not only one of the greatest pop singers of all time but a genuinely nice guy as well.

Of the four new researchers, we veterans of the staff knew Ruth Deutsch the best. When she applied for a writing position the previous year, Jules arranged for her to write on a freelance basis. She would write categories at home and from time to time come to the office to turn them in. The ones Jules liked he kept and used in the games and she was paid for those. A Californian from Pasadena, Ruth is an identical twin. She is into New Age and does fortune telling via smoke readings.

Carlo Panno is also a Californian, from Burbank. His dad is a fruit and vegetable wholesaler, and he would often bring baskets of fruit to the office. Unlike Steven, Carlo went so far as to make it on to the 1978 version of Jeopardy as a contestant and won one game. That wasn't all he won, however. While there he met another contestant, Debbie Dean, and later won her hand in marriage. They were married shortly before he came to work with us at Jeopardy and Jules attended the wedding. Carlo had previously worked on the Mark Goodson game show "Card Sharks."

Carol Campbell is originally from New York. Now divorced, she has two grown daughters, Kim, who later joined the Jeopardy staff, and Jennifer, a medical student. She lived in St. Louis for a while and was formerly a sales rep selling hospital equipment in Southern California and Arizona. Her brother, J. Kenneth Campbell, is an actor who has appeared in movies such as *The Abyss* and *Waxworks,* as well as the soap opera "Another World."

Anyone who knows Sean Wright knows he is very much into Sherlock Holmes. Sean heads up the Non-Canonical Calabashers, a society of Sir Arthur Conan Doyle devotees who from time to time enact mystery adventures. These have proven popular with people seeking entertainment off the beaten track and on the railroad track, as these "happenings" are often staged on board trains. Sean is a good writer and one time wrote a Mythology category for Jeopardy entirely in rhyme. Sean also hails from the Golden State.

The addition of these four researchers finally made it possible to lay down a policy that all Jeopardy clues should be double-sourced, with some exceptions. That second season we still had sufficient confidence in our encyclopedias that we accepted material from *World Book, Britannica* and *Encyclopedia Americana* on their word alone. We did the same with quotes from *Bartlett's Familiar Quotations*. By the third season we had found sufficient errors in the encyclopedias as to no longer accept them as single sources. As far as I can recall, we never found an error in *Bartlett's*.

Over the years, the system of double-sourcing the facts of a clue worked well for us, with very few exceptions. One exception I do recall was when we found two books that said it was General William Westmoreland who said of the enemy in Vietnam, "We'll bomb them back into the Stone Age." It was only after that clue aired on the show that a few viewers wrote to inform us it was actually General Curtis LeMay who had said that. Fortunately, that error didn't affect the outcome of the game.

The researchers, of course, did not have to double-source primary sources. A primary source is one that is so germane to the facts of the clue that those facts are absolutely certain. A tape of a movie proves a certain quote was uttered in it. If we say, "In his book, Frederick Cook claimed he reached the North Pole before Peary," all we need is a copy of the book. We found out the hard way that some sources that appear to be primary sources really aren't. A clue was written from the lyrics of the song *The Twelve Days of Christmas*. It was only after we'd used that clue that we learned there is more than one version of the song and if we ask what was given on, for example, the eighth day, there is more than one possible correct response, depending on which version of the song you use.

Finding a second source for some clues could literally take days and researchers could sometimes spend hours barking up the wrong tree, only to eventually find the writer's original source had been wrong all along. It's unfortunate but some of the most fascinating material we have found later turned out to be untrue. Truth may be stranger than fiction, but there is some pretty strange fiction out there masquerading as truth. Many people think the saying "Cleanliness is next to godliness" is from the Bible. But while the Bible certainly teaches cleanliness, that particular phrase is found no where in Scripture. Likewise, many associate the late actor James Cagney with the expression "You dirty rat!" but Cagney denied having ever said it in any of his 70 or so films.

At times, the researchers simply could find no further information on a subject one way or another. Jules then came up with two ways to get around the problem: We could provide the name of the one source we had in the clue as in this example: "According to the *Book of Lists*, this country's Queen Christina killed fleas with a tiny cannon." The only country with a famous Queen Christina is Sweden and that is the correct response. The other thing Jules would sometimes do if we couldn't find a second source would be to add the words "it's said" as in "It's said it took four plumbers with special tools to extricate this President from the White House bathtub." "Who was William Howard Taft?" Considering everything we knew about Mr. Taft's size we could assume we were on safe ground and there wasn't another president to whom this clue could apply.

We could not, however, say "it's said" about every clue and the researchers continued to complain that some clues were taking too much time. I then wrote a memo to Jules and Alex suggesting the following: If a researcher had spent 20 or more minutes on a single clue without finding who he or she was looking for, he should return it to the writer. If the writer wanted to keep the clue in the game, the writer would then come up with a second source. If not, the writer could submit a new clue to replace the original one. They thought that was a fair idea and it subsequently became Jeopardy practice.

We weren't far into the second season of the show when Michelle let everyone know she would be leaving. She and Gary were expecting for the third time. They already had two sons, Eric, who was then about 18, and Ben, who was around seven. Gary was making a good living as producer of "Scrabble" and so she could afford to leave a few months early to prepare for the blessed event. They subsequently had a lovely little girl named Samantha, whom everyone called Sam.

Michelle's leaving created a void in more ways than one. We all missed her because she was easy to get along with and was a good, prolific writer as well. She and I shared an office and got along well for a number of reasons. We were both good at cranking out the material, and although she is a Catholic liberal Democrat and I'm a Jewish conservative Republican, we found we did have a lot in common, stemming from our respect for religious values and traditions in general and our concerns for our children and family matters in particular. Inasmuch as all four of the new researchers wanted the writer's position that was open and none struck Alex as more qualified than the others, he decided to go with only four writers for the rest of the season. He was able to do that because we'd gotten a good jump in preparing material early for that second season with the 200 or so categories I was able to write during the hiatus. This saved them from having to hire another person. Sean took over Michelle's desk for the remainder of the season and we became office mates. Sean did not return the following season but when Jules later became co-producer of "Quiz Kids Challenge" in 1990, he enlisted Sean to work for him on that show.

PRODUCTION STORIES

Also that second season, Alex hired a new secretary, Penny Eaton. As soon as she spoke two words you knew she was British. She's outgoing and has a good sense of humor. Penny stayed with the show until the following season when she was offered more money to work for KTLA. She said Alex was a good boss and she would have stayed had Jeopardy just matched the salary offer.

Anne Burgeson moved from being Alex's secretary to working as a Production Assistant. She felt that would better position her to move up in the industry. One of her jobs was to "clear" the music to be used for Audio Daily Doubles. She also had to go out and buy the records. This was before CD's had become as popular as they are now and we still used mostly records and an occasional cassette tape. Clearing the song involved calling ASCAP or BMI to find out who currently had the rights to the song. She would then call Mort Lindsey, the band leader who is well known to those who used to watch the Merv Griffin Show. Mort has a lot of contacts in the music business and could usually get a good deal in terms of what the show had to pay to use a particular song. An Audio Daily Double on Jeopardy would use no more than 15 seconds of a song. In later years we would occasionally go to commercial between the Jeopardy and Double Jeopardy rounds, using a few more seconds of the Audio Daily Double music. For this, the show was generally willing to pay a maximum of $200. Occasionally Mort would encounter people who wanted considerably more than that, as was the case with the owners of the theme song of the old "Car 54 Where Are You?" sitcom, who wanted $1,200. In such instances we simply wouldn't use the song. Then there was singer/songwriter Paul Simon, who wouldn't let us use any of his songs because he felt it would demean the songs to have them used on a game show. Jeopardy also had to pay something to any record company whose record we actually used. As a result, we couldn't use any recording on Capitol Records or any of its many subsidiary labels the first year, although Mort was later able to work out a deal with them. To get around the Capitol ban, we sometimes found versions of the same song on other labels, particularly Sun records, where many of the big recording artists got their start. The Capitol ban meant dropping nearly half our audios; it was a relief when it was finally over.

Longtime fans of Jeopardy know that in the early years of the show we had an Audio Daily Double on virtually every program. In fact, a game wasn't really considered complete without one. Most people seemed to feel the music added a little something extra to the show. Occasionally we might have sound effects, a speech or poetry reading in place of the music. One of the things both Jeopardy contestants and viewers seem to like to do is to figure out where the Daily Doubles might be. In the case of the audios, the players would obviously expect to find them in music categories, which they sometimes did, and it was therefore fun to try to work them into other categories where they'd be least expected. One of my favorites was an audio in the category "Newspapers." The clue read "Newspaper in whose honor the following was written." We then played the music, which was by John Phillip Sousa. The correct response: What is *The Washington Post*? We of course played *The Washington Post March*. That, by the way, was written so long ago we didn't have to pay any royalties on it, as it is considered to be in the public domain. In a category on "Latin America" the clue read, "Country where this song originates." We then played *Guantanamera*. The term "Guantanamera" refers to a lady from Guantanamo and so the correct response was "What is Cuba?"

Some other audios I came up with over the years include:

"This aria from 'Pagliacci' gave him the first million-selling record ever." (Play "Vesti la Giubba" by Enrico Caruso.)

"Jack Norworth wrote this song in 1908 but never saw a game until 1941." (Play instrumental of "Take Me Out to the Ball Game.")

In a Brazil category I wrote, "City you'd go to to find the beach bunny's beach." (Play "The girl from Ipanema.") "What is Rio de Janeiro?"

Under U.S. History: "Episode in history with which this song is associated." (Play "Brother Can You Spare a Dime.") "What is the (Great) Depression?"

"This 1880 Italian song commemorates opening of a railway up Mount Vesuvius." (Play instrumental of "Funiculi, Funicula.") It was a funicular railway.

"Legend says this king wrote the following over 450 years ago." (Play "Greensleeves.") "Who was Henry VIII?"

"One of the foods mentioned in the following song:" (Play part of "That's Amore" by Dean Martin.) "What is pizza pie, pasta fagioli or wine?"

"River mentioned by name in a verse of the following song:" (Play chorus of "Michael Row the Boat.") "What is the River Jordan?"

Under TV Trivia: "Long-running CBS series mentioned in this song:" (Play "Flowers on the Wall" by the Statler Brothers.) "What is 'Captain Kangaroo?'"

In a Frogs category: "Name of the frog mentioned in this song:" (Play "Joy to the World.") "What is Jeremiah?"

Under Wild West: "He personally paid for many of the instruments & made this his soldiers' theme:" (Play "Garry Owen.") "Who was Gen. George Armstrong Custer?"

And under Wars: "War with which the following song was originally associated:" (Play "How Ya Gonna Keep 'em Down on the Farm?") "What is World War I?"

Occasionally in a Languages category I would write an audio asking the player to identify the language of a certain song, such as "Volare" or "Sukiyaki."

In our second season Steven Dorfman introduced Video Daily Doubles. These usually involved the use of a picture but could also involve some object Alex held up, such as a flag or an auto license plate (which the states of Minnesota and North Carolina were kind enough to supply). I later suggested the use of live Video DDs. (Perhaps it would have been more accurate to call it a *Visual* Daily Double.) We had JulieAnn bring her Yorkshire terrier, Bagels, on stage and, pointing out that they are popular with apartment dwellers because they require little exercise, asked the contestant to identify the breed of dog.

The following season I found a place that had exotic animals that could be rented, with the services of a keeper included, for $200. I wanted to bring out a live ocelot on stage and see if the contestant could identify it, but Merv and Bob vetoed the idea. Instead we were able to obtain some pictures of exotic animals free, courtesy of the Bronx Zoo and the National Geographic Society. The animals we used weren't easy. It wasn't like we asked players to identify a lion or a giraffe. One time we used a picture of an okapi. Another time we showed a picture of a wart hog.

Clearing pictures for videos was much simpler than clearing music for audios. Many of the pictures we used would be taken from the encyclopedia that was serving as our "source authority." From time to time Steven would go out and take a photo we needed and other staff members would also contribute photos. I recall Suzanne Stone borrowing a picture of Bob Hope's unique golf cart from a friend. Museums and government tourist offices were also good sources of pictures. For example, New York's Guggenheim Museum sent us a picture of their unique and easily recognizable building, while the Australian tourist office provided us with pictures of both the Sydney Opera House and Ayers Rock. When the San Diego Zoo wanted to charge us about $100 for the right to use a picture of an animal of theirs, we called the Bronx Zoo and got one free. All they wanted in return was a mention on the show, which Alex gave them. Overall, we found a great many people who were willing to give us the use of a picture in exchange for free publicity.

Later on, I pioneered the use of film clips for Video Daily Doubles. The first one we ever used showed Lou Gehrig's very moving farewell to the fans at Yankee Stadium on July 4, 1939, and it was provided to us courtesy of the New York Yankees' Publicity Department. We of course asked the contestant to identify the player seen and heard in the video. We also used some clips from National Geographic Society films and some old silent movies that are in the public domain. Anything newer was a problem, since the studios, actors, directors and writers would all have to be paid residuals. One time Steven found out studios' publicity departments will allow you to use film clips free during a film's first 60 days in release, since it helps promote the film, but we had to drop that idea when it was pointed out the shows could later re-run and that would of course be past the 60-day limit. When Merv Griffin Enterprises and Jeopardy later became part of the Columbia Pictures organization, we thought we might be able to use clips of their movies, but that didn't work out either. They still required the payment, even though it would be within the company to a large degree.

Anne Burgeson handled clearing the rights to the audios and occasional videos that second season but left the show shortly into the third season. I recall her complaining that she hadn't advanced enough in the organization and didn't think it was fair. Looking back, I would have to say if she wanted to advance farther she would have done well to keep the job as Alex's secretary, as that position would eventually evolve into a key power base at Jeopardy.

I continued to serve as a judge with Jules and carried on with all my other responsibilities that second season. From time to time I would catch certain problems. One writer wrote, "According to a Sunset Magazine poll, it's the most popular type of peanut butter." "What is crunchy?" This reminded me of the old saying, "There are three kinds of lies: lies, damn lies and statistics" and this was one of the latter kind. I've seen enough supermarket shelves over the years to know a lot more smooth peanut butter is sold than crunchy. We called Sunset Magazine, which is oriented towards the Western United States, and found the poll had indeed been limited only to certain parts of the West. And so we dropped that clue before it could get on the show.

Despite our efforts in the roundtabling sessions, unexpected alternate responses would still come up from time to time. One time the correct response was "What is the moon?" and a contestant said "What is Luna?" We called him wrong but at a commercial break the contestant explained he is a science fiction buff and, in science fiction, the moon is often called Luna. Alex decided we should give it to him and so we reversed ourselves. Another time we had a clue which in effect asked what ancient empire was ruled by King Nebuchadnezzar? The intended response was "What was the Babylonian Empire?" The contestant said "Chaldean." From my history background I remembered that Nebuchadnezzar's Empire had been dominated by the Chaldeans. In a flash I was able to nod "yes" in Alex's direction and he went on all the while maintaining his tempo. That was the kind of thing he liked. I guess that was why they had me down there judging. (By the way, there had been an earlier Babylonian Empire which it would have been wrong to call "Chaldean," but that was long before Nebuchadnezzar.) Steven thought so highly of Nebuchadnezzar that he later did an entire category about him.

Towards the end of the season, the researchers had an opportunity to each write a signature game. Of course those shows had to have the same diversity and balance among the categories as any other. When they were taped, Alex would usually announce the name of the researcher who had written the material. I think he saw it as a morale booster and it gave the researchers something tangible they could show a prospective employer in hopes of landing a better position. The writers also got to do signature games, though Alex usually didn't announce theirs, since they got to do two, three or more per season. On the whole, the signature games played as well as any other games. Some played quite well in terms of excitement and suspense due to close competition between the contestants. Some turned out about average and some were runaways, which we usually considered to be our poorest shows. In later seasons management banned all signature games. The reason given was that because they were entirely the work of one writer, the material wasn't sufficiently diverse and balanced. I personally didn't sense that nor do I believe did the viewers. I do believe it's hard to explain shows being "written" by one individual if the show was being billed as not having any writers at all.

One of the last games of the season would be a signature game by Jules. He didn't have much time to write but liked to get one of those in at the end of the season. A highly creative individual, Jules liked to include categories in his game that had never been done before. One of those that he came up with was Jews in Sports. Jules thought the category was rather easy. The $100 clue read: "This Dodger pitcher was the youngest man ever voted into the Baseball Hall of Fame." Unfortunately sports was not the forte of the three players for that game. The one who rang in said, "Who was Hank Aaron?" At that point Alex's face briefly took on a quizzical expression, as if he wasn't quite sure how to handle it. A second or two went by before he explained, "I'm sorry, but Hank Aaron was not a pitcher." (This incident got a short notice in *Sports Illustrated* under the heading "Who is Barry Latman?" Barry Latman was a Jewish pitcher who amassed a rather undistinguished record of 59 wins, 68 losses over an 11-year major league career.) The correct response was "Who is Sandy Koufax?" Back in Alex's dressing room after that taping, his wardrobe man, Alan Mills, whose father was black (one of the singing Mills Brothers) and his mother Jewish, asked Alex, "Does that mean I'm half a pitcher?"

Since his game played at the end of the season, Jules would always include some kind of "farewell" category. One year he wrote a category called "At Last," in which the responses were "The last straw," "The finale," "The end," "Swan song" and "All's Well That Ends Well." At the end of the last show the staff would rush on stage and mob Alex. Since we didn't have any Gatorade, Jules ended the season by dumping a bucket of used post-its on Alex's head. For those who may not know, post-its are those memo pads made by 3M in various sizes, which have adhesive on the back of each page. They seemed to have been invented just for Jeopardy, as we were constantly using them for suggested changes in the material.

We ended the second season with a wrap party on stage. There seemed to be a lot of partying at that time since it was shortly before Christmas. The staff put on skits and some of the women formed a dance group called the "Jeopardettes." We were entertaining the studio crew and a few people from King World and ABC Compliance and Practices. We got three volunteers from among the guests to play "Forbidden Jeopardy," an off-color version of the game utilizing the studio set. The clues were rather silly, such as using "Classical Gas" for an Audio Daily Double, but it was all just light-hearted, good-natured joking and people seemed to have a good time. There is a great deal of stress in working in television. Everything must be done on time and in as near-perfect a manner as possible and so there is from time to time a need to unwind and it was nice to have an occasional party or other social event. On the whole, however, we were a rather conservative lot and there was never the wild partying, drug use and the like which people tend to associate with Hollywood affairs.

And so the second season of Jeopardy ended. Jeopardy was of course engaged to return for a third season and the show had continued to improve both in content and in the ratings. Alex once told us he felt the success of the show depended 25% on the contestants, 25% on the host and 50% on the material. We had made important strides in all three departments. With the additional manpower in research and other changes that enabled us to be more careful with the material the shows proved to be more accurate, and we didn't have to bring back any contestants at all that year. The show's ratings continued to climb as more and more stations, mindful of the success our affiliates in Cleveland and Detroit were enjoying, moved the show into the access hour.

The entire year's tapings had been completed before Christmas. Plans called for us to move to another studio come next season, and Alex had the staff spend a couple of days packing, which gave us a couple of extra work days. For my part, I asked Alex if I could work at home through the hiatus as I had the previous year. It had proven beneficial to all and so I didn't think they'd say no but Alex had to check with Bob. Bob had already left for the holidays and it took a little while for Alex to get back with me. I'd been off work for a week when Alex told me I could go ahead and start writing again.

CHAPTER 5

JEOPARDY! GOES CORPORATE

Since we'd ended taping early, the second hiatus was considerably longer than the first and I ended up working at home for over three months in early 1986. Early one morning in February I got a call from my fiancee, Debby, before she left for work. "Guess what I just heard on the news," she said. "You've been sold."

"What?" I asked. I didn't quite get it. I felt a bit sleepy and must have missed something.

"It was just on the news. Merv Griffin has sold his entire company to Coca-Cola."

To me that sounded pretty good. Coke had a reputation as a prosperous and progressive company and I couldn't help but feel that the news was the harbinger of better days ahead. Of course the deal had not yet been closed as the details still had to be worked out. As I understood it, Murray Schwartz had been negotiating on Merv's behalf. What the deal called for was for Merv to sell Merv Griffin Enterprises to Coca-Cola for a substantial amount. Merv Griffin Enterprises consisted primarily of four syndicated TV shows: "Wheel," Jeopardy, "Dance Fever" and "The Merv Griffin Show." There were some administrative departments and a small development department mostly working on ideas for new game shows. Finally there was the TAV building in the heart of Hollywood, on Vine Street between Hollywood Boulevard and Sunset. The deal called for Merv to continue to operate Merv Griffin Enterprises as a separate unit within Coca-Cola Television, which included all the TV shows produced by Columbia Pictures that Coke already owned. All the employees would now be on Coke's payroll while, in exchange for his services, Merv would get part of the profits generated by Merv Griffin Enterprises.

Bob Murphy was named President of Merv Griffin Enterprises.

In the meantime, while I worked at home, Jules took a brief vacation, after which he and Alex began making plans for the third season of the show. Because of the long hiatus, Jules would have me come in every few weeks and meet with him in the TAV building to turn in my material. Everything seemed to be proceeding normally until one day I got a call from Alex. A group of women on the staff had come to him and told him they wouldn't be returning if Alex retained Jules in his position. They had complained of Jules losing his temper on various occasions, and Alex was asking me if it was true. It was, and I indicated as much although I felt funny being put in that position. Jules was, after all, my immediate supervisor. I suggested he talk to Nicky, his stepdaughter, since she did not report directly to Jules but would nevertheless have been aware of everything that was going on.

As previously indicated, there is considerable stress in television, and Jules had experienced a great deal of it. For my part, I had no idea as to the extent of that stress until I myself was in Jules' position a few years later. With the enlarged staff, Jules had 11 people reporting to him, which is, according to many books on management, more than one person should handle. Then there was the pressure of making sure the material was interesting and at the same time accurate (with even the slightest error certain to be pointed out in viewers' letters and phone calls) and all the while making sure we weren't repeating material—which is not easy when you're handling some 14,000 question/answers a season. Add to that the pressure of meeting taping deadlines in a tight season in which nine months' worth of shows were taped in four and a half months. That much I could perceive even back then.

From time to time during the previous season, Alex had indicated to Jules he felt a need for "new blood" on the writing staff. Jules didn't want to see any of the writers fired, and prevailed upon Alex to keep all four. It was eventually decided that one additional writer would be hired to fill Michelle's place on the staff for season three.

Alex reciprocated to Jules the mercy Jules had shown the writers. Jules promised Alex he would do all he could to curb his temper and Alex took him at his word. Alex then told the women what Jules had said and all agreed to return except Suzanne. Suzanne finally came back the following year to fill a vacancy in research, by which time Jules had been rather successful in keeping his promise. Unfortunately for Suzanne, she lost much of the seniority and salary status she would have maintained had she not left.

There were some improvements as a result of our becoming part of the Coca-Cola organization. For one thing, there was both a pension plan and a 401K retirement plan. If you joined the latter, the company would match every dollar of your contribution with a 50 cent contribution on its part. Coke also had a program where if you contributed to certain recognized charities, the company would match your contribution dollar for dollar. Finally Coke saw to it that from now on, provision would be made for us to get some vacation time *with pay*. And so conditions seemed to be improving.

As had been the case the previous year, some personnel changes were made prior to the start of the new season. Finding it impossible to live on $350 a week, proofreader Tina Levine left. Her duties were turned over to researcher Carol Campbell but she continued to be listed as a researcher on the show's crawl and she continued to earn a researcher's salary, which was somewhat more than Tina got. With Suzanne and Sean Wright not returning that left three openings in research. And there was the one opening for a writer to be filled as well.

MORE STAFF CHANGES

Alex and Jules ran an ad in the *Hollywood Reporter* and were swamped with resumes. If that wasn't enough, *USA Today* somehow got word of it and ran a story that Jeopardy was looking for writers. In all, something like 1200 resumes must have come in. There was nothing Alex and Jules could do with the applicants from out of town. The ones in the L.A. area were all invited to come in and take the Jeopardy contestant test as a way of narrowing the field. I would guess some 200 job applicants actually took the test.

Out of that group a petite, ebullient, blonde woman named Kathy Easterling scored highest. Kathy had gone to USC but is from the Petersburg, Virginia area. One of the other real high scores belonged to Jim Kearney, originally from New Jersey. They and some others were then invited to submit writing samples. Both Kathy and Jim were impressive as writers but Kathy was quite strong in Literature and it was felt she would best fill Michelle's slot, thereby helping to maintain the balance in the writing staff.

Jim Kearney was designated head of research. The idea was to have the other researchers reporting to one head researcher thereby off-loading Jules of the pressure of so many people reporting to him. It was intended that Jim do some research as well and like the other researchers, he was also promised some writing time. That still left two openings for researchers.

As soon as the current version of Jeopardy started getting popular, it was decided there should be a home, box game version of Jeopardy, as had been the case with the old version of the show. A licensing deal had been struck with Milton Bradley whereby Merv Griffin would provide answer/question material and of course the use of the Jeopardy trademark. Now Jules had done some work to provide material for the home game during the first season but he increasingly had his hands full with the TV show. When Michelle left to have the baby she indicated she could work at home. As she is a good writer, it was decided to turn the home game project over to her and she was authorized to hire people to help her.

Two of the people Michelle hired were Steve Tamerius and Frederik Pohl IV.

Like Michelle, Steve is from Nebraska (in his case the small town of Fairbury, near Lincoln). He'd attended the University of Nebraska where he majored in music. One of his interests is the late (we believe) Elvis Presley and Steve's written a number of books about The King of rock 'n' roll. These include *Elvis: His Life From A to Z* and *All the King's Women*. He's also quite a trivia buff, having published his own trivia magazine, and has worked with Fred Worth, author of three "Trivia Encyclopedias." Fred Worth and Steve had been responsible for all the material on "Trivia Trap," a daytime game show that came out in the fall of '84, at the height of the mid-eighties trivia craze (which helped bring back Jeopardy), and lasted for a season. He'd worked on a number of other shows as well but was between jobs when Michelle picked him up.

Fred Pohl is from Red Bank, New Jersey and attended Syracuse University where he had a double major in Anthropology and film. If you haven't guessed, he's the son of the well-known science fiction writer of the same name and co-authored *Science Fiction: Studies in Film* with his father. He'd also done some work in TV in New York and later California when Michelle hired him to work on the home game. The home game was just about finished when Michelle heard the show was looking for researchers and recommended Fred and Steve. Both were given the contestant test, which they easily passed, and they joined the research staff.

At the last minute it was decided *not* to move to a new studio as had been planned. Jeopardy was about to move to the old Zoetrope Studios lot on Las Palmas Avenue in Hollywood but management decided to stay on the KTLA lot instead. (It wasn't until 1991 that the show finally moved to the Las Palmas site which is where it remained for two years.) And so we had to unpack and reshelve the library but kept the same old offices. The office furniture was provided by the management of the lot and had been around. The carpet on the floor appeared older than we were. The buildings were creaky and we feared for earthquakes. But everyone was nevertheless glad to get back to work in early April.

Shortly afterwards, Alex's secretary, Penny Eaton, resigned to take a job with KTLA. She was replaced by Rocky Schmidt. Originally from North Dakota, Rocky had been a contestant on the show the previous year and had won two games. He and Greg Muntean became friends, and it was through Greg that Rocky learned of the job opening at Jeopardy. Rocky is a lawyer by profession, having passed the bar, and it seemed strange to see a lawyer take a secretarial job that hadn't paid the previous occupant enough to keep her from leaving.

Our new receptionist that third season was Amy Reed, a lovely young brunette from Buffalo, New York. Also, the contestant department was enlarged to three with the addition of Glenn Kagan, a tall, handsome guy from Brooklyn, who had attended the University of Miami.

For us in the writing/research areas, things did not get off to a good start that year. Jim Kearney's interests and abilities clearly lay in the writing area and he was spending as much time as possible writing and as little as possible on his other duties. There was some friction in the office and the research staff seemed leaderless and directionless. It was finally agreed that Jim should leave for the good of all. Jules then went back to having the researchers as well as the writers report directly to him. The vacancy in research was then filled by Victoria Haselton, one of the earlier applicants. Originally from the San Francisco Bay area, Victoria had been teaching English as a second language to immigrants. She was working in a junior high school just down the street from the Jeopardy studio and continued to teach part-time to augment her income.

Jules had to spend extra time with Kathy, teaching her the ropes. It is hard for a new writer at Jeopardy since that person isn't as familiar with what we've used in the past. As had been the case the previous year, Steven and I were the workhorses of the writing staff.

While there were lots of new faces on the Jeopardy staff that third season, there were also some old ones that were leaving. After many years on the air, "The Merv Griffin Show" had been cancelled. Merv wanted to keep his stage manager, John Lauderdale, and associate director Kevin McCarthy in his employ and therefore decided they should replace Jeopardy's stage manager, Keith Richmond, and associate director Robin Felsen.

TEEN TOURNAMENTS ARE BORN

Kathy was gradually learning the ropes as a writer and our shows continued to improve. The 1986-87 season saw the introduction of the Jeopardy Teen and Seniors Tournaments. The Teen Tournament was something of a last minute decision as a result of which Greg and his assistants had a limited time in which to find contestants. The Teen Tournament is of course for high school students. The ones who make it on to Jeopardy are of course quite bright. Still, they have not had the time in life to acquire as much knowledge as adults and it was therefore necessary to come up with easier material. In addition, there were various recent history, nostalgia and pop culture categories which worked quite well for adults who remembered the '60s, '50s and '40s. But here we would be dealing with kids who weren't really old enough to remember the war in Vietnam and Watergate. And so we would need more up-to-date material as well as easier clues. We hastily assembled a contestant test that met those criteria and Greg, Ingrid and Glenn quickly hit the road as it was arranged with a number of Jeopardy affiliates in various parts of the country to sponsor teen testing.

While they were looking for players, we had to create the material for the games. Since that first Teen Tournament hadn't been planned for, Jules was still under pressure to crank out the regular games. In addition, it had been decided to extend the regular Jeopardy season from 39 weeks of shows to 46, leaving only six weeks for reruns instead of the previous 13. This was done for a number of reasons. For one thing game shows that were on the networks in daytime never ran reruns. This had been the case with the old Jeopardy as well, and many in the Jeopardy audience were therefore not used to nor did they expect or enjoy the reruns, since many remembered having seen the contestants before. In many ways, rerunning a game show is like rerunning a sports event. In addition, some of the clues, which were true at the time of the first airing of a program, were no longer factual at the time of a rerun. Political conditions change around the world, as do sports records and various awards, etc. There was little doubt therefore that the affiliates would be happier and the program could therefore command a higher price with more first-run shows. For the staff it meant Jeopardy would now be a year-round job for all of us and the end of unpaid "hiatus." Since Coke was already committed to paid vacations for us, it wouldn't cost management all that much more and they stood to gain a far larger return. I believe Alex was the prime mover behind this change and was pleased that it went through.

The addition of the two new tournaments gave us a total of six weeks of tournament games to rerun. The tournaments were, in many ways, the highlights of the season, and besides, each tournament was a self-contained two-week entity. Rerunning a limited number of old regular shows always meant there would be some kind of break in the continuity. The best you could do was to end the reruns with a five-time champion winning his fifth game. Then the viewers would expect three new players on the next show but what they'd get would be two new players plus the returning champ from the last show of the previous season. Rerunning just the tournaments solved that problem for us.

And so we had seven weeks, or 35 additional shows, to write. This included 13 Teen games (of which Compliance and Practices would select 10). Likewise, we would need 13 Senior games and, in addition, 15 extra regular games. It happened that Barbara, Gary and Kathy shared a large office that Jules had dubbed the WASP's nest, since they were all Protestants and most of the rest of the writing/research staff was either Catholic or Jewish. After consulting with Alex, Jules decided to turn the Teen Tournament over to the three of them while Steven and I would keep on writing material for the regular games. He concluded that for the teens, the Double Jeopardy round should be no harder than the first round in a regular game while the Jeopardy round in teen games should be extra easy. Because the games were for kids, Jules told the writers they could include more light, off the wall and fun categories than we normally use.

With Compliance and Practices' approval, Jules was able to arrange the games where the six easiest ones would be designated preliminary games and C & P would choose five of those for the first day of taping. The four next-hardest games were designated semi-finals; C & P was to choose three out of those four, the three toughest games would be designated finals, and two of those would be used. This would leave us with three games remaining after the tournament, which Jules planned to toughen up to use as regular games. Using those games with their "kiddie" categories as regular games seemed to be something of a mistake, and we didn't do it in future years. In addition, the need to differentiate between the difficulty of preliminary, semi-final and final games did not seem necessary. After all, the game of baseball isn't any harder in the World Series. It's just that the competition is tougher. And so we were later able to reduce the pools for tournaments to 11, with five of six for the first tape day and five of the remaining six for the second day. That way there would be only one leftover game which we would save for the corresponding tournament the next year, and we would update the material in that game as needed.

The three WASPs had the Teen Tournament all written and the categories assembled into games before Christmas. One day shortly before the holidays, Alex assembled the troops to give us Christmas gifts. He indicated he'd been very pleased with Jules' progress and had arranged that from now on Jules would be designated an associate producer. The room broke into applause. We were all happy for Jules as he had worked quite hard. (Jules' title was later changed to editorial associate producer when Sherry Hilber, who had held the title of associate producer since season two, indicated she thought it unfair.) That year, Alex gave me a sundial for our new back yard and he gave us all some time off with pay.

We came back after New Year's to tape the Teen Tournament. It aired in February, during the second major ratings sweeps period of the season and was a resounding success. The show enjoyed its highest ratings ever, 16.6. And this was a show that was still on in daytime in many of the biggest markets. To give you an idea of what a 16.6 rating means, when compared to the ratings of various shows in September and October 1992, it is higher than the ratings for the Miss America pageant, the first game of the World Series, Monday Night Football and the ever-redoubtable "Cheers."

SENIORS TOURNAMENT IS BORN

We finished the tapings for the '86–'87 season in March, with the Seniors Tournament, which was slated to air during the third sweeps period, in May. Finding contestants was not difficult since all Greg had to do was take players who were over 50 (the minimum age for the Seniors Tournament) from the pool of contestants for regular games. However, the emphasis was on much older players. The idea behind the Seniors Tournament, which was largely Alex's, was that in the Seniors, you had players who knew a great deal, but whose reflexes in ringing in on the signalling button would be slower, putting them at an unfair disadvantage against younger players. Thus was born Jeopardy's third tournament.

In some ways the Seniors Tournament was the opposite of the Teen Tournament. Here we could emphasize nostalgia categories, although there was no reason to exclude current material. In the first few Seniors Tournaments we ran categories on Big Band music, since Merv had started out as a Big Band singer and that was a favorite subject of his.

When the Seniors Tournament aired in May, the ratings were not nearly as good as those of the Teen Tournament and the Tournament of Champions and, as a result, the Seniors Tournament over the years became a *bete noir* at King World. For a while there was even talk of cancelling it. My own feeling is that in May, unlike November and February, we are in Daylight Savings Time. Not only are the days longer, but the weather is warmer and people spend more time outdoors and less time watching TV. I don't believe any tournament run in May can compete with those in November and February. In any case it was later decided to run a Jeopardy College Tournament in May. The Seniors Tournament was continued, but aired in July as the last original programming of each season. I don't believe the College Tournament ratings proved appreciably better than those of the Seniors Tournament.

ALEX IS FIRED . . . AS PRODUCER

About the time we were writing the first Seniors Tournament, rumors began to fly that Alex would not be producing Jeopardy the next season. The staff thought this incredibly strange. For in that third season, the show had truly come into its own. The ratings could hardly be better as Jeopardy had become the second-highest rated strip (the industry term for a show on five days a week) in the history of U.S. syndicated television. The show had a solid hold on second place in the ratings competition among all syndicated shows and was second only to "Wheel" so Merv Griffin Enterprises and Coca-Cola Television were totally atop the heap. As for Jeopardy profits, they were climbing.

We asked Alex if he would be coming back as producer for the fourth season and at first he indicated he didn't know, since the matter was still undecided. Then Alex announced he'd signed a contract to co-host a program called Value Television, or VTV for short, along with Meredith MacRae. It was primarily a home shopping program, but the show would also have guests that the two co-hosts would interview and in that sense it would resemble a talk show. Alex said he liked the idea of doing a talk show. Alex seems to have the makings of a good talk show host. His intellectual curiosity is such that he keeps very much abreast of what is going on. One reason he's been so successful hosting Jeopardy is that his knowledge and range of interests are so broad.

In part, it was precisely the success of the show that now made Alex expendable as producer. But the King brothers were not about to allow Alex to be dropped as host. This, after all, was a man of whom his fellow game show host Jim Lange ("The Dating Game") had said, "Frankly I think he's the best in the business. He's bright, quick and good-looking." Jefferson Graham, author of *Come on Down: The Game Show Book*, said of Alex: "The cliche host is a cross between your son-in-law and a used car salesman. But Trebek could play James Bond in a movie. He brings a classy tone to a classy show." However, with the profit level as high as it was, Merv could go on paying Alex as much, if not more than before, just to host the show and still afford to pay another man to be producer.

For his part, Alex made it quite clear to his staff that he very much regretted having to give up the job of producing Jeopardy. Becoming a producer had been one of his main career goals for a long time. He'd gone through arduous negotiations to get the job in the first place and, once he had it, he took his production responsibilities quite seriously. He was visibly moved when he said farewell to the staff on the occasion of the final day of taping that first Seniors Tournament. That night he began speaking to us collectively to thank us for our contributions when he became so overwhelmed emotionally that he couldn't go on. It had been his first producing opportunity and it had been a highly successful one. The next day he sent us each a note of thanks and farewell that ended with one of his favorite signoffs, the New Testament admonition "Go and sin no more."

That Biblical quote seems to say a lot about Alex. He's no saint and can curse like the proverbial sailor when he's angry or upset. But he does have a sense of right and wrong and seems to have a sense of personal integrity. That came through very clearly in his role as producer. For three years he ran an above-board operation, and while there was lots of good humor in the Jeopardy offices, it never descended to the level of hanky-panky or sleaze. The pay may not have been the best but at least there was an atmosphere of decency and camaraderie in the office. I think in many ways Alex felt like a father figure to the staff; I know many of us regarded him that way.

As a manager Alex was very much a take-charge guy, was quick to make decisions which a producer must often do, knew why he was making those decisions and stood by them. He obviously had a stake in the success of the show in terms of his own long term employment, financial fortune and prestige. He's not a maudlin or overly emotional man by any means but he nonetheless managed to let you know what you were doing was appreciated. He realized there was such a thing as employee morale and did try to maintain it to the degree that he could. This is not to say he was the perfect manager. He'd occasionally get uptight and say something he'd later regret having said. But overall, it seemed to me his heart was in the right place. No matter how tired he might be, and I've seen him *very* tired, I never saw him turn down a request for an autograph or some similar personal favor.

A major part of Alex's personality is a deep and abiding social consciousness. Over the years he's done a great deal of work for many worthwhile causes. One of the main charities for whom he's done yeoman work is World Vision, a Christian organization dedicated to fighting hunger and disease around the world, particularly as they afflict the world's children. He's given not only of his time and energy but has undergone considerable personal discomfort and even risked danger in working on behalf of World Vision. He's travelled to remote areas in Nepal, Africa and Brazil among others in order to help bring to the public's attention many of the difficulties and afflictions faced by children and adults in poor countries and what we might be doing to help. As someone who's adopted a number of Third World children through World Vision programs, Alex is one charitable spokesman who indeed practices what he preaches.

Alex has also been an ardent supporter of the United Negro College Fund and has worked on their annual telethon for a number of years. He's quick to use his fame and position as Jeopardy host to do as much as he can to support the cause of education and teacher recognition.

As much as it was relevant, Alex even carried over his sense of social consciousness to our work at Jeopardy. He was pleased when I wrote Jeopardy's first Black America category, as well as categories dealing with ecology, the environment, and physically challenged people who had overcome their disabilities.

Though I know Alex took it hard, I'm convinced his being dropped as Jeopardy producer was far more the show's loss than his own. For us and for Jeopardy, a three-year era had ended. We faced the future and the fourth season of the show with feelings of uncertainty as to whether things might get better. One thing was sure. We were definitely in store for change.

CHAPTER 6

JEOPARDY! CHANGES

From the moment we knew Alex would no longer be the producer, there had been speculation as to who his successor might be. Some of the names bandied about included Peter Barsocchini, who had been producer of "The Merv Griffin Show." Now that Merv's show was history we figured Peter would be available but it turned out that Merv preferred to keep Peter employed in other capacities. Others mentioned included Paul Gilbert, who had produced "Dance Fever," another Merv Griffin Enterprises production that had not been renewed for the coming season, and John Tobyansen, who had previously produced "Headline Chasers" for Merv, as well as other game shows. In the end it turned out to be neither of them as well.

The new producer, we were told, would be none other than the man who said he'd never work for Merv again, George Vosburgh. In fact Merv had been trying to lure George away from "Sale of the Century" for quite some time because he saw in George someone who would monitor the material closely for him and respond to his every request.

The story on George was that he was supposed to have a real good feel for precisely the kind of material Merv wanted to see in the Jeopardy games as well as what he wanted excluded from the games.

When Merv really wants something (as would later be the case with the Resorts International hotel and casino in Atlantic City) he goes after it. In this case, he really wanted George Vosburgh and he obviously met George's price. The first day on the job at Jeopardy, George pulled onto the KTLA studio lot in a brand-new, shiny black Jaguar.

George had previously been producer of the ill-fated 1978 version of Jeopardy. And though that show had only lasted some six months on the air, that didn't matter to Merv as the current version of the show was fully established by now. Merv was comfortable with George as producer in a way that he'd never been with Alex. George was quick to respond to all of Merv's requests, and wasn't one to make waves. Whereas Bob Murphy often addressed Merv as "Chief," George referred to Merv as "the Big Chief."

It appeared that Merv at last had the man he wanted to mold the show more to his liking. And so George Vosburgh was coming on board to take charge of an established show with a staff all intact and all of whom had been hired by his predecessor.

He met with Jules and in order to help him handle the transition it was decided to give the staff three weeks vacation, two weeks with pay, one without, just as George was coming in to take over. This was in March 1987. March isn't the greatest time to take vacation if you have children in school and so I pretty much spent the three weeks just hanging around the house and attending to some things that needed fixing. I did go into the office one day to pick up my paycheck and was told by Amy the receptionist that George was in. And so I went in to see George and reintroduce myself. We chatted for just a few minutes and I found him to be cordial but at the same time rather reserved. One could sense he didn't yet feel sure of himself.

We were all back in the office at the beginning of April, prepared to see what life would be like under the new regime.

CHANGES AT THE HELM

As we began preparing for the fourth season of the show, it wasn't too long before George Vosburgh began making his presence felt by instituting some of the changes for which he'd been brought in.

With the coming of every new season, one of the first responsibilities facing the Jeopardy writers is to prepare new contestant tests. Since some individuals are prone to try out for the show more than once, we made up two new tests each year, as well as a new teen test. In later years we made up new sets of tests twice a year. Up until this time, the tests contained a balanced assortment of questions designed to reflect the kind of material used on the show. When our group put together two new tests following the pattern we heretofore were using—15 academic, 10 lifestyle, 15 pop culture and 10 word play questions—George rejected it, saying it had too much pop culture and word play. We cut the pop culture back to 10 and the word play to five, increasing the academic and lifestyle material, but even that was still too much. When we got down to just five pop culture and two word plays, George finally said OK. He seemed to feel that pop culture and word play material somehow cheapened the integrity of the show.

Now in order for a contestant test to be of any value to us in selecting contestants, it had to accurately reflect the content of the program. A test with many literature questions would be of little value if literature rarely appeared as a category on the show. From the way George had redone the tests, it appeared we would be using very little pop culture and word play on future shows. George indicated he did want them significantly cut back, but would still allow for some pop culture and word play categories in the games. When you have to come up with 12 *different* categories per game, there is obviously a need for some variety. I've always felt the mixture should be as diverse as possible, with something for everybody so to speak, thereby making the show attractive to as wide a circle of viewers as possible.

Jeopardy has always been a serious quiz show with emphasis on the weightier, academic subjects, with pop culture and word play used to round out the games and give the show a lighter touch. Up to that time a show might have had two word play and as many as three pop culture categories, although it was usually just two. From now on the shows would generally be limited to just one pop culture and one word play. For example, if there was a TV category you couldn't have Movies or Pop Music of any kind in the same game. Furthermore, TV and Pop Music were seen as especially lightweight subjects never worthy of the larger dollar amounts in Double Jeopardy. Henceforth no matter how hard the individual clues in a Pop Music or TV category, it had to go in the Jeopardy round. Sports was likewise limited to the first round from now on but that was because it was viewed as a "male" category and giving it the higher dollar amounts of the Double Jeopardy round was seen as hurting the chances of female contestants.

CHANGES EQUAL PROBLEMS

Jules, of course, began carrying out the changes as ordered. It was difficult for a number of reasons. First, we had some games left over from the previous season, which would now have to be reassembled with pop culture and word play categories pulled out, and new material put in which would then have to be rechecked for any possible conflicts with material already in the game. Then Jules still had to put together games with some kind of variety and balance in them. No one wanted to see American Literature, Poetry, Novels, Mythology and Shakespeare all in one game, but whereas formerly you would most likely have seen only one of those in a single game, now you would be more likely to see one in each round. Finally, the five writers we had were all used to working a certain way. Since I seemed to be the most academically oriented of the writers, the change was probably easiest for me. But the others all enjoyed doing pop culture and word play, and Jules would always have a backlog of pink and yellow categories and a shortage of blues and greens. And so he was constantly calling for more academic categories and we kept cranking them out for him.

But there was a problem with the contestant test George had revised to reflect the cutback in pop culture and word play questions. Formerly, when there were 15 pop culture questions on the test, you weren't likely to pass if you didn't know a thing about pop culture. Now, with pop culture reduced to five, you could easily pass. When we asked George about this he said it didn't matter.

With regard to word play it's more or less true. Generally speaking, bright people can handle our word play clues which a player can often figure out without having to draw on considerable specialized knowledge. It doesn't usually work that way with pop culture. I for one consider myself reasonably intelligent yet pop culture is not an area in which I excel. I like to read and see only a limited amount of movies and TV. What began to happen that fourth season is that on some occasions, pop culture categories simply would not play. That is, none of the three contestants would know the response to any of the five clues in a pop culture category, regardless of how easy the material might be. And I mean basic questions, like identifying Elvis as the singer of *Don't Be Cruel* and James Dean as having starred in *Rebel Without A Cause,* were being missed. And why not, since that knowledge was no longer necessary to get on the show. In future seasons, we suggested revising the test to include more pop culture so as to eliminate this problem, but George wouldn't hear of it.

The show is, after all, taped in Hollywood and from time to time people would manage to get on who had some knowledge of or even expertise in the show biz fields, particularly individuals who earned a living in the entertainment industry. Such a player would then tend to go for the lone pop culture category as quickly as he could get to it; since his two opponents might not know anything about show biz, there was a good chance he might run the entire category. And so every time a player who was strong in pop culture won, word went out to be sure to even further limit that sort of material. Even references to show biz in, for example, a word play or an In The News category had to be purged.

All the while that was going on, we were receiving precisely the opposite message from King World, the company that distributes Jeopardy. The King World people hated dry academic categories like Chemistry, Physics and Mathematics. They liked lively, up-to-date material especially in pop culture and would get word of that to us through associate producer Sherry Hilber, the person on staff who was most often in contact with them. You obviously can't have it both ways and since the King World people weren't our bosses, we chose to ignore *them*.

MATERIAL CHANGES

Prior to season four, we writers could give our creative instincts free rein to a large extent. While the bulk of each program has always consisted of serious categories, the idea had been to round out each game with some lighter material. In addition, we tried as much as we could to come up with brand new, off-the-wall categories in order to make every show as unique as possible. In most cases Jules would place the new, unusual category in the right-hand column of the board in the Jeopardy round. Most of the new fun categories were thought up by Steven, undoubtedly the most creative writer of the group. Steven's creations ran the gamut from "Famous Pigs" to "In Other Words," in which the clue for a well-known saying was given in alternate words such as "Cheerful like one bivalve" for "Happy as a clam." Long-time Jeopardy fans will also be familiar with: "How to . . .," for which each response should begin with "How do you . . ."; "Letter Perfect," for which the correct response consists of just one letter of the alphabet; "Approximate Weights and Measures," for which the responses were inexact weights and measures such as "king size," "hunk" and "bunch"; "Act It Out" and "Point It Out." For "Act It Out" the player had to act out the correct response, while "Point It Out" entailed saying "What is . . ." and then pointing to the correct place. For the clue "It's where an Indian woman has her bindhi." In that case the contestant correctly pointed to his forehead.

Then there was "Stupid Answers," for which the responses tended to be obvious and were usually found in the clue. But not all stupid answers clues are that easy. Try this one: "The main campus of the University of Mississippi is in this town." "What is University?" Or this one: "This war for the French throne was fought by Henry of Navarre, Henry of Guise and Henry IV." "What was the War of the Three Henrys?"

Here's a Stupid Answers category I wrote back in the third season:

Stupid Answers
$100   Wyoming's only university.
$200   Voltaire said it was "neither holy, nor Roman, nor an empire."
$300   Much larger town located just south of Porcupine, Ontario, Canada.
$400   Reason men do not tend to marry their widows' sisters.
$500   In 1956 TV's "The Ford Show" was sponsored by the Ford Motor Co.
        & starred this country singer.
Extra   In "Charlotte's Web," it's what Charlotte is.

And the responses:

$100   What is the University of Wyoming?
$200   What was the Holy Roman Empire? (Do not accept Roman Empire.)
$300   What is South Porcupine?
$400   What is that men who leave widows are dead?
$500   Who was Tennessee Ernie Ford?
Extra   What is a spider?

Not all that easy, but on the whole a light, fun category of the type we would put in the right-hand column of the Jeopardy round in an attempt to add a bit of humor to the shows. Other categories in that game besides Stupid Answers included The Human Body, Quotes, Argentina, 1959, Botany and U.S. Cities, so it was by no means a lightweight game overall. But in those days we made a determined effort to inject a bit of humor into every game.

One time a writer turned in a Poetry category that included the following clue: Carl Sandburg said of this city, "I have seen your painted women luring the farmboys." At about the same time I turned in a Music on the Map category with this clue: "To Frank Sinatra it was 'My Kind of Town.' " Jules thought it would be fun to have both those clues in the same game in the Jeopardy round. And though we usually don't run two clues with the same response in the same game, we did it in this case for the sake of the joke. Of course we were taking a chance because in order for the joke to work the Poetry clue needed to play before the music clue. But you always take a chance when you try to inject a bit of humor and that time it worked. The correct response for both clues: "What is Chicago."

Another time Jules was in the process of assembling categories into a game when he noticed something interesting. As a result he came up with a Jeopardy round board that contained the following $100 clues:

Potent Potables
$100   When his name is used to describe a brandy, it usually means it's over 5 years old.

Cards
$100   This general used playing cards as ration cards during the French Revolution.

Rulers
$100   He said, "I have never loved anyone for love's sake, except perhaps Josephine—a little."

Movies
$100   Recently revived 1927 Abel Gance film, so big it takes 3 screens to show it all.

Proverbs
$100   When the cat's away, what the mice will do.

Just Desserts
$100   Rich treat composed of layers of puff pastry filled with cream, custard or jelly.

The responses:

Potent Potables: Who was Napoleon?
Cards: Who was Napoleon?
Rulers: Who was Napoleon?
Movies: What is *Napoleon*?
Proverbs: What is play?
Just Desserts: What is a napoleon?

The fact that the contestants had some fun with that inspired me to write this category, which Jules used in season three:

Famous Napoleons
$200   The world's greatest detective told John Watson that this man was "the Napoleon of crime."
$400   The Napoleon in Disney's 1970 film "The Aristocats" was this.

$600   Self-styled "Napoleon of the West," this Mexican general managed to lose half his country to the U.S.

$800   Cinco de Mayo commemorates the 1862 Mexican triumph over his forces.

$1000   Self-help author Og Mandino considers this man's "Think & Grow Rich" the best how-to-succeed book.

Extra   Though he did it in 1901, Napoleon Lajoie set a league record that still stands in this sport.

The correct responses:

$200   Who was Professor Moriarty?

$400   What is a dog?

$600   Who was (Antonio Lopez de) Santa Anna?

$800   Who was Napoleon III? (Accept: Louis Napoleon.)

$1000   Who was Napoleon Hill?

Extra   What is baseball? (Lajoie hit .422 setting the American League record for a single season.)

One time Jules' mother suggested a category dealing with punch lines from common children's riddles, and he passed the suggestion on to me. Of course we weren't sure how it would work, but we thought it was worth a try. Here's what I came up with:

Punch Lines

$100   Looks like the backstroke to me, sir.

$200   When it is ajar.

$300   Why, is there one missing?

$400   From the huge footprints in the jello.

$500   Heat, because you can catch cold.

Extra   Pull the plug out.

No extra effort was needed to put the responses in question form since riddles always start out that way:

$100   [Waiter,] What's this fly doing in my soup?

$200   When is a door not a door?

$300   Did you take a shower [this morning]?

$400   How can you tell an elephant's been in your refrigerator?

$500   Which travels faster, heat or cold?

Extra   What should you do if you find a horse in your bathtub?

I came up with some suggestions of my own for fun categories which included the following:

Mad Scientists

$200 Many mistakenly think it's the name of the monster, but it's really the name of the scientist who made him.

$400 Peter Sellers played an RAF captain, the President of the U.S. and this mad scientist in a '64 film.

$600 Noted for "Heh! Heh! Heh!" laugh, mad scientist Dr. Sivana was this comic book superhero's arch-rival.

$800 Audio Daily Double
Singer who portrays a mad scientist in the following song:
(Play beginning of "Monster Mash.")

$1000 While Ed Norton was probably his foremost fan, mad scientist Dr. Pauli was his foremost enemy.

Extra He created the novel in which Dr. Jekyll goes a little mad and becomes a little dwarf.

Bald is Beautiful

$100 He first shaved his head to play Pilate in "The Greatest Story Ever Told" before doing it for "Kojak."

$200 Of the 4 main characters on TV's "I Love Lucy," the bald one.

$300 He wore a toupee while playing "Adam" on "Bonanza."

$400 Mustachioed wrestler whose baldness is apparent when he takes off his keffiyeh.

$500 Son Erik said Gypsy Rose Lee had an affair with this producer "just for the purpose of conceiving me."

Extra Screen & stage star who described himself as "a nice clean-cut Mongolian boy."

Gobbledygook

$100 The Pentagon has described it as a "wood interdental stimulator."

$200 The government describes these as "human resources."

$300 "Predawn vertical insertion" referred to the Grenada landing using this type of soldier.

$400 "Learning resource centers" on college campuses were formerly known as this.

$500 At some colleges, a department of "human kinetics" has replaced this department.

Extra "Experienced cars" is an automotive euphemism for these.

Now for the correct responses:

Mad Scientists
$200   Who was Frankenstein?
$400   Who was Dr. Strangelove?
$600   Who was Captain Marvel?
$800   Who is Bobby "Boris" Pickett?
$1000   Who was Captain Video?
Extra   Who was Robert Louis Stevenson?

Bald is Beautiful
$100   Who is Telly Savalas?
$200   Who was Fred Mertz? (Accept: William Frawley)
$300   Who is Pernell Roberts?
$400   Who is The Iron Sheikh?
$500   Who was Otto Preminger?
Extra   Who was Yul Brynner?

Gobbledygook
$100   What is a toothpick?
$200   What are people? (Accept: personnel)
$300   What is a paratrooper?
$400   What are libraries?
$500   What is physical education?
Extra   What is a used car?

After Mad Scientists worked well, I thought it would be fun to follow it up with this one:

Frankenstein
$100   At age 16 this author of "Frankenstein" ran off with married poet Percy Bysshe Shelley.
$200   He played the monster in the original 1931 "Frankenstein" & the master in 1958's "Frankenstein-1970."
$300   In Mel Brooks' "Young Frankenstein," Gene Wilder preferred this pronunciation of the name.
$400   "Frankenstein Meets the Wolf Man" was the only film in which this Hungarian played the monster.
$500   The full title of the book is "Frankenstein or the Modern" this.
Extra   Scientist Frankenstein's first name.

Now see how much you knew about Frankenstein:

Frankenstein
$100   Who was Mary (Wollstonecraft) Shelley?
$200   Who was Boris Karloff?
$300   What is Fraunk-en-steen?
$400   Who was Bela Lugosi?
$500   Who was Prometheus?
Extra   What is Victor?

Sometimes it wasn't so much the contents of the category that were especially funny as the category title itself, or just the *concept* of doing a Jeopardy category on a specific subject. One of the first categories we ever did dealing with a specific U.S. president was the following one I wrote for the second season. It got its best laugh when Alex first introduced the category title:

Millard Fillmore
$200   In the chronology of presidents, Fillmore fills this lucky number.
$400   Fearing jokes about his lack of education, Fillmore turned down an honorary degree from this English University.
$600   Under Fillmore, a treaty was signed with Peru regarding the use of these bird droppings found off its coast.
$800   Many believe the phony H. L. Mencken story that Fillmore installed the first one of these in the White House.
$1000   When his party didn't run him for a second term, he joined this one which seemed to favor ignorance.
Extra   In 1850 it became the only state to join the Union during Fillmore's presidency.

Here are the facts about Fillmore:

Millard Fillmore
$200   What is 13th?
$400   What is Oxford?
$600   What is guano?
$800   What is a bathtub?
$1000   What was the Know-Nothing Party?
Extra   What is California?

The following category, which we used in our first Tournament of Champions, sounds serious enough but the gimmick worked well:

Bodies of Water

$100   Narrow, Biblical sea between Saudi Arabia & Africa that's an intense blue-green in color.

$200   China's Huang Ho River carries large amounts of straw-colored earth into this sea.

$300   The name of this sea is said to allude not to its dark water but its storms.

$400   Icebreakers now keep port of Archangel, on this appropriately-named sea, open in winter.

$500   Dutch settlers named this longest river of South Africa not for its color but for their royal family.

The correct responses:

Bodies of Water

$100   What is the Red Sea?

$200   What is the Yellow Sea?

$300   What is the Black Sea?

$400   What is the White Sea?

$500   What is the Orange River?

From time to time we would try to come up with an interesting gimmick for an entire round. One Jeopardy round board which I wrote contained the following six categories: Start at the "top" (which meant all the responses contained those three letters), followed by The Middle East, The Midwest, The Middle Ages, Middle Names and finally Bottoms Up (our alternate name for Potent Potables).

One interesting game board Jules assembled had these categories: Cowboys & Indians, Cats & Dogs, Sickness & Health, Medals & Decorations, Myths & Legends and finally Odds & Ends. Another board, used in our first Seniors Tournament began with The Brain, followed by The Military, The Movies, The Bahamas, The Olympics and finally just "The" for which all the correct responses began with that word.

Another gimmick we occasionally used was to have *all* the categories in an entire game start with the same letter. The following signature game was one in which I had all the categories built around the comparatively uncommon letter "H." Keep in mind the material dates back to 1987:

JEOPARDY ROUND

Starts with "H"

$100   By definition, a golfer who averages par for his game doesn't have one.

$200   In the '20s, Americans created this word to replace the French "coiffure."

$300   When the bicycle became popular about 1890, upward-curving mustaches came to be called this.

$400   Figuratively, it can refer to a small person; literally, it's 1/16th of a gallon.

$500   At these early American events, a young man who found a red ear of corn got to kiss the girl of his choice.

Holidays

$100   Type of pudding most associated with Christmas.

$200   Waubeka, Wisconsin, not Philadelphia, was where the annual observance of this June 14 holiday began.

$300   While this day is hardly noted in Mexico itself, it's a major holiday among Mexican-Americans.

$400   The 2 months in which Ash Wednesday can fall.

$500   Shakespeare's "Twelfth Night" may have first played on the eve of this holiday also called 12th Night.

The Honeymooners

$100   Though it was rarely mentioned, this character, Norton's wife, was an ex-stripper.

$200   He composed the music for "The Honeymooners'" theme.

$300   While Art Carney gets no money for today's reruns, this actress asked for and gets "residuals in perpetuity."

$400   The Grand High Exalted Mystic Ruler of this Lodge had three tails on his hat.

$500   This New York Street is the principal route along which Ralph drives his bus.

Horticulture

$100   Term for raising vegetables for market regardless of whether one owns a pickup or a Mack.

$200   Plant breeder said to have added over $1 billion to the world's wealth by developing the Idaho potato.

$300   All orchid blossoms have this many petals.

$400   When shopping for this salad vegetable, you can get an English one
        that's 2 feet long.
$500   Huckleberries are often confused with this other berry that has much
        smaller seeds.

Hit Tunes
$100   A Dolly Parton-Sly Stallone movie bomb, "Rhinestone," was based on
        this 1975 Glen Campbell hit song.
$200   Top hit of 1960, this movie theme by Percy Faith is considered the #1
        instrumental single of the rock era.
$300   Singer who had both the first and last songs to reach #1 in 1957 with
        "Don't Forbid Me" and "April Love."
$400   *Audio Daily Double*
        Heard here, Billboard says he'll always be known as "The Father of
        Rock & Roll":
        (Play "Shake, Rattle & Roll" original version.)
$500   Only '80s song to top Billboard's pop charts for 10 weeks is this Olivia
        Newton-John hit.

Hints From Heloise
$100   You can buy the pink variety of this fish & add red food dye to make
        it appear like the more expensive kind.
$200   You can find spices quicker if you realize most stores display them in
        this order.
$300   Refrigerator odors can be eliminated by cleaning shelves, bins & walls
        with this on a damp sponge.
$400   Cooking meat soup a day ahead and refrigerating it makes it easy to
        remove this.
$500   Scraping corrosion from both ends of these with an emery board can
        extend their lives.

DOUBLE JEOPARDY

History
$200   Some claim the modern era began with this 14th-century epidemic
        which devastated medieval society.
$400   In 1869 the president of the Dominican Republic offered to sell his
        country to this country.
$600   Ben Bella overthrew Ben Khedda right after this country gained inde-
        pendence from France.
$800   In 1968 Albania became the only country ever to withdraw from this
        alliance.

$1000   Japan's government didn't approve the 1931–2 conquest of this part of China but couldn't stop the army.

Health & Fitness
$200   It's believed the first diagnosed victim having this muscle strain was a lame race horse.
$400   Exercises promoting bodily use of oxygen, they include rowing & swimming as well as jogging.
$600   After applying "dynamic tension" exercises, this former "97-lb. weakling" took the name of a mythical giant.
$800   The initials in the name of this popular product stand for mineral oil.
$1000   The scientific name of this root, panax, is related to panacea & many Chinese consider it a cure for many ills.

Highways & Byways
$200   Football team whose offices are at 1265 Lombardi Avenue.
$400   Famous landmark bordered by Houston St., Bonham St. & Crockett St.
$600   U.S. routes are designated by a number on a sign shaped like this.
$800   Temple Street intersects North Temple Street at this city's Temple Square.
$1000   In 1961 part of this city's Stalinallee was renamed Karl-Marx-Allee.

Hippies
$200   The expression "Haight is love" referred to this place.
$400   Learned individuals regarded as "high priests" were often referred to by this Hindu term.
$600   Song which spoke of "mystic crystal revelation & the mind's true liberation."
$800   Diminutive name for the youngest teenage hippies who didn't understand the philosophy but liked being "hip."
$1000   Timothy Leary urged, "Turn on, tune in, drop out" at the famous San Francisco "Human be-in" held there.

Hopeful Quotes
$200   Some 160 years B.C., the Roman dramatist Terence wrote, "While there's" this, "there's hope."
$400   Completes Alexander Pope's quote, "Hope springs eternal" there.
$600   *Daily Double*
         On the night before Christmas, "The stockings were hung by the chimney with care, in hopes" of this.
$800   St. Paul wrote the Corinthians that along with hope, one should have these 2 virtues.

$1000   Charles Revson said, "In the factory we make" these, "in the store we sell hope."

Hodgepodge

$200   Though few have it as the family name, over half this country's population are Flemings.

$400   *Daily Double*
         Some Indianans are miffed that Webster's 3rd defines this as an "awkward person" or an "ignorant rustic."

$600   When Khrushchev visited the U.S., this man wanted to show him his own sub fleet—the world's 8th largest.

$800   Greater Cincinnati International Airport is in this state.

$1000   It's reported Egypt's Nasser offered him his daughter in marriage, but Elijah Muhammad was against it.

FINAL JEOPARDY

Category: The House of Representatives
Last decade in which the Republicans at any time had a majority in the House of Representatives.

Here are the correct responses:

Starts with "H"

$100   What is a handicap?
$200   What is hairdo?
$300   What are handlebar mustaches?
$400   What is a half pint?
$500   What was a husking bee?

Holidays

$100   What is plum pudding?
$200   What is Flag Day?
$300   What is Cinco de Mayo?
$400   What are February & March?
$500   What is Epiphany?

The Honeymooners

$100   Who was Trixie?
$200   Who was Jackie Gleason? (Accept: Bill Templeton—the co-writer.)
$300   Who is Audrey Meadows?

$400   Who were the Raccoons? (International Order of Friendly Raccoons)
$500   What is Madison Avenue?

Horticulture
$100   What is truck farming (or truck gardening)?
$200   Who was Luther Burbank?
$300   What is 3?
$400   What is a cucumber?
$500   What are blueberries?

Hit Tunes
$100   What is "Rhinestone Cowboy?"
$200   What is the "Theme From 'A Summer Place' "?
$300   Who is Pat Boone?
$400   Who was Bill Haley?
$500   What is "Physical?"

Hints From Heloise
$100   What is salmon?
$200   What is alphabetical order?
$300   What is baking soda?
$400   What is fat?
$500   What are batteries?

History
$200   What was the Black Death (bubonic plague)?
$400   What is the United States?
$600   What is Algeria?
$800   What is the Warsaw Pact?
$1000   What was Manchuria (Manchukuo)?

Health & Fitness
$200   What is a charley horse?
$400   What are aerobics?
$600   Who is Charles Atlas?
$800   What is Haley's M-O?
$1000   What is ginseng?

Highways & Byways
$200   Who are the Green Bay Packers?
$400   What is the Alamo?

$600   What is a shield?
$800   What is Salt Lake City?
$1000   What is (East) Berlin?

Hippies
$200   What is (the) Haight-Ashbury (section of San Francisco)?
$400   What is guru? (Accept: maharishi)
$600   What was "Aquarius?"
$800   Who were the teenyboppers?
$1000   What is Golden Gate Park?

Hopeful Quotes
$200   What is life?
$400   What is "in the human breast?"
$600   What is "that St. Nicholas soon would be there?"
$800   What are faith & charity (love)?
$1000   What are cosmetics?

Hodgepodge
$200   What is Belgium?
$400   What is a hoosier?
$600   Who was Walt Disney?
$800   What is Kentucky?
$1000   Who is Muhammad Ali?

FINAL JEOPARDY

What was the fifties (1950s)?

Besides Hippies, I did categories on other social phenomena such as Yuppies and the following category about Beatniks:

Beatniks
$200   Geometric term for that which the beat generation considered old-fashioned & outmoded.
$400   Seeking the depths of their individuality, many beatniks turned to this meditative Buddhist sect.
$600   If, like, a real hepcat laid some "geets" on you, this is what you got.
$800   Traveling man who wrote, "Where we going, man? I don't know, but we gotta go."
$1000   In April 1958, this San Francisco columnist coined the term "beatnik" in his column, "Baghdad-by-the-Bay."

Extra   Beat poet who assured his country, "America, I'm putting my queer
shoulder to the wheel."

Like what follows now are the right questions:

Beatniks
$200   What is square?
$400   What is Zen?
$600   What is money?
$800   Who was Jack Kerouac?
$1000   Who is Herb Caen?
Extra   Who is Allen Ginsburg?

Noted columnist Herb Caen was referring to this last category
when he mentioned Jeopardy in his April 5, 1987 column in the *San
Francisco Chronicle*. He wrote:

Fortunately for me, I am a humble person and proud of it. Therefore,
my ego remained unscathed a few days ago when a question on the TV
show "Jeopardy!" required the contestants to identify the columnist who
coined the word "beatnik" in his column, "Baghdad-by-the-Bay." Usually there is lively guesswork when the contestants are stumped, but
this time they just sat there, looking blank. They looked even blanker
when they heard the answer. I ascribe part of this to the fact that the
show is produced in Los Angeles, but only part. In at least two places
in L.A., my name is a household word and I owe money to both of
them.

EVERYTHING'S A POSSIBLE CLUE

Occasionally you'd come across a fact just begging to be turned into
a Jeopardy clue. A perusal of National Football League records resulted in the following clue: "Quarterback Eddie LeBaron holds the
record for the shortest one in pro football—just 2 inches." Before you
say it, know that the correct response was, "What is a (forward) pass?"
Other cute clues included these:

• "Jackie Wilson hit that sounds like a fitness program for infants."
"What is 'Baby Workout?' "
• Under Animals we asked for the "Animal for which the Canary Is-
lands are named."

"What is the dog?" (from *canine*—canary birds are named after the islands, not vice-versa.)

- Another memorable clue: "It's what his constituents did to Ivory Coast Senator Victor Biakabodo while he was campaigning among them."
  "What is they ate him?"
- Then there was this one in a Presidents category: "Presidents often spend the night here, in the middle of a public park in Frederick County, Md."
  "What is Camp David?" (It's in the middle of Catoctin Mountain Park.)
- Under Golden Oldies we had, "Jerry Lee Lewis' 'Great Balls' and Johnny Cash's 'Ring' were made of this."
  "What is fire?"
- And also under Golden Oldies, "In the title of a 1956 hit, Pat Boone almost lost it."
  "What was his mind?"
- In a Sports category there was this clue: "Lightweight champ Benny Leonard made it a point to always call her right after every fight."
  "Who was his mother?"
- A World History clue read: "Until the 19th Century, this Asian country's 'Foreign Ministry' was called 'The Hall for the Governance of Barbarians.' "
  "What is China?"
- In a Fifties category we had the following: "After posing for pictures she was asked what she had on & replied, 'The radio.' "
  "Who was Marilyn Monroe?"
- Under American Indians: "If you told a woman she had a lovely papoose, you'd be referring to this."
  "What is her baby or child?"
- "The tribe calls itself 'Dakota' which means 'allies' while others call them 'Sioux' meaning this."
  "What are enemies?"

While the above represent some of my contributions toward making the shows a bit lighter, more colorful and sometimes funny, it was Steven Dorfman who contributed most of the humorous, lighthearted material. In the early years of the show, Steven tried to have certain running gags recur from time to time. One had to do with references to "spineless jellyfish." Another, and probably his best known one, was a series of categories dealing with "Wood." The first one was simply called "Wood" but it was followed by "Son of Wood," "TV

Wood," "Biblical Wood," "Deadwood," "Wood Lives," "Literary Wood," "Historical Wood," "Hollywood," etc. until Merv had George put a stop to it.

MAKE 'EM LAUGH

As anyone who has ever worked in comedy knows, anytime you try to contribute a little humor, you take a chance. The joke might go over great or it might fall flat on its face. Judging from the reactions of studio audiences we had our share of both. There were plenty of good laughs but there were also occasional groans. By the time Alex came to Jeopardy he'd been in the entertainment business long enough to know that's how it worked. If something that was supposed to be humorous looked like it would work, Alex was willing to take a chance on it. From time to time he was willing to try something different like swallowing a certain gas and letting it affect his voice so that the player would come up with "What is helium?" Sometimes when a would-be joke would fall flat on the show, Alex would complain to the audience and the viewers saying something like, "There go our writers getting cutesy again." But you could tell he was saying it in such a way that he wasn't angry but rather wanted to acknowledge the effort while at the same time try to excuse the fact it hadn't gone over well. On one occasion Alex told an interviewer, "There are times you do what Johnny Carson does in his show: You leave a bad joke in because you're going to get more mileage out of the take you'll follow with." Not that the writers always got their way by any means. If Alex didn't find something particularly funny or if he had reason to believe it might be offensive to someone, he'd axe it and that was that.

In an interview for the Jeopardy press kit for season three, the last season he would be producer, Alex said, "The main difference, I think, between our show and the original Jeopardy, which was on NBC for 12 years, is the element of humor. We have a lot more humor on our program than those shows did." As Shakespeare's Hamlet lamented, "Aye, there's the rub."

If there was one thing Merv and Bob definitely were, it was nostalgic about the old Jeopardy. To them it represented the epitome of a successful quiz show. It may have been serious but it had staying power, and on TV that counts for a lot. They may have felt that the more serious style played a major role in contributing to that show's success and that a show with more humor was more likely to burn out sooner.

Not that Alex had gone overboard on humor. Not by any means. In the press kit interview he'd gone on to say, "In the Double Jeopardy round we get more serious, because there's more at stake — a lot more money — and by then we feel our contestants have relaxed enough with the lighter fare in the earlier going and the bit of an interview I do with them. So now they're really ready to bear down and get serious about this and win some big bucks and become a champion. We try, at this point in the competition, to stress knowledge as opposed to frivolous trivia-type material."

DON'T MAKE 'EM LAUGH

What limited humor we had on the show was now to be sharply cut back, and George Vosburgh, who had worked on those old shows back in New York, was given the task of making the current program more closely resemble the old Jeopardy. The lighthearted material was to be severely reduced and categories that had been deliberately written to be funny, such as Stupid Answers and Punch Lines, were eliminated altogether. From now on Jeopardy would be a much more serious show, like the old

"G.E. College Bowl" stressing more *significant* categories and clues rather than the merely trivial. Incidentally even the use of the term "trivia" in a category title was banned for a time.

In retrospect, I would say our most balanced programs were in seasons two and three (which aired from September 1985 to June 1987). Fun and humor were an integral part of the show without its losing its integrity and its serious side. Ironically, at the same time the shows were funnier, the material was also more difficult and, believe me, the contestants back then were no slouches.

Not that George intended to eliminate *all* humor. It was essentially that Merv wanted the show to have a more serious overall appearance and the result was simply fewer funny incidents far less often.

The show, under Alex, had been enjoying extraordinarily high ratings and so George at first took a cautious, gradual approach to instituting change. Besides, after having done it for three years, the writers and Jules were largely used to working a certain way. And so season four was something of a transition year. We were constantly being told to cut back on the lighter fare but, being creatures of habit, we still wrote some which managed to find its way into some of the shows.

Early in season four, I managed to write one of my all-time favorite categories, Biblical Parties. For some reason I found the idea that they had parties back in Biblical times to be intriguing and managed to find enough of them to create this category:

Biblical Parties

$200 Genesis tells us Abraham made a great feast the day this child was weaned.

$400 King Solomon sacrificed 120,000 sheep & 22,000 oxen for a gigantic 14-day feast at the dedication of this.

$600 When Herodias' daughter danced at Herod's birthday party, he lost his head.

$800 At the banquet she threw, Haman fell on her bed & the King thought Haman was about to ravish her.

$1000 Babylonian King Belshazzar's party came to an abrupt halt & his knees started shaking when he saw this.

Extra At his birthday party, this ruler decided to pardon his chief butler & hang his chief baker.

The correct questions:

Biblical Parties

$200 Who was Isaac?

$400 What was the Temple?

$600 Who was John the Baptist?

$800 Who was Esther?

$1000 What was the handwriting on the wall?

Extra Who was Pharaoh?

So much for a category you don't see on TV game shows every day.

Occasionally it would be contestants who quite inadvertently would lighten up the show. In a City Nicknames category a clue read, "In 'The Frisco Kid,' Gene Wilder called it 'The city where all the brothers love each other'" (that being his character's way of saying "the City of Brotherly Love"). The first contestant who rang in responded, "What is San Francisco?" It was either the second player or Alex who gave the correct question saying, "What is Philadelphia?"

One time a Mythology category contained the following rather tough clue: "He gave his name to a class of snakes." The contestant remembered the study of reptiles is called herpetology. That made him first think of the mythological Hermes, but Hermes didn't sound like it went with herpetology. And so he rang in and said, "Who was Herpes?" What we were going for was "Who was Python?"

Then there was the time we asked for the name of Dagwood's dog to which a contestant responded, "Who is Blondie?" Certainly, Blondie wasn't that bad. The actual dog was Daisy, usually seen with four or five pups in tow.

And of course we had our in-house jokes. I once wrote the following for an Animals category: "Because this wild dog is a scavenger, it's used as a street cleaner in some Asian and African cities." The correct response: "What is a jackal?" To which Steven replied, "They have signs, you know. 'No parking Wednesday—Day of the Jackal.'"

UNDER PRESSURE

At the time I had little idea as to how much pressure Jules was now under in having to learn to dance to the new music after having done it differently for the first three years. Later it became my responsibility for three years to assemble the games. When I took a vacation, I arranged for Fred Pohl (who later became a writer and judge on the show) to assemble some games in my absence. He did his best and we managed, but when I came back he said to me, "Harry, I don't know how you do it, putting those games together." Truth be told, to this day I don't know how I did it either.

As in past seasons, we spent April, May, June and July writing away, trying to provide Jules with as much material as possible in order for him to assemble sufficient games for us to choose from, once taping began and our supply of games would begin to be used up. Since he had been brought in to more closely monitor the material and he didn't seem to trust Jules, George decided early on that the writers should report directly to him, with only the researchers reporting to Jules.

Jules used to keep track of how much material each writer had turned in and when. When he needed more categories he'd call for the writer he hadn't met with for the longest time and go over the material. By the third season duplicating material had become so much of a problem that Jules began requiring at least seven written clues per category based on the assumption that one of the clues would most likely deal with something we'd done before. If there was more than one duplicate or some material didn't meet his standards he wouldn't use it and the writer would have to rework the category.

WORKING WITH GEORGE

Going over material with George was something else again. If you were going to wait until *he called you,* you'd have a long wait indeed, as Gary found out the hard way. The rest of us were more eager to turn in material, and we would always be asking George when he could see us. The best time to see him was in the morning, but he seemed to prefer meeting with us in the afternoon, usually for lunch.

What he preferred to do was to sit in his office and read the *Columbia* one-volume encyclopedia or an atlas in between watching the stock market reports on a cable TV channel. But he realized the material had to be processed, and so he'd meet with you on an average of one time for every three requests you made. Gary seemed to sense George's discomfort and was in turn uncomfortable asking to see him. As a result, he fell way behind in turning in his material.

Turning material in with George was virtually the complete opposite of doing it with Jules. I would hand in my clues in the order of difficulty I perceived them as having. Jules might have kept them in that order or he might have changed it. Other writers didn't bother with an order of difficulty, since Jules was going to arrange one anyway. If he thought a clue could be written in a better way, he'd rewrite it. Sometimes I'd agree with his changes and sometimes I wouldn't but since he was in charge his changes went in. With George there was, quite surprisingly, virtually no criticism of the material other than the fact that he thought some clues might be too difficult and the writer would have to make them easier or replace them. As for the order of difficulty, he deferred to each individual writer, and the writer would then number the category cards in the order of difficulty he or she perceived, one through five plus an "E" for the extra. George also let the writer decide if the category should be designated for the Jeopardy or the Double Jeopardy round. What really surprised me was that he didn't even want to initial a category after he'd approved it, the way Jules used to, and so we writers would put down a "G.V." on the top card. At first even that made him uncomfortable and we had to put the "G.V." on a post-it attached to the cards. Since they kept falling off, he finally let us put it on the card itself.

HEAVY ON ACADEMIA

Considering all George's concerns about the different types of categories and his reactions to Merv's wishes and complaints, I would have thought he would have been far stricter than Jules as to what he would accept and what he wouldn't but in fact, quite the opposite was true. When you went over material with him, George would accept virtually everything the writers gave him. He then left it up to Jules to organize each game in such a way as to meet his and Merv's wishes. That really put the pressure on Jules. One result was that Jules usually had too many show biz and word play categories and not enough of the heavier academic ones, so he had to keep asking the writers for more and more of those and less of the other. But since the writers were getting virtually all their material accepted by George, there wasn't as much incentive to do what Jules asked as there should have been. Kathy, in particular, kept writing a lot of celebrity and show biz material, which led to some tension between her and Jules.

At that point I virtually stopped writing anything but academic subject categories, and most of the other writers did the same. That in turn caused the researchers' workload to increase somewhat. Academic clues tend to be harder to research (and often have more aspects to them) than do show biz or word play clues. (Show biz clues were often researched by calling the agent of the celebrity in question for confirmation.) In addition, since Carol had given up the proofreader's job, those duties had been spread among the five researchers. Each week a different researcher would serve as proofreader. That did not prove to be a particularly good idea. Carol had put together a rudimentary Jeopardy style book but there were still some questions of punctuation that were open. Also, some people are simply better at spotting errors than others, and as a result some grammatical and spelling errors slipped through.

When some of the researchers began to complain of too heavy a workload, Jules ordered the writers to double-source their own material from then on. That did not sit well with some of the writers, including me. I felt I was doing all I could just to handle my extra responsibilities and at the same time write a full quota of material. Most seasons I would come in second only to Steven in number of categories turned in and used on the show. I complained of this to both Jules and George, pointing out that if the writers provided their own second sources all the researchers would have to do is reread those sources to make sure the writer had understood it correctly, which would hardly require a staff of five researchers! Both Jules and George agreed with me, and I was told I didn't have to double-source my material. This decision left the other writers free to make their own arrangements with Jules and George. Steven and Kathy, for their part, continued to double-source some of their clues for the remainder of the season.

THE FOURTH SEASON

The first tape day that fourth season had to have been strange for both Alex and George: Alex because he was no longer producer, and George because he now had to make decisions regarding the man who had formerly been in charge. Where he previously had the biggest office on staff, Alex came in that morning unsure of where to even sit down. George eventually had him use a sofa and coffee table in what was now his office. At the meeting to go over the material to be taped, now attended by Alex, Jules, myself and George, there was a certain unease, at first on the part of both George and Alex, with nobody about to propose any changes in the material unless *absolutely* necessary.

At the tapings Alex no longer took time to brief the contestants on how best to handle the material, since it was no longer his place as producer to do so. For whatever reason, George didn't want to do it himself, and so that responsibility now fell to Greg, the contestant coordinator, and his assistants. Between shows Jules and I, as we'd previously done, used to join Alex in his dressing room. There we'd discuss anything unusual in the show just completed, as well as go over anything we felt we should remind Alex of for the upcoming show. We expected George would join us as well, but he preferred to go out for a smoke between shows. Alex, a non-smoker, would have been annoyed to have his dressing room resemble a smoke-filled meeting of back-room politicians. Along with Alex in the dressing room, there would be his make-up man, Larry Abbott, and his wardrobe man, Alan Mills. They're both first-rate professionals, excellent at what they do. They have been with Alex from the start, and their joking and banter have always helped relax Alex between shows. Larry has won a number of Emmys for his work in makeup on various TV shows. As for Alan, he took care of all the wardrobe provided for Alex's use by Mr. Guy, a Beverly Hills clothier, who did that in exchange for a mention on the show's crawl. (Another clothier now provides his wardrobe.)

Overall, the 1987-88 season was the turning point, the year in which Jeopardy would take on the form and style it has maintained to this day. Alex would come in only on those 46 days of the year on which shows were taped. Much of his time would then be spent familiarizing himself with material he was now seeing for the first time. He would go over each clue carefully, deciding which words needed to be emphasized in order that the gist of the clue come across clearly to both viewers and contestants. In addition, he would make sure he had the right pronunciation for each word. If he wasn't sure of a name or foreign word, he would ask a researcher to look into it and make any necessary phone calls. He might occasionally suggest a category to the head writer but otherwise his input was now minimal.

The aim was to produce a serious quiz show on which the Q & A material was clear and accurate. Whether or not a competing show might have done it better, we would not know since at that time, when it came to quiz shows, Jeopardy was the only game in town.

CHAPTER 7

FURTHER UPHEAVALS

As we got deeper and deeper into that fourth season, it became clear Jeopardy would never be the same. Jules seemed quiet and subdued as he went about his daily tasks. Personally, I tried not to let the office atmosphere bother me as my chief concern was taking care of my family.

We were not a bunch of happy campers that season. Of course there were some exceptions. Steven has always been content just being at Jeopardy and he always had his radio contests as a diversion. Kathy seemed to be enjoying herself for reasons I'll explain later. But that was about it. For the rest of us it seemed things couldn't get any worse, which is of course when they did.

Greg Muntean had written a book entitled *How to be a Game Show Contestant* that was being published. In it Greg played heavily on his experiences at Jeopardy, as the book's cover proclaimed him to be the show's contestant coordinator. He also got Alex to write a brief introduction to the book. Generally speaking, an author needs to establish as much credibility in his subject field as possible. If you're offering the reading public a book on how to be a game show contestant, identifying the author as contestant coordinator of the second-highest rated syndicated TV series of all time doesn't seem like a bad idea.

It happened Greg had not arranged to take any vacation as yet that season and therefore had, under Coca Cola rules, two weeks coming to him. At the beginning of the season he was busy lining up contestants, and by the fall he'd had the entire season's contestants arranged for though taping was not yet over. His publisher wanted him to go on a two-week tour to publicize the book. Greg asked George for the time off and George agreed.

FIRED BY THE BOOK

But word of the book tour got back to Bob Murphy, who then called Greg telling him not to go or he'd be in danger of losing his job. Greg had already made all the arrangements with the publisher and didn't see how he could go back on his word and so he took the chance and went anyway.

As soon as he returned he got word he was being fired for taking unauthorized time off. He asked George to explain to Bob that he had gotten permission to take off in advance and George said he would. But whatever George did or didn't do didn't help and Greg was gone.

Luckily for management, Greg had already arranged for the remainder of the season's contestants in advance. Ingrid and Glenn, who were familiar with everything, remained in place. If somewhere out there there's a better contestant coordinator than Greg Muntean, I can't imagine it. His ability to give us contestants who were not only great Jeopardy players but also interesting, memorable personalities seemed matchless. Another era had ended on Jeopardy, never to be repeated.

Ingrid and Glenn, who had been working under Greg as assistant contestant coordinators for two years or more, approached Bob to ask if they together could take over Greg's duties in hopes of the higher title and a little higher salary. After all they knew everything that was going on in the contestant area and had trained under a master. But George had other plans for that position and so they were turned down.

Susanne Thurber is a nice, middle-aged lady who is a friend of George's. She'd worked on some shows but never in the contestant area. Having inherited Alex's people, George apparently wanted some close allies on staff and Susanne clearly filled that need. They seemed comfortable around each other and would occasionally go out drinking together.

Relying on Ingrid and Glenn and the contestants that had been arranged for beforehand, Susanne could easily coast through the remainder of the season. The next season however was her ballgame. Unlike Greg, who used his instincts and intuition and seemed to have a sense of who would do well on television, Susanne played it more conservatively and relied more heavily on the contestant test. That is to say, she seemed to be much more enamored of applicants with very high scores on the written test. As a result, the contestants tended to be somewhat duller than before, although there were of course some exceptions. In fairness to Susanne, it should also be pointed out that the longer the show is on the air, the harder it becomes to find good contestants, since those who are most eager to get on the show have by and large already tried out. Susanne is a cheerful, outgoing lady who always has a smile for everyone; the Jeopardy atmosphere needed someone like that.

Though she was never credited for it, it was Ingrid who came up with the idea of an annual contestant search on U.S. military bases overseas to be sponsored by the USO, which we started doing the following year. Jeopardy has, for many years, been carried by Armed Forces Television and the show is quite popular with our men and women in uniform overseas. Alex liked the idea from the outset. Then when I wrote a Final Jeopardy going for the foreign country in which the most American soldiers are stationed, that clinched it. In conjunction with and under the sponsorship of the USO, it was decided our first such contestant search would be held in what was then West Germany, with stops in some of the neighboring countries. Alex of course went along with the contestant people, since he is the big draw. He senses that any connection with home can be an important morale booster for the troops and likes helping out in that way. Having come from Canada I think he also appreciates how good the U.S. has been to him, and he is pleased to try to repay some of that. The following year they went to the Far East. Each year they arranged for a number of good contestants to come on the show. All TV game shows consider contestants in uniform quite desirable, as viewers tend to readily identify with and root for them. And so if you've ever thought of going on a game show and are in the service, consider that a word of encouragement.

CHRISTMAS

As we got into the 1987 Christmas season the atmosphere did lighten up a bit. George gave each person on staff a silver Tiffany pen, which was a nice gesture on his part. It was the first and last time he gave gifts to the whole staff, which numbered about 25 people. Like most people, I've always felt it's not the cost or even the nature of a gift that matters so much as the thought behind it. When I was in sales, the sales manager usually gave us a bottle of liquor or wine. Now I'm not much of a drinker, but it didn't matter. What mattered was the warm "thanks for a job well done" which came with the gift and for which the gift was only a symbol. Any sales manager worth his salt knows it's the hard work and achievements of his sales staff that play the key role in his success and provide his income. Any good manager is bound to express his appreciation.

One day Alex came by with gifts for the entire staff. That was unusual in that he was no longer in a managerial position. Other game show hosts were not known to do that kind of thing. He obviously valued our work, which was, after all, helping to make it possible for him to earn a handsome living. Alex understood the importance of morale on the Jeopardy staff and wanted to contribute something to it. He continued to do the same thing every Christmas, year after year.

Merv again had his annual Christmas party. He was no longer using the tent but rather rented out a private club, since the number of people under his management was much smaller following the Coca Cola deal and the cancellation of "The Merv Griffin Show" and "Dance Fever." We also had a small office party at which gag gifts and white elephant items were exchanged. Finally, we got the days between Christmas and New Year's off with pay, all of which helped raise everyone's spirits.

XTRA

One day in February, I was sitting at my desk in the office I shared with Steven and working away. Suddenly he yelled out, "Dial 1-800" followed by three more numbers and the letters XTRA. By then I'd been sharing an office with him for a year and a half and was used to this. A contest was on and what did I have to lose? As I dialed, I asked Steven what I had to answer, since many radio contests require you to answer a question of some sort.

"Nothing," he said. "Just be the sixth caller."

Instead of the usual busy signal or overloaded circuits announcement I got a ring. Soon a voice answered. It was none other than celebrated DJ Wolfman Jack telling me I was the sixth caller and had therefore won $69 from radio station XTRA. XTRA is a radio station aimed at the San Diego market whose tower is just across the border in Tijuana, Mexico. Unlike ours, which begin with "W" or "K," the call letters of Mexican radio stations begin with X. Like many other Mexican border stations, it has a powerful signal and could easily be heard in Los Angeles. Its frequency on the AM dial is 690, which is why the prize money was $69. In those days they had a Golden Oldies format and Wolfman Jack would do a daily program for them out of a studio in his home in Beverly Hills. XTRA later went to an all-talk format. I later wrote a Jeopardy clue about him indicating his real name is Robert Weston Smith and got to know him a little bit over the phone when I called to confirm the fact.

That XTRA contest was being run once a day throughout the month of February, which had 29 days that year. Besides the $69 dollars, each winner would get his name entered in a drawing for "the fantasy vacation." That meant airfare and lodging for a week for two to your choice of London, Paris, Switzerland, Rome, Kenya, Tahiti, Australia, New Zealand or Tokyo. I won the day the contest began, on February 1. Later in the month Steven and Ruth Deutsch also won.

All the winners were later invited to a party in San Diego during which the drawing was to be held. Unfortunately, the party was on a Monday night when we were taping, so I couldn't go. Debby didn't feel like going without me. Steven was also helping out at the taping that day and that ruled him out, but Ruth was able to go and represent the three of us. I forgot to tell Debby Ruth would be in San Diego that night, and when I got home from the taping, Debby told me about an unusual phone call she received earlier. It had been the operator saying she had a collect call from Ruth in San Diego. Debby replied she didn't know a Ruth in San Diego when Ruth blurted out "It's Ruth Deutsch! You won the contest! You won the contest!"

TAHITI

The next day I took Ruth to lunch; it was the least I could do. Debby and I now had a difficult decision on our hands. We thought about choosing England as our destination, as that country has so much in the way of cultural offerings. But we finally settled on Tahiti. It's so far off the beaten track we concluded we'd probably never see it if we didn't take this opportunity.

Tahiti is in the tropics, but late May and early June are part of its cooler, drier season, so the weather was ideal. In all we spent eight nights and nine days there, half on Tahiti and half on the neighboring island of Moorea. Moorea was the island on which James Michener based his fictional *Bali Hai* in his *Tales of the South Pacific*. On Moorea we stayed at the Club Bali Hai hotel. Owned by three Americans, the Club Bali Hai is located deep in Cook's Bay, a stunning inlet of the sea. The scenery all around us was nothing short of breathtaking. Equally spectacular, neighboring Opanohu Bay is less developed and was the sight of the Tahiti landing in the 1963 version of *Mutiny on the Bounty* starring Marlon Brando.

Tahiti was equally enjoyable, with both islands offering pretty beaches, snorkeling, jungle hiking and superb Polynesian, French and Chinese cuisine. The people were most friendly and seemed so genuine. You could drink the water and everything seemed clean and sufficiently well ordered. The Polynesians are not rich but they seem to have a dignity about them that is both inspiring and refreshing to see. Family values are important to them, and all the children we saw looked clean and well cared for. But I've gotten ahead of myself.

THE NEW EDITORIAL ASSOCIATE PRODUCER

Back at Jeopardy it was still March 1988 and the taping season was moving towards a close. There were two weeks of taping to go and season four would be history when on a Saturday afternoon I got a phone call at home. It was George. I was surprised to say the least, since he'd never called me at home before. He was calling to tell me Jules would no longer be working on Jeopardy and to ask if I'd be willing to take over his responsibilities.

"What happened?" I asked. I could sense he wasn't comfortable talking about it, but said Jules had lost his temper again and this time he'd gone so far as to strike Kim Grunenfelder. Kim is Carol Campbell's daughter and was the show's runner at the time. George said he could no longer have Jules in the office. I said I was sorry to hear that and agreed to take the editorial associate producer position.

All this came as quite a shock to me. Here I had been under the impression that Jules had pretty much succeeded in controlling his temper. I couldn't recall a single problem that season. With my heavy work load at Jeopardy and my family responsibilities I was one who came in to work, did his job and went home with little time to spare for office politics and intrigues. On top of all that we were now planning a wedding and at the same time trying to decide where to take the trip we'd won. What happened to Jules and my being offered his job was the last thing in the world I expected to happen at that time.

Most people would welcome a promotion at work, and I'm no different in that regard. It's obviously indicative of the fact that management has some respect for the work you've been doing and believes you can handle additional responsibility. As far as that goes I felt honored in being chosen for the job, but there was no pleasure in getting it under these circumstances. Here Jules had been with the show from the very start, having even written the pilots. He was instrumental in my being hired and had taught me a great deal, and now to have it end like this. How much better it would have been for me to get a promotion at the same time he was getting one.

I got back to work on Monday morning, which was a tape day, and I had my hands full. As always, Steven had come in early and I got him to do many of the things I'd previously been doing. Since he had been the most prolific writer and was quite knowledgeable in pop culture, an area in which I was weak, I suggested he serve as the other judge, and George agreed. When Alex came in he said he was sorry about what happened to Jules but felt he'd brought his problem on himself. In the meantime we had to get on with the tapings.

The ten shows of that day and the next came off without a hitch, other than the fact Steven said he felt uncomfortable in a judge's chair. From time to time Alex would look to us for a nod of yea or nay; we had to respond almost instantaneously. We handled it all smoothly those two days, although the tension and pressure were always there. The pressure comes with the realization you can be called upon for a spontaneous ruling on anything that might come out of a contestant's mouth. Having of course prepared the material, we could handle most unforeseen contestant responses all right. Occasionally, however, there would be one which threw us for a loop, and we'd either have to stop tape or later reverse a decision that was made too hastily. Judging on Jeopardy is a humbling experience, which ultimately tends to make any person realize how little he actually knows. Steven quickly concluded it wasn't for him, and I asked George if it would be OK with him to have Fred as the other judge in place of Steven. It was fine with him. Fred is well educated, well read and is stronger than me in the sciences. He has an excellent vocabulary and is excellent with definitions of words, which can often be a factor in dealing with contestant responses regardless of the category. Neither of us is particularly strong in pop culture, but that didn't seem to be a problem since George was constantly looking to cut back on that aspect of the show (Alex knows a great deal in that area anyway). By the end of the seventh season our weakness in the pop culture area was starting to show a bit, and it was decided that Kathy, who is quite strong in movies, TV and celebrities in general, would join us at the judges' table.

Fred worked out fine those last two tape days of season four, both as operator of the switches that control the players' signalling buttons and electronic pens and as a judge. He has been serving in those capacities ever since.

The season's last taping session was followed by a wrap party, which is customary in the industry. It turned out to be the last wrap party we would ever have, as they were later cut out, apparently to save money. At the party JulieAnn presented me with a giant pair of plastic scissors symbolic of cutting out and assembling the various category strips into Jeopardy games. It seems everyone came up to me and indicated how much they were looking forward to working with me in the future. With the upcoming wedding as well as my promotion, I too was looking forward to the future. But that night at the party what I mainly felt was a tremendous sense of relief at having come through those tapings okay after having been suddenly and unexpectedly called upon to take responsibility for the material.

CHAPTER 8

A NEW BEGINNING

When George had first taken over as producer, he made no formal announcement as to any changes in format or procedure but simply made changes whenever he felt like doing so or when Merv or Bob asked him to. Most of the procedures we'd developed in the early years of the show were still in place. With George's changes being introduced one at a time the show seemed to be evolving gradually. The only procedural change George had in store for me in making me editorial associate producer was that he indicated that both the writers and researchers should report to me, as they had to Jules prior to season four.

I however was eager to institute a number of changes up front as I was quite aware of various problems in the writing and research areas from my four years as a writer. I began by calling a meeting of the writing and research staffs. The first thing I said was I was looking forward to working with all of them on a professional basis and wanted to maintain an atmosphere of professionalism in the office. I went on to indicate I felt we should all enjoy what we're doing and that the job should be fun but did not wish to see the atmosphere degenerate into one of silliness, pettiness, immaturity and backbiting. Our task was to provide usable material for 230 shows; no more, no less. A complete season of 230 shows meant a total of 2,760 regular categories plus 230 Final Jeopardies. With five writers on staff that came out to 552 categories per writer for the season plus 46 finals. I could be the most lenient guy in the world but there was no way I could settle for less than that. Likewise, I could be the meanest S.O.B. but I wasn't going to demand more. I reminded the writers that their quota was 15 categories per week. Allowing for holidays, vacations, visits to the doctor, dentist, etc., it should not be a problem for any writer to do his share since at 15 categories per week, 552 categories could be written in less than 37 weeks out of a 52-week year. As for the Research Department, between taking turns proofreading, occasionally writing and constantly complaining about the work load, it pretty much struck me as rather chaotic. Amazingly, the researchers had never been assigned an output quota and there was therefore no way of knowing for sure just how much each individual researcher was contributing. I was well acquainted with the research job since in the past, whenever we were behind in research, which was fairly often, Jules would assign all the writers to do research for a day or two. In doing research I saw it wasn't all that difficult to do from six to eight categories per day provided you stuck to the principle of not allowing yourself to get bogged down on any single point of fact for more than 20 minutes or so.

QUOTAS

The idea of having a different researcher serve as proofreader for a week on a rotating basis had not worked out. Some were better at it than others and one result was a lack of consistency. Some people caught certain errors while others let them go through. In the past I had suggested we hire a professional proofreader and through a friend had located a person with years of experience. The woman came in for an interview but didn't hit it off with Associate Producer Sherry Hilber under whose jurisdiction the matter of proofreading the Chyron computer system fell. In any case, I was now determined to go with one proofreader rather than six. That would leave five researchers. I saw no reason why each one couldn't handle a quota of 18 categories a week and told the researchers so. If I had to research 18 categories a week, I'd get it done in three days and spend the other two at the beach.

Fred had indicated that since he now had additional duties on tape days, his quota should reflect that. I agreed with him as I don't feel it's fair to expect a person to do two jobs but only get paid for one. Since we began keeping tabs on the output of each researcher, we've had numerous researchers able to make their quota with ease and it was later increased to 20 a week. Unfortunately, we also had our share of game players.

I didn't institute the research quota because I wanted to be a harsh taskmaster. More than anything, I wanted to be able to recognize and reward those who were carrying their share of the load and doing a good job. In this regard I was totally naive.

One of the first things I did after being named editorial associate producer was to request some kind of expense account in order to occasionally take a staffer to lunch or have a staff luncheon in the office. I thought taking someone out to lunch from time to time would be a nice way of thanking them for some extra effort on their part. It can also help promote or maintain a good working relationship. I felt taking a subordinate to lunch occasionally was the right thing to do and so I did it out of my own pocket.

Keeping track of each person's overall output helped me at the end of each season to write a comprehensive evaluation of each person on my staff. This is fairly standard procedure in the business world and I did so in the hope that these evaluations would be taken into consideration in deciding pay raises for the following season. Naturally, I wanted to see those who had done more rewarded for their extra efforts. This idea, too, was all for naught.

For each new season, management gave all the writers and researchers the same pay raise regardless. That is, if they were going to give them any pay raise at all. Perhaps management kept the raises the same because they were afraid of being charged with unfair discrimination.

In any case, my evaluations had no effect but I still took the trouble to do them from year to year. As far as I was concerned, each employee I managed was a human being whose individual contributions were worthy of noting. I felt that George and those above him *ought* to be aware of the specific contribution and role played by each worker regardless of whether they were willing to do anything about it or not. After I saw how unconcerned George was with regard to these evaluations I have to admit I felt awkward doing them but something in me told me to keep on doing what I believed to be the right thing regardless. Neither Jules before me nor Terry McDonnell, who was to succeed me bothered to write up individual job descriptions and evaluations and I can see why. In talking to the Merv Griffin Enterprises personnel manager some three years later, I was amazed to learn that it is a company that doesn't even keep job descriptions of its employees on file in the personnel office.

I informed the researchers that I did not think it right for the writers to have to double-source any clues. If the writers did that, all the researchers would have to do is go over the writers' work and for that you didn't need four or five researchers. One or, at most, two would be quite sufficient. In the interests of keeping their jobs, none of the researchers complained. Prior to the meeting I had gone over that point with George. For his part, he didn't think the researchers should have to go over what the writers had already read and reminded me that on the old Jeopardy they did without researchers altogether. I pointed out we from time to time had instances where writers misread something and since the writer was citing his source, it wouldn't take the researcher much time to check it out. The bulk of the researchers' time has always been spent finding or trying to find that second, confirming source.

One of the things I was able to arrange with George from the outset was to allow for individual vacation time. I hadn't much cared for having my vacation time selected for me the previous year and had no desire to do so to others. Just as I needed some time for an upcoming wedding and honeymoon, others had their personal needs as well. By now Coca Cola's Entertainment Business Sector no longer existed and Merv Griffin Enterprises had been made a part of Columbia Pictures, which Coke then owned. Columbia rules allowed for a third week of vacation after you'd been employed for four years, which gave those of us who had been with the show from the start an extra week. George agreed that people should be allowed to take their vacations any time outside the taping season. This meant people could arrange for their time off anywhere from April through the end of July, which was something we'd never known before.

ENTER ROCKY SCHMIDT

Rocky, you will recall, had started out in season three as Alex's secretary. When George took over Rocky was able to arrange to have a double job with extra salary. He would continue to take messages for Alex, who would of course continue getting calls on a private line at Jeopardy (to which Rocky would answer "Alex Trebek's office") even though he no longer had an office there. And he would work as George's secretary as well.

The advent of George was an opportunity Rocky could hardly miss seeing. It wasn't very long until Rocky had made himself absolutely essential to George. His job title was soon changed to Assistant to the Producer. That in turn became Assistant Producer. Rocky came across as quite ambitious and Associate Producer Sherry Hilber thought he was after her job. Assistant Producer is an uncommon title in television so it was hard to figure out what to make of it. For his part Rocky seemed content for the time being to simply consider himself our equal even though Sherry and I were managing the entire staff other than the contestant department.

One of Rocky's duties was to answer the letters that came in to the show. A computer with the WordPerfect program was quite helpful to him in that regard. Now many of the letters that came in dealt with mistakes or alleged mistakes in the Jeopardy material. In the vast majority of the cases it was the viewer who misheard or misunderstood something on the show. Merv Griffin policy nonetheless required that every letter be answered. But that created a lot of work for Rocky and the higher the show's ratings and the more viewers we had, the more letters that came in. You would think that most people are too busy to spend much time writing letters to TV programs but some obviously have the time to write letters of four, five, or more pages in length and Rocky had to deal with them all.

It seems he directed much of his annoyance at the researchers. On getting a letter alleging an error or inaccuracy in the material, Rocky would track down the original card on which the clue had been written and seek out the researcher who had initialed the card indicating he or she had checked the facts. More often than not the researcher would explain to Rocky how it wasn't we who had slipped up but the viewer who misunderstood. But there were instances where we were wrong and under George and Rocky, the researcher had to bear the full brunt of that.

PROOFREADING ERRORS

When Alex had been producer, he seemed to view everything as a team effort and if something was wrong it wasn't just the researcher's fault but also the writer's, Jules', mine, the proofreader's, Alex's and anyone else's who had seen the material and let the error get by. As a writer I had prided myself on being accurate but I had made my share of mistakes. One time I described the Biblical Esau as "Jacob's hairy son." I'm fairly familiar with the Bible and I know Jacob was Esau's twin brother and Isaac was their father. But sometimes your mind plays tricks on you and whether I misread or misthought, it didn't come out right on the typewriter and the mistake managed to get into a game and on television. We're not perfect and we've done everything humanly possible to keep errors to a minimum. That's why the research staff was enlarged from originally one person to six.

Inasmuch as the researcher's primary task is to make sure everything in a clue is true and accurate, they obviously bear a major responsibility in this area of accuracy. But now Rocky began keeping tabs on how many errors each researcher was responsible for and his tally showed that Ruth and Suzanne's work contained more errors than that of the others. That was the reason George wanted to fire them

and he furthermore pointed out that Jules had agreed (prior to his being forced out) that they should not be retained for the next season. I
told George I wanted to think about their situation.

I went through what seemed to be a representative number of the
category cards that had been written the previous season. They seemed
to confirm what I had suspected. The reason Suzanne and Ruth had
more errors in their work was because they had done far more work
than the others to begin with. Someone who researched 50 categories
without a flaw may have batted 1.000 but someone who researched
700 categories while making three or four errors contributed a lot more
to the show and if that latter person had stopped at 50 categories they
might very well have likewise had no errors at all. It's too bad Rocky
could only keep tabs on the number of bad clues that got through as
opposed to the number of good, flawless categories each researcher
turned in. Of course the figures I cited in my example are somewhat
extreme but it did turn out in later seasons that Suzanne, who was
then our most productive researcher, literally did more than twice as
many categories per season than our least productive researcher.

I also went to see Sherry to discuss the proofreading situation.
Proofreading at Jeopardy was originally a double job with the proofreader first making sure the final copy of the game was accurate as
regards punctuation, spelling, typos and the like and then proofing the
Chyron to make sure the Chyron operator hasn't made errors in trans-
ferring the material from the game sheets to the computer which con-
trols the game board you see on your TV. Patrice, the Chyron operator reported to Sherry and worked with Sherry's production assistants
and the proofreader. Sherry therefore had an idea as to who among
the researchers who shared last season's proofing duties was a good
proofreader and who wasn't. Ruth, it turned out, was one of the good
ones according to Sherry while some of the others had been so poor
at it you could readily tell which had been their week to do it. Sherry
eventually came to depend on the production assistants to help proofread the Chyron. She said as far as she was concerned, the PAs could
proofread the Chyron all the time as they had enough time to do it.
That gave me an idea and so I went back to see George.

First, I pointed out the flaw in Rocky's reasoning as to why
Suzanne and Ruth should be fired. I then explained that Sherry felt
the PAs could proofread the Chyron and said I'd like to have Ruth
proofread the game copy as her primary job and do research in the
remaining time. George agreed to that arrangement and was willing to
keep Suzanne for the time being as well but indicated he would consider both "on probation" for at least six months after which he would

reconsider their status and give them a raise if they warranted staying. I told him I would, for the first time, be monitoring the output of each researcher and would keep him posted.

BAD NEWS

Next, I had to break the news to Barbara, Gary, Ruth and Suzanne. At first I thought, "Well, I've managed to save their jobs at least for the time being and hopefully they'll be appreciative," but I quickly realized better. I now had to tell four veteran employees, all of whom had worked at Jeopardy for three or four years that they wouldn't be getting a raise this year, at least not for the time being, were in danger of losing their jobs and were now "on probation." I may have gone to some lengths to save their jobs but as soon as I would apprise them of the situation the reaction was sure to be one of anger or at the very least disappointment. After all, they'd never received a warning of any kind and had no inkling of what was going on.

That was precisely what happened as I now had four angry and disappointed people on my hands. All had been looking forward to a raise and what I had to say was the last thing on earth they expected to hear from an associate producer they considered a friend. I, of course, talked to each one privately and in every case offered to assist them in any way I could to do their best on the job. In that way they could hopefully remain at Jeopardy and would later get that pay raise as well. Of course, each individual's situation was somewhat unique.

BARBARA HELLER

Barbara Heller had come in as a researcher but was made a writer early in the first season. Despite that her salary had never been brought up to par with the other writers and as a result Jules agreed to allow her a smaller production quota of categories. I told her that at this point she would have to work at full quota and the work would have to be of sufficient quality in order for her to remain on staff. If that were to be resolved satisfactorily, I agreed to then do my best to have her salary issue dealt with fairly.

We all knew Barbara's first love is country music. In the past she'd appeared as an opening act for major country stars in venues ranging in size from small clubs to Houston's Astrodome. She's also done her own shows featuring both singing and comedy in restaurants, clubs and auditoriums. Barbara is a good singer and a superb songwriter. She even wrote a song especially for Debby and me which she sang at our wedding reception. Her recording of it is one of our most cherished possessions. Unfortunately, the country music industry is dominated by men. That's because most of the fans are women who are apparently more interested in male performers than those of their own gender. In addition, most country stars write a lot of their own songs which makes the market for other songwriters an extremely tough one to crack. But Barbara is one of the best and maybe one day soon she'll get a break.

Barbara's marriage had come apart while she was working at Jeopardy. She'd turned her back on her performing career because that's what Stan, her husband, wanted and when the marriage didn't work out she undoubtedly had her regrets about leaving country music. She remained at Jeopardy until July (1988) when she left to return to the music world. She lived briefly and performed in Park City, Utah before moving on to Nashville. Thomas Wolfe said "You can't go home again" and it hasn't been easy for Barbara. She came back to California to nurse Stan when he was dying of cancer. Stan was one who liked to burn the candle at both ends and lived the life of the big spender but when it was all over he had nothing to leave Barbara but debts and she's had a hard time dealing with those. Once again known as Barbara Hart, she's now back in Nashville in the ranks of those who come to that city trying to fulfill their country dreams.

GARY LEE

Over the years Gary Lee had given us some of the best clues we ever had on Jeopardy. Some of his material was so good and/or funny it was selected for the clips of the show we submitted to be used in judging the show for consideration for a daytime Emmy award as Best Game Show. His tastes and interests are somewhat eclectic and not all the material he submitted was what you would necessarily call mainstream. I've often thought that having Woody Allen write for Jeopardy probably wouldn't be all that different from having had Gary. George seemed to want the kind of material that would play in Peoria and much of Gary's material came across as too "off the wall." Gary is something of a perfectionist and he therefore tended to work slower than the others, devoting more time to each clue but that considerably lessened his overall output. I told him he would have to meet quota from now on and that I'd work with him to try to produce the kind of material George wanted.

Gary now realized his job was on the line and he began working extra hard to try to save it. I explained to him and showed him the kind of material we wanted and he seemed to be gradually adjusting his style in that direction.

When I would turn in the games I had assembled for George to go over, George asked me to point out which categories had been written by Gary and Barbara and I would note that on a post-it for him. He continued to be rather critical of them and I thought maybe the process wasn't fair. I then suggested George go over each game without knowing who wrote which categories and simply point out what he didn't like. A considerable amount of that turned out to be Gary's material, and George made it a point to let me know when the three months were up. I would have liked to continue working longer with Gary as I felt progress was being made. I pointed that out to George but I think he'd made up his mind from the outset and his patience had now run out.

Telling Gary we were letting him go was the hardest thing I ever had to do at Jeopardy. I arranged for us to meet in a restaurant as I respected his sensitivities and thought it would be better than discussing it in the office. He had made a genuine effort and had worked up to and even exceeded the quota in those last three months. We worked together for four years and I considered him a friend. He's not just a fair weather friend but is the type of guy a person can depend on when they need help and so it really hurt. I told him he wasn't coming up with the kind of material we were looking for. He certainly has writing ability but it just didn't seem to mesh with Jeopardy. I wished him nothing but the best for the future and offered to help him in any way I could. By the time our meeting was over I wished to God I would never have to go through something like that again.

One conclusion I later drew from this and many other incidents is that staying on a job where one is not appreciated for whatever reason is worse than being unemployed. I know that's contrary to the conventional wisdom that says one should avoid unemployment at all costs since it makes one appear less attractive in the job market besides creating numerous financial problems. But if a person is smart enough to put his health before his finances he will realize it is psychologically and probably psychosomatically damaging to remain in a job where you are not wanted. I have never in my life seen anything good come out of such a situation.

As for Gary, he went on to become a writer, and later Head Writer, on the Q&A show "Trump Card," which aired during the 1990–91 season.

RUTH DEUTSCH

Like the others, Ruth Deutsch was quite surprised when I talked to her about her situation, and she wasn't sure if she should take the proofreading job. She didn't fully grasp the gravity of the situation at first and I explained to her she'd be on more solid ground if she took that job and excelled at it. Ruth is a highly creative person who wanted to write but, like Gary, her tastes are somewhat eclectic. Proofreading isn't very creative but neither is research which was of course what she had been doing. It was the best I could offer her and hopefully she'd make the most of it. Her work as our proofreader proved to be more than adequate in my opinion and she remained with Jeopardy for over two more years.

SUZANNE STONE

When I spoke to Suzanne Stone, she immediately understood the situation but was deeply hurt. She was the show's original researcher and had personally trained just about every researcher on staff. They were always taking problem clues to her but she never got any official recognition as head or senior researcher. She was making less than most of the other researchers, having lost her seniority when she left at the beginning of season three, while doing considerably more work than any of them. I'd gone to George and told him that Rocky was dead wrong in her case, but George wouldn't agree. Rocky was rapidly becoming a power to be reckoned with in the office. The best I could do was to arrange to monitor every researcher's work output from here on, so that output could be compared with the number of errors each one made.

As I expected, Suzanne proved me to be correct in her case. Her output continued to far exceed the others and her error average (flawed material getting through versus number of categories done) was among the very lowest on staff. I was then able to convince George to put in for a pay raise for her and Ruth which finally came through the next February. I later asked George to officially name her Head Researcher as Alex had done with Jim Kearney but he demurred saying he felt that would offend Fred, who though also a researcher was serving as a judge at the tapings. I didn't agree but failed to convince George and it went no further. During my tenure as editorial associate producer Suzanne served as a virtual right arm to me, as I found her always willing to take on extra work and totally dependable. She is still with the show and has remained the *de facto* if not *de jure* leader of the research staff.

ADDITIONAL CHANGES

In those early days as editorial associate producer, I instituted some other changes as well. I eliminated the use of Latin scientific names of animal and plant species as well as other foreign terms that we'd been using to "pin" down the correct responses to clues. I felt the right response should be pinned down by the facts in the clue with the facts clearly understood by the player and viewers. A Jeopardy clue should not have to depend on strange terms not in common usage.

I felt that whether a clue was hard or easy and whether the viewers knew what the right response was or not, they should always know what we're talking about. It's a point I constantly emphasized to the writers. As much as possible, I preferred short, snappy writing to long, convoluted clues that were hard to follow. As a writer I came up with the "Presidential Middle Names" category which consisted of just a single word for each clue. But even with that you could have a little fun as we had "Woodrow" (Pres. Wilson's *middle* name—his first name was Thomas) followed by "Wilson" (Pres. Reagan's middle name). I felt the one-word clues helped diversify the games and was always on the lookout for creative ways to make the shows a bit more interesting. Of course the short clues also helped Alex to clear the board.

We later introduced all-audio categories in which the monitor screens on the game board came up blank and the clues consisted solely of music. One of those categories was "Big Band Themes" in which we played the themes and the contestants had to name the famous big band leaders with whom they are associated. We knew it was a subject Merv liked and we appropriately saved it for the Seniors Tournament.

I also wanted to do an all-video category in which each clue would have consisted entirely of a picture but was told it would create too many technical difficulties. In general I always liked the idea of adding a little "color" to the show but George took a much more reserved approach and preferred to stick to "meat and potatoes." Occasionally he would be willing to go along with a creative new idea we generated but for the most part he would nix them.

Up to this time we had been using a four-color coding system in organizing our categories: blue for academic, green for lifestyle, pink for pop culture and yellow for word play. To this I now proposed adding orange for categories about people—politicians, famous women, movie stars, athletes, doctors, lawyers, teachers, businessmen, famous people born under specific signs of the zodiac, etc.—and George agreed. I was impressed by the great success *People* magazine has enjoyed from its inception. People, especially women it seems, are interested in knowing about other people and I felt a greater emphasis on people in the material would be attractive to the viewers, make the shows more interesting and perhaps even help narrow our "gender gap."

Unfortunately, this idea never really caught on at Jeopardy. Among the writers Kathy was the only one who turned out these orange categories with any consistency and since most of her people categories were in the celebrity-pop culture realm, I could only use them on a limited basis. Once writers are used to writing a certain way, it is very hard to re-orient them. If you're ever going to produce a question and answer game show, first keep in mind the kind of material you want on the show and then go out and find the kind of writers who can give it to you. If you start with the writers first, you may have a hard time getting the material you want.

With Carol moving to the writing side we were now short one person in research. Since becoming editorial associate producer I'd made it a point to have lunch from time to time with Sherry, the other associate producer. We seemed to have a good rapport and Sherry, having dealt with George as his direct subordinate for a lot longer than I, was able to advise me in certain matters. For example, she pointed out that George preferred significant communications to be generated in writing via memo, rather than orally, which was how Jules did most everything with Alex. Sherry told me that Kim wasn't all that busy as the show's runner and she had expressed interest in becoming a researcher. We worked out an agreement where Kim would work half time in research doing half quota and the remainder of the time as the show's runner. We took this to George and he approved.

With the addition of Kim half time, Ruth researching when she wasn't proofreading and increasing the research quota to 20 categories a week I was confident we could do the job without having to hire someone new and without putting an undue burden on anyone.

When the researchers turned in material I would keep a running total and at the end of every month check how much each person had contributed for the month. I also kept track of the type of categories each was researching (how many blues, how many greens, pinks, etc.) because I know some types of categories tended to require less work than others. Some researchers had a tendency to go for the easier-to-research pinks and yellows, leaving the harder material for the others in order to make their numbers look better. I brought that up in a meeting and asked that people not hoard large numbers of categories.

With Barbara and Gary having left within a few weeks of one another, I suddenly found myself short two writers. By now I had learned a few lessons. I had just seen the risk in hiring comparatively inexperienced writers and what could result. Also Carol was not working out as well as I had hoped. Month after month she would come in way behind quota-wise. Where I was expecting fifteen categories a week I was getting seven or eight and had to make up the shortfall. But at that point in time I was hopeful she would eventually improve. However, I made it a point to tell George we simply couldn't afford any more inexperienced writers. What I wanted were experienced professionals who could work under the pressure of having to make their quota week in and week out. He agreed and told me to see who I could find. I asked what the company would be willing to pay for experienced pros and he told me they'd been paying Gary $700 and Barbara $650 and he was hoping to keep the salaries at that level.

STEVE TAMERIUS

One of the people I was interested in bringing to Jeopardy as a writer was Steve Tamerius. I of course knew Steve from his days as a researcher with us in season three. I remembered he'd left on good terms (having given ample notice and explaining his reason) in order to take a writing job at "Card Sharks," a Mark Goodson production. I knew he had approximately five years' experience writing for game shows. I also knew he hated leaving Jeopardy because he enjoyed working with our tougher material but that the move to Mark Goodson represented a substantial salary increase for him.

From time to time Kathy and Steven would exceed quota by two to four categories a week, which helped. I was able to write a few categories myself but the remainder I owed to Steven's somewhat unorthodox system of working. When the other writers got back say, three clues in a single category that had been unused in a previous game, they would write four more and turn the seven in as a new category. Steven didn't do that. He wrote all his complete categories new from scratch and saved all the old recycles for an emergency. By doing that he'd amassed four large card files of unused leftover clues. The rainy day had arrived and Steven and I went through his files of leftovers and put quite a few categories together. That more than anything else helped carry us through the crunch.

STEPHANIE SPADACCINI

I was still looking for one more writer and when I told Steven about it, he suggested Stephanie Spadaccini, a lady he knew who had previously been managing editor of *Games* magazine and had also written for some game shows. Steven had written some puzzles for *Games* as well as an article about Jeopardy and spoke highly of Stephanie. I called Stephanie and asked if she might be interested in writing for Jeopardy. She was and so I asked her to submit a writing sample, much as we had been asked to do when I was first considered for the show. I was impressed by her material and George wanted to see it as well.

When George read it he couldn't believe it. He was aware Steven knew Stephanie and said he must have helped her. He figured Stephanie must be some young girl in whom Steven had taken a personal interest and now wanted to bring on staff. When I pointed out Stephanie was a middle aged woman with grown sons George calmed down. She came in for a pleasant interview, met George and agreed to join us for the $650 salary that had been offered. Both she and Steve started working the last week of September.

The arrival of Steve and Stephanie was like a breath of fresh air. I now had four writers on whom I could depend to meet quota. Stephanie and Steve turned out to be very much the professionals I'd hoped they would be. I'm not a martinet or one to stand on ceremony, but Steve and Stephanie always treated me with the kind of deference with which one would expect a manager to be treated. In fact, that was true of every person we brought in from the outside to join the writing and research staffs. On the other hand, a few of the "old timers" couldn't get over the fact that I'd once been "one of them" and it was apparent in their attitude towards me.

Stephanie is a lovely lady—pleasant, friendly and originally from New York. Stephanie likes word play but could write Jeopardy clues in just about any category. She was divorced and one of her three sons had recently been killed in a tragic traffic accident. She stayed with us a little over a year before moving up to San Francisco where she preferred to live and pursue a career as a freelance writer. Before she left she told me how much she had appreciated the opportunity to work at Jeopardy which came shortly after her personal tragedy. Enabling her to perform work she was good at and found meaningful, she told me, helped her to cope with her loss. I never forgot that and it has meant a lot to me.

I've talked about Steve before. As a writer he was pretty flexible though word play wasn't his forte. He could do sports and show biz but I asked him to limit those since George didn't want to see too many of them in the games. So mostly he did the academic and lifestyle ("meat and potatoes") categories. Occasionally George would complain Steve's material was too "male." I don't see how you can ask a male to stop being male, though you certainly can request the inclusion of some categories and the exclusion of others. Unfortunately all I ever received were lots of exclusionary requests (cut back on TV, Movies, Sports, Pop Music, Wars, Weapons, Politics, and even The Queen's English—our British English category). Inclusionary requests that were positive in nature were extremely few and far between. I failed to see why this male–female material business should be a problem, as our writing staff now consisted of three women and only two men. From time to time George would point to some category in a game and complain it was "too male" and must have been written by Steve, only to have me point out it had been written by a woman.

As I continued to collect and edit categories from the writers I kept on trying to add a little color, a little humor, a little life to the material as much as I could, though this was of little concern to George. He seemed to fear that such things would not go over well with Merv. Occasionally I'd put some categories alongside one another for fun such as "Soap" followed by "Water" or "Bells" followed by "Books" and "Candles" or "Wine" "Women" and "Songs." If I found myself with six or eight categories that all began with the same letter, I'd request a few more and put together a game in which all the categories, including the one for Final Jeopardy, began with the same letter, such as "A" or "M." Every time I did that George would suspect I'd put together a "signature game"; that is one that had been written entirely by one writer, something he didn't approve of, and I'd have to assure him that wasn't the case.

As we began taping our fifth season of shows, I was somewhat nervous in that it was the first time we would be using material for which I'd been responsible. Fortunately the shows turned out quite well. The contestants seemed to handle the material well and there were comparatively few runaway games. There also seemed to be fewer controversies regarding individual clues than there had been in the past.

Alex's "VTV" show that he'd co-hosted with Meredith MacRae the previous season had not done well and was cancelled. But Alex was picked up by Mark Goodson to host the revived version of "Classic Concentration" and so he was managing to keep quite busy.

Back in 1988 there was yet another personnel change to deal with. One of our researchers, Victoria Haselton, had previously married Dr. Daryoush Jadali. He is an immigrant from Iran and when they married in 1987, it was the first time I'd ever been to a Muslim wedding. Daryoush was taking his medical residency in New Jersey and so Victoria was leaving us. I spoke to George and arranged to run an ad for a researcher in *The Hollywood Reporter*, only this time it would be a blind ad, using only a box number rather than giving out the employer's identity.

As the responses started to come in, one person was smart enough to figure out the ad had been placed by Jeopardy and began calling me regularly. She was a young lady named Sandy Sycafoose and she finally convinced me to let her come in for an interview. We gave her the contestant test which we were planning to do with all the applicants we wanted to seriously consider. She passed. In fact she was so persistent in going after the job, I asked that she be hired and George approved. I'd never seen anyone pursue a job with such enthusiasm and desire.

Sandy left us after two years to move to Portland, Oregon. She's originally from Massachusetts and everyone was advising her to tell the folks in Oregon she's from Massachusetts rather than California. We'd all heard there was such a large influx of Californians into the Pacific Northwest, they were becoming rather unpopular. Sandy is now the executive assistant to the producer of the Claymation animated puppets. In 1992 they won an Emmy Award for their Claymation Easter Special.

WINNING AN EMMY JEOPARDY! STYLE

Back in the second and third seasons of the show, Alex had submitted our names to the Academy of Television Arts and Sciences for consideration for a daytime Emmy award for writing. Since there is no longer a "Best Writing for a Game Show" category, game show writing now falls under "Writing—Special Class," which is a catch-all miscellaneous category for shows that don't fall under the other specific genres. In 1974, the only year in which there was a "Best Writing for a Game Show" category, that Emmy went to the writers of "Hollywood Squares" who were always coming up with those terrific gag answers for the celebrities. The Academy then dropped the game show writing Emmy apparently figuring that in some seasons there might not be enough game shows employing writers to make for fair competition since many game shows such as "Price Is Right" and "Let's

Make a Deal" have formats that don't require writers in the conventional sense.

Since Alex saw Jeopardy as a team effort, he included not only Jules and the writers but also the researchers, most of whom at that time did do some writing (but not enough to qualify under TV Academy rules), and even JulieAnn, who never wrote so much as one category, as "writers." Both times, a sufficient number of members of the writers' branch of the Academy saw fit to vote for us, and the result was that we were twice nominated for an Emmy. We didn't win either time. One year we lost to a special about artist Marc Chagall called "Chagall's Journey" and the second time none of the nominees had enough "yes" votes to win. Still it was an honor to have been the only game show writers even nominated in those years.

For the show's fourth season ('87–'88) we couldn't even be nominated; we had fallen through a crack in the rules. For a show to be considered for a daytime Emmy it had to be on before 6:00 P.M. in at least half its markets. By that time we were on in the access hour in most markets, which in effect made us a prime-time show, but there were no categories into which we could fit for consideration for a prime-time Emmy. However, the following year the rules were changed so as to allow all game shows to be eligible in the daytime Emmy competition, regardless of air time.

WE WON!

In June of 1991 the Jeopardy writers won Daytime Emmys. Ironically, the awards ceremony that year was held in, of all places, Merv Griffin's Beverly Hilton hotel. It was only the second time ever that game show writers had been so honored and the first time in the wide-open "Special Class" category. Though I had left Jeopardy a few weeks before, at the end of May, I nevertheless considered it a personal triumph.

This time the Jeopardy writers did receive acknowledgments of congratulations from Columbia as well as King World. It is customary in the TV industry for production companies to take out ads in the Hollywood trade papers thanking the members of the Academy when the latter have seen fit to honor those working for them with an Emmy. Kathy Easterling placed a big ad in the *Hollywood Reporter* on her own to thank the Academy for her award.

Prior to my leaving Jeopardy in '91, I had edited and assembled 65 shows for the upcoming eighth season of the show. I therefore ended up having worked on a full 75% of all shows that aired in the eligibility period for the 1992 Emmys. Someone at Jeopardy nonetheless saw to it that my name was excluded from those submitted for Emmy consideration that year. When the Jeopardy writers were once again nominated, I protested my exclusion to Academy officials, who saw to it that my name was included among the nominees. We didn't win that year, however, having lost out to an environmental special on the Disney Channel.

At Jeopardy, from the start back in 1984, we were encouraged to include any explanatory or humorous comments for Alex with our clues and they were always marked with an asterisk. On tape days it was my job, and later Fred's, to transfer those comments to Alex's copy of the game. This was an integral procedure and policy throughout my seven years with the show. I cannot recall a single game that didn't include some comments for Alex. In that sense alone we did more than just write questions and answers.

Writing for Jeopardy is not like writing questions and answers for a show like "Sale of the Century," "Joker's Wild," "Tic Tac Dough" or "Card Sharks." For one thing, and as any Jeopardy fan can tell you, you don't write questions and answers for Jeopardy as the program's format *does not allow it!* The idea behind Jeopardy is "we provide the answers—you provide the questions." To a contestant playing the game the "answers" are actually the questions and vice versa. What this means for the writer is that the material must be put into this unusual, backwards format in which usual questioning words such as who, what, when, where, why and how cannot be used. This requires a degree of mental agility on the part of the Jeopardy writers that goes beyond merely writing questions and answers.

All Jeopardy material must be written *in categories.* Each category is, in effect, a theme around which that material is based. Some categories, such as history, geography and literature, are quite broad. But every Jeopardy game requires 13 *different* categories which means a considerable number of categories must, of necessity, be quite narrow in scope. For example, a category on South Dakota would require a writer to come up with at least six clues about that state to which a reasonably bright, well-educated player could correctly respond.

In addition, each Jeopardy writer had to provide clues with *varying degrees of difficulty.* A $100 clue is supposed to be easier than a $500 or a $1000 clue. You couldn't just turn in six easy clues or six difficult ones.

Unlike nearly all other quiz shows, Jeopardy clues are displayed on the TV screen. Each clue must fit into a box on the Jeopardy game board. These boxes contain seven lines with about 15 spaces per line. I say about because O's, M's and N's are wider, I's, T's and L's narrower and so we could never be sure. The clues had to be written to fit within the allotted space and we weren't allowed to hyphenate individual words except in rare and extreme cases. In journalism this is called copyfitting. It requires rewording and rephrasing clues time and time again until you got them to fit within the space you had.

Finally, because Jeopardy clues are shown on screen, attention must be paid to proper spelling and punctuation. This, too, is a matter that writers of "questions and answers" for other shows don't have to deal with.

CHAPTER 9

THE INNER WORKINGS OF JEOPARDY!

Jules Minton had left his position at Jeopardy in March 1988, after almost four full seasons with the show. The following year, in April 1989, it was the turn of the other associate producer, Sherry Hilber.

I was sorry to see Sherry go, not only because of the personal pain she experienced but also because she was the one person in a managerial capacity with whom I really had a good rapport. Contestant coordinator Susanne Thurber was always pleasant but it wasn't the same thing as being able to talk to someone with whom you could share your problems.

Sherry had on a number of occasions voiced the fear to me that Rocky was after her job. Rocky, it turned out, didn't need her job since he was pretty much a power in the office right where he was. Sherry's job would have meant giving up the connection to Alex, which he liked. All Rocky lacked was the associate producer's *title* and it wasn't long before he got the similar-sounding title of Assistant Producer.

Instead, Sherry was quickly replaced as Associate Producer by Lisa Broffman (now Finneran). Lisa had spent years in the Merv Griffin organization starting out as a secretary and working her way up. She was known to be a favorite of Bob Murphy's.

NO RIGHTS TO THE RIGHTS

On a couple of occasions Merv and Bob struck deals with computer software companies to produce computer game versions of Jeopardy. Not only did they sell them the rights to the show's format and trademark, they also sold them the game material, which was the same material we'd written for and used on shows that had already aired. I was twice retained to reassemble the games for the software companies. This entailed replacing all the audio and video daily doubles as well as clues that were out of date, had more than one correct response or might not work well on the computer for other reasons. I assembled some 40 games each time, which entailed working evenings and weekends, and was paid $1000 for each group.

Some of the other writers and I asked to be paid something for the reuse of our material but management refused. In copyright law there is a concept known as "work made for hire" and according to it, employers have felt they have perpetual right to written or other creative material produced by those in their employ. In June 1989, there was a case that went to the Supreme Court (Committee for Creative Non-Violence v. James Earl Reid) in which the Court's decision seemed to imply that this might no longer be the case. Many experts in copyright law were concluding that the 9–0 ruling implied that unless a writer specifically signs away his rights to his work, he still retains such rights, even when in the employ of others. Many attorneys including those at Columbia concluded it would be necessary to have their employees sign over their rights to the company. The Jeopardy writers and researchers were therefore given the following statement to sign:

> The undersigned agrees that JEOPARDY PRODUCTIONS, INC. (JPI) shall have the ownership in perpetuity throughout the universe of the copyright in all media, markets and for all uses of all materials (hereinafter collectively "Works") without exception, which have been or will be created and/or written pursuant to or by reason of your retention by JPI to prepare and research materials with respect to Jeopardy or any Jeopardy related purpose. Any such Works shall be deemed a work made for hire for JPI under all applicable law. To the extent such Works are not deemed transferred to or owned by JPI pursuant to the provisions of your employment by JPI and/or any other agreement between you and JPI, by operation of law or otherwise, then you hereby assign and transfer all rights in and to such Works to JPI.

Not long afterwards, Merv Griffin entered into a deal with HarperCollins Publishers to provide them with *The JEOPARDY! Book,* to be written by Alex Trebek with help from Peter Barsocchini. The book would be marketed as purporting to provide readers with a "behind the scenes look" at the show.

In fact, Alex wrote very little of the book. Merv and George wrote a short chapter each and Peter (who had never worked on Jeopardy but was a former producer of "The Merv Griffin Show") compiled the rest from interviews and some written submissions from the Jeopardy staff. Well over half the book consisted of our material on pages resembling the Jeopardy game board, with clues on one side and the correct responses on the back of the page, while Final Jeopardies took up an entire page alone. Since the book wasn't constructed like those musical greeting cards, Audio Daily Doubles were out. Overall the book, which went for $12.95, consisted largely of blank space and could easily be read in its entirety in less than two hours. All told, some 250,000 copies were sold.

Since the first book had proven so cost effective, management subsequently had the staff put together another book, this one titled *The JEOPARDY! Challenge*. Merv must have regretted giving Alex solo top billing on the previous book, as this new one was marketed as being "by Alex Trebek and Merv Griffin." Actually it is by Steven Dorfman, Gary Lee, Barbara Heller, Kathy Easterling, Steve Tamerius, Stephanie Spadaccini, Michelle Johnson, Harry Eisenberg and some others, since 98% of it consists of our material.

Ironically, most of the material in *The Book* consists of "fun" categories—pop culture and word play—the sort I was under constant pressure to sharply cut back on in assembling games. Hence much of it is from the second and third seasons of the show when Alex allowed a category balance that was about 25–30% pop culture and 10–15% word play.

Then on page 39 of *The Book* George Vosburgh makes this strange statement:

> While some of the researchers (*sic*) and some of the production assistants have knowledge of some of the completed games, no individual in research or production has knowledge of all the completed games.

In fact all of the writers, a.k.a. researchers, had access to all of the games, either during the roundtabling meetings when a group of them, led by Fred Pohl, went over the games looking for alternative correct responses, or afterwards when the games were accessible to all the writers in order that they replace any unusable clues. Our proofreader, Ruth Deutsch (and later Billy Wisse), who was also listed on the crawl as a "researcher," had to go over all the material. I of course did the same as the one who edited and approved all the categories.

HOW JEOPARDY GETS ITS MATERIAL

And so, to set the record straight let me now run down the complete path taken by a Jeopardy category from its inception to the time it appeared on the show.

People often ask, "Where do the Jeopardy writers get their material?" To that, let me respond in the form of a question: Where *don't* we get them from? In the past I'd gotten ideas for clues from the radio while driving in the car. Material dealing with the news, music, occasionally sports and celebrities and even history (from Walter Cronkite and Charles Osgood's features on CBS radio) as well as the obvious musical Audio Daily Doubles have all come from there. Newspapers, magazines, encyclopedias, almanacs, books of every type, sheet music, visits to museums, airports, foreign countries, historic sites, gambling casinos, sporting events, supermarkets and stores of every type; zoos, amusement parks and home video rentals have all proven to be significant sources for us. The whole idea is to be alive and alert to the fascinating world around us.

I recall writing a clue that read, "The first word uttered by a man on the moon was the name of this Lone Star city." I was reading the AAA Tour Guide for Texas while planning a trip to Houston in order to attend the convention of the National Association of Television Programming Executives when I came across that bit of information. The correct response, of course, "What is Houston?"

While dating my wife back in 1986, I was waiting for her to get ready to go to dinner and noticed a copy of *Savvy* magazine (a magazine for working women) on her table. I started thumbing through it and came up with this Final Jeopardy under the category Women in Business: "The largest publicly-held U.S. firm headed by a woman publishes this daily newspaper." The correct response: "What is *The Washington Post*?"; the reference, of course, was to Katharine Graham.

As a writer I would keep a pad and pencil in the car and on my nightstand, as there was no telling when inspiration might strike. After hearing songs by Paul Simon and Paul Williams played back-to-back on the radio, Barbara came up with a "Small Pauls" category. While hearing "I tawt I taw a puddytat" on TV my 10-year-old daughter suggested a "Cartoon Quotes" category.

Most of the time the five writers were generally free to write any category they wanted but within certain parameters. As I mentioned, in later seasons we had to severely limit show business, sports and word play categories. I also had to put moratoriums on other categories, say Opera or Shakespeare, if I already had too many of them. Once a week each writer would meet with me to turn in their quota of material. We would then carefully go over each category, slowly, one clue at a time.

THE CLUES

Many clues were good enough as they were but a significant percentage required editing. Often that entailed taking a clue that was relatively convoluted and putting it into a shorter, snappier form. For example (and you'll pardon me if I use a pop culture clue), under The Sixties a clue originally read, "This was the name usually used when referring to model Lesley Hornby." That was changed to "Model Lesley Hornby was better known by this name." The correct response (for all you nostalgia buffs): "Who was Twiggy?"

Sometimes a clue had to be changed in order to pin down its correct response. A clue under Fruits and Vegetables originally read, "Common name for the love apple" but was changed to "Most common name for the love apple" in order to avoid unexpected alternate responses. The correct question: "What is the tomato?"

As I was going over the material in a category, I was also looking to create a viable, workable and fair order of difficulty among the clues. Often that meant easing up a clue. Under Lawyers a clue originally read: "Life magazine called him the 'king of torts.'" I changed it to "Life magazine called this San Francisco attorney the 'king of torts.'" to ease it up a bit but still considered it a level five (bottom of the game board) clue. The response, by the way, "Who is Melvin Belli?" Another clue that was eased up originally read, "The 2 members of George Washington's original cabinet besides Jefferson and Hamilton." That was simply eased to "1 of George Washington's original cabinet appointees besides Jefferson and Hamilton." The correct response: "Who was Edmund Randolph or Henry Knox?" That also remained a level five clue.

Back when I was a writer I once came across what struck me as a fascinating quote: I decided to submit it as a Final Jeopardy clue under the category "U.S. Presidents." It read, "He said, 'I am the last president of the United States.'" I knew it was tough, so I suggested it for the Tournament of Champions. Jules and Alex thought it was too tough even for the Tournament, so I suggested changing the category to "Democrats," figuring that would significantly narrow the field, since the majority of presidents belonged to other parties. They still thought it was too tough. I still liked the clue and really wanted to use it so I said, "How about calling the category 'Nineteenth Century Democrats?' " That narrowed the field to where they agreed to use it. It was the Final Jeopardy of the last game of our third Tournament of Champions, in 1987.

In its eased-up form all three players got it. The correct response: "Who was James Buchanan?" He said it as the Union was breaking up at the end of his administration, shortly before Lincoln's inauguration.

Sometimes we needed to go the other way and make a clue tougher.

A clue under "Palaces" first read, "Paleis Huis Ten Bosch, the Dutch Royal Palace, is in this city." I edited it to read "To see the Paleis Huis Ten Bosch, home of Queen Beatrix, go to this city." "What is The Hague?" I also felt it was slightly more interesting in the edited form. That, by the way, was a level four clue.

Some clues just need to be edited for clarity and to avoid giving viewers the wrong idea. In its original form one clue read, "Joe DiMaggio had the longest one in baseball." Period. To which were added the words "—56 games." All we were going for was "What is a hitting (or batting) streak?"

Material had to be rejected for being too easy or too hard when neither the writer nor I could come up with a way to modify it. Sometimes I'd tell a writer, "You have two or three ones here." "Ones" meant level one clues, the easiest we used, which appear on the top horizontal row of the game board. I'd tell the writer to save the extra "ones" to be used in future categories. Likewise there could be too many really hard "fives" and I could only take one. Some clues were simply too esoteric or too hard period, and occasionally you'd get one that was ridiculously easy.

I usually found enough good material in a category to accept it. When I accepted one I would decide if the category was of the easier sort and mark it "J" for the Jeopardy round or, if it seemed harder, "DJ" for Double Jeopardy. Exceptionally difficult categories were set aside year round for the next Tournament of Champions. In editing the clues I made sure the writer was in agreement with whatever changes I made. After all they had read the original source and I assumed they generally knew something about the subject.

When I was finished going over a writer's material I would tally up the number of categories that had been accepted. I also kept track of how many were "J" and how many "DJ" as well as the number of each type of category they'd turned in (blue, green, pink, yellow, orange). This gave me an overview of each writer's contribution and helped me to try to fairly allot the number of pink and yellow categories we could do among the several writers, since most liked doing them.

After we finished going over the categories, the writer would take his material into our conference room where each writer had a clipboard with sheets on which they would write in the name of each category. They would then deposit their categories, each of which consisted of six 3 by 5 cards clipped together, into a box where they would be picked up by the researchers.

THE RESEARCHERS

The researchers would take the categories they wished to work on from the box, signing them out by initialing the writers' sheets. This enabled us to keep track of each category. The researcher then set out to double-check the writer's original sources and then find second corroborative sources for all facts on the card. If the core of a clue proved false the researcher would take it to the writer for one or more possible replacement clues. The researcher would then run the replacement clues by me. After I'd settled on whatever replacement clues were needed, the researcher would research those as well.

I met with each researcher at least once a week at which time they'd turn in all their completed categories. We'd run down the categories one at a time and the researcher would recommend whatever changes, if any, might be needed. At this point these were usually modifying frill aspects of a clue to conform with the true facts of a matter. For example, a clue under Italian Idioms read, "Literally 'pity,' it's a picture of the dead Christ being held by the Virgin Mary." Though the original source said it's a "picture," the researcher found that "representation" would be more accurate and so "picture" was changed to "representation." The response to this level one clue: "What is a pieta?"

After going over the material with each researcher, I would tally up his or her categories and enter the amount, also keeping track of the type of categories involved. I encouraged each researcher to try to work on categories in which they felt some degree of expertise, but ultimately, of course, all the categories had to get done. Word play categories tended to be the easiest, and sometimes less mature individuals would hoard those in order to augment their total output.

After the categories were researched I would hand them over to JulieAnn who would enter them in the computer and print them out on appropriately colored strips—blue, green, pink, yellow or orange. Each strip would be marked "J" or "DJ" depending on how I had designated the category. JulieAnn then gave me the strips while she held on to the category cards.

Once I had enough strips that were sufficiently diverse in nature, I could assemble a game. My goal was to be able to assemble one or two games each non-taping day, which I generally could as we were doing everything humanly possible to keep the material flowing smoothly. I would lay out the strips and would go over in my mind what it would sound like to have Alex read them off in order. Once I settled on an order that sounded good, I would paste the strips onto large sheets that resembled the game board, six strips per sheet with one sheet for the Jeopardy round and one for Double Jeopardy. I would then clip the two large sheets together and *voila* another Jeopardy game was born.

Assigning the game a four-digit game number was the equivalent of giving the new "baby" a name. The first of the four digits represented the season of the show we were in and it was followed by the number of the game in that season. Thus 7077 was the seventy-seventh game assembled in season seven. Any games left over at the end of a season were assigned a new number to be used the following season. The only other thing remaining for me to do was to select clues to serve as Daily Doubles. I'd need to select three: one for the first round, two for the second, less any Audio or Video Daily Double that might already be in the game.

GETTING APPROVAL

The new game's next experience of its young existence was to be presented to George for his comments and approval. If a particular clue bothered him he ordered it replaced. For some reason he hated references to hamsters and gerbils; he seemed to consider those creatures obscene and so that was out. Other no-nos included references to Donald Trump, the quiz show scandals of the Fifties, and mentions of Zsa Zsa Gabor. (Merv was good friends with Eva Gabor but the two sisters supposedly did not get along.) George was also uncomfortable with references to other game shows (except "Wheel," of course) as he didn't like crediting the "competition" in any way.

He always made sure there wasn't too much pop culture or word play in the games and usually wanted them eased up in some way. We even had a few in which a single clue was not missed. For my part, I was striving for *balance*. I certainly didn't want the shows to be too hard but I didn't want them to be too easy either. I thought the rule of thumb we'd been given at the outset of the show which said the ideal balance was a show in which Alex ends up giving the correct response in five to seven out of the sixty clues was good. At the tapings I made it a point to always keep track of the number of clues for which Alex had to give the correct response. It seemed to me that shows in the five to seven range or even four to eight played best and generally had good competition.

COMPETITION

Tough games with more than eight "misses" tended to favor the most knowledgeable of the three contestants and were therefore more likely to be one-sided "runaways." Games with fewer than four "misses" on the other hand were so easy they became little more than contests as to which player had the fastest reflexes to ring in and you could often see the looks of frustration on the faces of those players who also knew the correct response but couldn't ring in fast enough.

Those easy shows, however, did not *look* nearly as bad as shows in which the three contestants would "stand and stare" a lot. That is, the players found the material so difficult they were afraid to ring in and even try. This is what George desperately wanted to avoid. Of course a lot depended on the contestants and they, like the material, came in cycles.

Everyone wanted close, highly competitive games. The contestant coordinators would try to match up strong players against other strong players, weaker players against similar ones, all based on their scores on the contestant test. When I was assembling games there was no way I could know which contestants or even which *kind* of contestants would be playing a particular game, nor should I have known. It was only on a tape day itself, once ABC made the pick of which games would be played, that we first learned when a game would be used. Games with low game numbers, indicating they'd been assembled early in a season, could go, and sometimes did, for months without being picked.

On tape days George and Rocky saw the list of contestants invited to play on the show that day along with the test score of each. On days when we were going to have weaker players George set about in the morning meeting to ease up the material in order to help it play better. We therefore would have lots of last-minute changes to put into the Chyron. Alex never did that sort of thing when he was producer.

In fairness to the Contestant Department, they couldn't possibly come up with players who were equally strong all the time so matching them up with comparable opponents was the best they could do. The result was that some strong players were quickly beaten by other strong players while some weak players had multiple wins by defeating players who proved to be weaker still.

But back to the procedure. After George saw the games and indicated via post-its what he wanted done to specific clues and categories, I got them back and would give them to Fred for the roundtabling session. About a third of the games would come back to me with no comments from George. He either didn't make the time or didn't feel like doing them but could not hold up the pipeline or the Production Department wouldn't get the material in time. At first that didn't bother me as I thought it indicated he had confidence in my judgment and was content to go with it. But later I'd occasionally find myself being sharply criticized in front of everyone in the tape day morning meeting and felt very much undermined. Then we'd have to put in extra last-minute changes George required in the games.

ROUNDTABLING SESSIONS

In any case, Fred led the roundtabling sessions. These meetings included three other writers and/or researchers who would take turns doing that since it pulled them away from their other work. The games would be reviewed for alternate correct responses, clues that give away responses to other clues, repeat material and clues that didn't play well for other reasons such as not being pinned down. At first individual writers and researchers would take turns reading the material and leading the sessions but some of the writers were very defensive about their own material when others criticized it. I quickly concluded it would be best to have Fred lead those sessions.

Fred was a researcher at the time and therefore couldn't be accused of favoring his own material. Since he was a judge at the tapings I felt his being at the roundtabling meetings would help familiarize him with the material. Even when he later became a writer he seemed much less emotionally attached to his own material than some of the other writers and he continued to do an outstanding job leading the roundtabling sessions.

After games were reviewed in a roundtable meeting, they were left in the conference room for a day in order to enable all the writers to submit whatever changes both the meeting and George's notes called for. Hence all the writers and researchers had ready access to all the material.

PROOFING

Following that I would go over all the changes the writers had submitted. I would edit and/or replace anything that did not sit right with me. I would then turn the games over to our proofreader whose job included researching the new clues that had been introduced to the game as a result of the roundtabling meeting and George's instructions. That research was handled in the same way as all other research and the games would be turned in to me when the research was completed. I would make any changes due to the research before handing over the game to JulieAnn.

JulieAnn would enter all the changes in the computer and could now assign the game number to each category in the computer. That enabled us to later look up material by key word and immediately know which game a particular clue was in. She then printed out "clean" strips which she pasted up on the large sheets keeping the categories in the same order in which I originally had them. Working copies of those sheets were then made and submitted to the proofreader.

After proofing the games the proofreader went over any proposed changes with me. After those were settled, JulieAnn made her final changes with new strips replacing the former ones on the game sheets where needed. JulieAnn would then gather all the clue cards together for each individual game. A production assistant or the receptionist would enter the game number on all the cards for each individual game after which the cards would be bound up with a rubber band and filed away to be available as needed on tape day.

GAME CARD

JulieAnn then created a "game card" which was an eight by five blue index card on which she listed the game number and all the categories in the game. She then gave me the game card which indicated that game was available to be used at any future taping while the game sheets were passed on to the Production Department. One other thing that JulieAnn did was to write out the wording for any Audio Daily Doubles and arrange to have the rights cleared for us to use the music.

CHYRON

Once Production got the game they would arrange for Chyron computer system operator Patrice Long to come in to enter the game onto a floppy disk. That would enable each clue to turn up in its proper place on the game board when we taped. A production assistant would join her to proofread her work. Owing to the peculiarities of the Chyron, we would occasionally have a clue we thought would fit that didn't. We worked from the premise that we had 15 spaces per line but it wasn't quite so. M's, W's and O's would take more space than usual while I's and L's took less. So from time to time I'd get a call from the Chyron booth saying a clue didn't fit. Since Merv hated abbreviations that was rarely a solution. Generally I had to reword the problem clues so as to make them fit. Where there's a will there's a way and we always found a way to fit them in somehow.

For years we had been talking about linking JulieAnn's computer directly to the Chyron, thereby saving this step. It was finally done after I left the show, but someone still has to check the Chyron to make sure each clue was properly picked up. For the first seven years of the show the Production Department would order printed cards with the category titles. Those would be put on top of the game board by a member of the studio crew who had to climb a ladder. It seemed like a link to the old Jeopardy. Occasionally a card wouldn't turn out right or would go astray. If the "PENNSYLVANIANS" card was missing, we could call the category "PENNSYLVANIA" and Alex would explain it was about people from Pennsylvania. One time we had a category called "MISSING" about people and things that had disappeared. When the category card did the same we used the blank side of another category card. It seemed apropos that the title over the "MISSING" category was missing. The category played fine. Now the category titles are entered on the game board electronically just like the rest of the material.

FINAL STEPS IN A LONG PROCESS

Steven would take the game cards from me to see which games were available, in order to create pools of games for ABC Compliance and Practices to pick from. Using JulieAnn's computer, he would run printouts showing how often and where each category appeared in a pool of say 20 games. Working together, Steven and I would eliminate the games that gave us the most category duplication and narrowed the pool down to the 13 games with the greatest variety. Steven would then run a key word printout for those 13 games and would also obtain working copies of those games from Production.

Working with a different writer each week, Steven and the other writer would go over the printout looking for all key words mentioned more than once. Clues sharing the same key word, even though they were in different games were carefully examined. Two mentions of Europe in the same pool really didn't matter since it's a broad area but two mentions of Michael J. Fox did and one would have to be replaced. Usually the extra would suffice even if it meant re-ordering the category as regards the relative difficulty of the clues. Occasionally the writers would have to provide a new clue.

Steven would go over his proposed changes with me. Once those were agreed to the researchers would check out any new clues. Some games would emerge from this process unscathed but one or two changes per game seemed to be the average. Steven would then type up a memo to the Production Department to have them enter the changes on their master copy of each game.

FINAL JEOPARDY

Steven would also select and assign a Final Jeopardy clue to each game in the pool. The procedure for Final Jeopardies was somewhat different and worked like this:

The idea behind Final Jeopardies is that they should be "thinkers"—clues that require a bit of thought to come up with the response, thereby justifying the 30 seconds of "think time" the contestants are given. Occasionally we had situations in which all three players came up with the response and put down their pens so quickly it looked like a waste of time to play the "think music" to the end. Most of the time though the clues have required some thought, which is what we wanted. Here are a few examples:

Presidents:
First president who was not a signer of either the Declaration of Independence or the Constitution.

Here you have to think of which future presidents signed which documents. Jefferson obviously signed the Declaration since he wrote it. John Adams helped edit it and signed as a delegate to the Continental Congress from Massachusetts. James Madison is known as the

Father of the Constitution and so he obviously signed that document, while George Washington presided over the Constitutional Convention. The man who served as president after those four individuals was James Monroe, which is the correct response.

Marylanders:
Slaveholders posted rewards totaling about $40,000 for her capture.

Here one asks oneself what woman would slaveholders have disliked so much that they wanted so badly to capture her. Perhaps a woman who was helping many of their slaves escape and had once been a slave herself. The correct response: "Who was Harriet Tubman?"

Historic Names:
Slave trader, land swindler and notorious brawler known as a hero of the Alamo.

This one works by process of elimination. Only three heroes of the Alamo are well-known: Davy Crockett, the commander William B. Travis, and Jim Bowie who was second in command. Only one of the three was associated with a weapon—the Bowie knife—which might lead you to conclude he was the "notorious brawler." Incidentally, during the siege of the Alamo Jim Bowie was described as "roaring drunk" and in no condition to fight.

Once a week I would get together with the writers for us to collectively go over all the Finals that had been written that week. Each writer would read the ones he or she wrote and the rest of us would try to respond correctly. What we were looking for were not only clues that required some thought but also those that were neither too easy nor too hard. We wanted Finals whose degree of difficulty was such that of the three players, one or two would get it right and one or two would miss.

That would make the Final Jeopardy round interesting and it would have a bearing on the game, provided of course the game was not already a runaway. If all three contestants missed the Final, the outcome of the game might still be interesting depending on the betting but we really didn't prefer that, as it tended to make the players, even the champion, look weak and ended the show on a somewhat negative note. On the other hand, a Final that was gotten by all three players did nothing more than reaffirm the standings in the game at the end of Double Jeopardy, and outcomes in which all three get the Final right are therefore the least interesting.

If a Final didn't "work" for us in the meeting, that is, it was too hard or too easy, it was dropped right then and there. If it didn't require much thought—a situation where you immediately know it or you don't—I would suggest using it as a regular clue in a regular category. Those Final Jeopardies which managed to pass muster at our meeting were handed over to George for his approval.

George would accept about a third of the ones we gave him. He didn't want any in categories that seemed too "lightweight." That eliminated all word play and nearly all those having to do with entertainment. Pop music and TV were pretty much out as subjects for Finals though an occasional one about the movies could be acceptable while Theater was okay. At the same time he didn't want any that struck him as too difficult. To George a Final that was missed by all three players was far more disastrous than one that had been gotten by all three.

I would put a "G.V." on each Final Jeopardy card he approved, while the ones he turned down were returned to the writers to be modified in some form for possible use as regular clues or to be kept as souvenirs. The approved ones would then be put in the box to be researched. Those that cleared that hurdle finally made it into the stack of usable Finals.

In assigning a Final to each game Steven would make sure its category was sufficiently different from the 12 regular categories already in that game. He would then look up all the key words in each Final against the key word printout he had covering all the games in the pool to make sure there was no conflict between the Final and any material in any of the games. Some conflicts could be handled by controlling the order in which the games would play. For example, a Final which read, "This president served the shortest time in office. Who was William Henry Harrison?" could play before (but not after) a game with this clue: "William Henry Harrison and Zachary Taylor were the only men elected President from this political party." That's because this latter clue contains the correct response to the Final, whereas if the Final played first, it wouldn't necessarily help the contestants come up with the correct political party (the Whig Party).

SELECTING THE GAME ORDER

The JEOPARDY! Book claims ABC Compliance and Practices selects not only the games to be played but also the order. This is untrue as we were always allowed to select the order ourselves and have always done so. Steven would make a list of which games needed to play before or after other games within specific pools so as to not have some clues tip off the correct response to others. If that were not done we would have had to replace even more material. If a conflict between a Final and a regular clue couldn't be resolved by controlling the order and we didn't have another Final to put in place of the one we were using (we were perpetually short of Finals) we would either replace the regular clue with the extra or put in a new one altogether and Steven would add that change to his memo to the Production Department.

After I looked over the Finals with Steven, we would ask George to approve them. He would usually have second thoughts about one or two he previously approved, and we'd have to replace those. The numbers of the games in which the Finals were to be used would be written on their cards. Steven would photocopy the Finals and turn the copies over to Production while I would hang on to the original cards containing the source information should a need arise to refer to them.

One of the production assistants would enter the changes from Steven's memo onto the master copy of each game. He or she would then add the Finals onto the game sheets making each game complete. At that point the P.A. would make multiple copies of each game to be set aside to be used on tape day. The other production assistant (we usually had two and they would take turns) would meet with Patrice to enter both the Finals as well as the changes from Steven's memo into the Chyron. All this was usually done a couple of days before taping.

TAPE DAYS

On tape days things were hopping. We had to be in at 9 A.M., at which point Steven would take the call from whoever Compliance and Practices had assigned to work with us that day. Assisted by Fred, he would set an order for the five games that had been picked to be played. I would look it over to make sure it made sense to me and then give Fred the OK to take the game numbers in order to production coordinator Linda Smith and later Joel Charap. (The production coordinator's duties included overseeing the P.A.s and serving as the associate producer's right hand.) The production coordinator would then assign each game a show number which was its number in the order of being taped and aired going back to the outset of this version of Jeopardy. Show 001 was the first one we taped and aired back in

1984. By the time I left the show the show numbers had exceeded 1600.

Fred would obtain four copies of the games; for George, Alex, himself and me. Carlo and later Suzanne Stone would get the original clue cards for each game that had been picked and pull out all those with asterisks indicating the writers had included explanatory comments for Alex to make in connection with certain clues. They would give those to Fred and he'd go over them writing the ones he thought best onto Alex's copies.

The four of us would go over our copies. Alex was prepping himself for reading the clues aloud on the shows and would underline the words he wanted to emphasize. He would also do his utmost to make sure he was pronouncing the names of people and places as well as any foreign terms accurately. His knowledge of French, Ukrainian and the closely related Russian have proven invaluable in this regard. If he couldn't find the pronunciation in the office, Alex would ask a researcher to make whatever phone calls might be necessary to get the correct pronunciation.

Apart from that, we were looking for any flaws which may have eluded our previous scrutiny as well as clues which might have become outdated between the time they'd been written and now or which might be out of date by the time the show aired. Once a game was selected and assigned a show number we would know the precise date on which it would first air. On average we were taping about three months ahead. The Tournament of Champions and Teen Tournament were taped just a couple of weeks ahead while other shows were taped as much as five months in advance. In reviewing the games George would also play the music for any Audio Daily Doubles we might be having in order to make a final judgment on them as well as to familiarize Alex with them, if indeed they were going to be used.

After we had all gone over the games the four of us would meet in the conference room for a final discussion of the material. In later seasons Kathy managed to add herself to the meeting and we then felt Steven should be included as well since he was the senior writer. Carol who seemed to like Fred's company, then joined the meeting too as did Ruth who felt it necessary to be there in order to defend her work, with which Kathy was prone to take issue. In addition, we had a researcher present to look up any information we might need from reference sources. (In seasons four and five Carlo was the designated researcher. Then, for a time, the researchers took turns while later it was always Suzanne.)

A MATTER OF STYLE

Dubbed by Alex "The Comma Queen," Kathy would each week insist we needed to add commas in various places. To her it was a matter of following the rules of punctuation as she understood them, while I saw it as a matter of *style* and believe the use of commas is optional in many instances, depending on whether you follow the more traditional style (which used more commas) or the current style (which I preferred) which calls for less. By sheer force of her personality Kathy almost always got things her way. I really didn't care except it bothered me to be wasting all that time on trivialities.

George also had a grammatical quirk. He insisted adverbs always follow the verb they are modifying rather than fall between the noun and the verb. A $1000 History clue originally read:

He bankrupted his country and fell from power in 1955; in 1973 he was again made president.

George had that changed to:

He bankrupted his country and fell from power in 1955; in 1973 he was made president again.

The significance of that change somehow eludes my comprehension. (The correct response by the way: "Who was Juan Peron?")

Neither did George care much for the location of the adverb "soon" in the following $1000 clue in an Opera category:

After learning he'll soon go to jail, Baron Von Eisenstein goes to a ball in this Strauss operetta.

But putting the adverb after its verb here would have given us the phrase "After learning he'll go soon to jail." Since that sounded weird he simply removed the adverb "soon" altogether. (The response here was, "What is *Die Fledermaus?*")

Here is an example of a clue in which there was no place to move the adverb "traditionally" nor could it be removed from the clue (because to do that could have unpinned the clue and opened it up to unexpected alternate responses). The category was "Last Lines":

Jimmy Durante traditionally ended his shows by saying good-night to her.

The answer?: "Who was Mrs. Calabash (wherever you are)?"

The adverb game went on for all four years I worked under George and goes on to this day. He never explained his reasoning as to why an adverb must follow its verb except to say he wanted it that way. I figure he either got it from Merv or a stubborn English teacher back in high school.

Meanwhile the tape day morning meeting had gone from a three-person, 20-minute final check to a nine-person, hour-and-a-half ordeal. The morning meeting, which tended to begin around 10:30 or 10:45, now ran into the afternoon!

Once the ordeal was finally over, Fred would inform Rocky and someone from Production of the changes that had been decided on. Rocky would later inform the Compliance and Practices representative when he or she arrived to cover the show and Fred would head for the Chyron room where he would have tape day Chyron operator Doris Diaz Montes enter the changes. Since he was entering the changes for all five games to be taped that day, it could take a while and the scheduled 1:30 P.M. start of taping was usually delayed 15 minutes to half an hour or more.

We generally had to make and enter all our changes before taping started. Once we began taping there was so little time between shows (usually about 15 minutes) that we tended not to make changes then, except if they were absolutely urgent.

At times, the need for last minute changes between shows did come up. Between games, Johnny and Alex would come out to talk to the audience and sometimes one or the other might inadvertently start talking about something that also happened to be mentioned in the next game, say a trip to Nepal (where Alex went on behalf of World Vision) or Mexico's Yucatan Peninsula, where Johnny once went on vacation. Then we'd have to take a few minutes to replace the clue in question before going on to tape the next program.

Shortly after Fred was finished director Dick Schneider would call out "Places, please." Fred and I would take our seats at the judges' table. Fred had his control switches, which activated the players' ring-in devices and electronic pens as well as a box containing the index cards on which were all the writers' original material for that day's shows in case we had to check the sources of any particular clue. In front of me was a buzzer. Alex had built it himself when the show had been new and it always reminded me of a school science fair project. It was to be used to grab his attention for a judgment call.

RESOURCES

Also in front of us were five or so reference works to be used if we quickly needed to look up something. These included a *Random House* one-volume encyclopedia, a two-volume *World Book* dictionary, a *Webster's Third International* unabridged dictionary (which George liked and was quite useful for our purposes), and George's one-volume *Columbia* encyclopedia. We formerly had an *American Heritage* dictionary as well, which Alex liked because it included biographical and geographical listings and pronunciations but which George very much hated and insisted it not be used at the tapings. George was the boss and the *American Heritage* dictionary was banished from the studio. Alex, however, still kept one in his dressing room.

THE HOTLINE

Finally, in front of me there was also a telephone, which was used when necessary to call up to the writers and researchers in the office. While we were taping they would sit in the conference room and watch the proceedings on a TV monitor. They had easy access to our reference library and if some question of judgment arose of which we were uncertain (usually involving an unexpected contestant response) I would reach for the phone and they would quickly check out the matter. Since I had the original clue cards with me, I could tell them where to go for the original sources and they could look elsewhere as well. By way of an example, we once had a clue that read, "Title four of the U.S. Code states its length must be exactly 1.9 times its width." While all we are going for was the American flag, the contestant responded, "What is the union of the flag?" That didn't seem right as the union or canton (the upper left hand corner of Old Glory) looks to be about square. And so we nodded "no" to Alex and he told the player, "I don't think we can accept that. I'm sorry." But to make sure, I got on the phone and checked with the researchers upstairs. Carlo found a copy of the flag per the flag code, measured the union's length versus its width and found the width was only 1.02 times the length and so we were fine on that score.

Sometimes we had to make phone calls out. When a contestant questioned the matter of the buzzards returning annually to Hinckley,

Ohio, we called Hinckley and spoke to the town's one-woman Chamber of Commerce to make sure.

Then there was this story I shared with *Boston Globe* reporter Susan Bickelhaupt: We once had a clue dealing with the fact that Federal judges were appointed for life. When we asked for how long they are appointed, a player gave a fixed term in years and was ruled incorrect. At the commercial break he challenged our ruling. As it was already 6:00 P.M. in California we decided to call the Federal court in Honolulu for verification. When Susan asked who was right I just smiled. "We were," I said.

THE CONTESTANTS

Prior to the start of taping the contestants would be briefed. The players would be encouraged to try and be as relaxed as possible. They were not to plug products, organizations, causes or even to name the corporations for which they worked, although it is permissible to name a government agency. In responding to the material, they'd be told that when in doubt, give the most obvious response in that we weren't trying to trick them.

Each contestant would be placed behind a lectern to see how they looked on camera. If height adjustments were necessary, boxes would be placed behind the lecterns for the shorter players to stand on.

Over the years we made accommodations for as many different types of contestants as possible. On those occasions when we had contestants with physical infirmities which made it difficult for them to walk, we would open the show with all three players already on stage behind their lecterns.

There was an occasion where we had a contestant who had just come off a diet during which he'd lost some 100 pounds in a comparatively short time. He seemed to play the game well enough but when we got to Final Jeopardy he passed out just as the think music was being played. We immediately stopped the tape. It happened that one of the other contestants that day was a nurse. In addition there were paramedics on the studio lot because the California State Lottery's "Big Spin," in which players spin a wheel in an attempt to win $1,000,000, was being taped on the same lot. Because of the tension involved in possibly winning the million, the State required the presence of paramedics. They were quickly summoned. The contestant was revived and turned out to be okay. Taping was resumed and the game was finished. The tape was edited in such a way that the viewers had no idea what had happened in the studio.

Another time we had a contestant whose eyesight was so poor she was considered legally blind. The fact that Alex reads all the clues makes Jeopardy a show that can be easily followed and enjoyed by the blind. (The show is also closed-captioned for the hearing impaired.) Our contestant happened to play in one of those comparatively rare games that included a Video Daily Double. And, as luck would have it, of the 3 players in the game she happened to be the one to hit on it. In what was one of the more painful moments I remember on the show, there was nothing we could do but rule against her when she couldn't identify the picture. The contestant, I must add, took it very graciously.

We all have certain weaknesses and we all face certain challenges in life. I'm reminded of a category I wrote for the show back in season three:

Physically Challenged

$200   Though paralyzed in both legs, he was elected Governor of New York as well as President.

$400   *Audio Daily Double*

He's gone through life remembering his mother's words, "You've lost your sight, not your mind." (Play part of "Unchain My Heart.")

$600   He overcame polio as a child to become the dean of game show hosts.

$800   In 1933 this one-eyed Texan became the first man to fly solo around the world.

$1000   Severely burned in a fire at age 8, he set a world record running the mile in 1934 despite a toeless foot.

Extra   Unable to walk at age 7, she went on to win 3 gold medals in track in the 1960 Olympics.

The responses:

Physically Challenged

$200   Who was Franklin Delano Roosevelt?

$400   Who is Ray Charles?

$600   Who is Bill Cullen?

$800   Who was Wiley Post?

$1000   Who is Glenn Cunningham?

Extra   Who is Wilma Rudolph (Ward)?

It's always inspiring to learn of people who overcame physical disabilities and other difficulties. This is a category I'd like to see many more times on Jeopardy.

MORE MEAT & POTATOES MATERIAL

George continued to make his demands for more "meat and potatoes" categories.

I kept on doing all I could to encourage the writers to keep the material as lively and interesting as possible. Only rarely would George approve a lively or gimmicky category. Here are two categories that were rejected:

Bodies of Water

$100 Called the sea of reeds in Hebrew, it separates the Arabian Peninsula from Africa.

$200 It provides much of the Texas-Oklahoma boundary before finally joining the Mississippi in Louisiana.

$300 Both Hanoi and Haiphong are on this river, northern Vietnam's main one.

$400 You can sail from Fargo, North Dakota to Winnipeg, Manitoba along this river.

$500 Wisconsin's oldest city is on this body of water whose name it shares.

Now the correct responses:

Bodies of Water

$100 What is the Red Sea?

$200 What is the Red River? (Accept: Red River of the South)

$300 What is the Red River? (Accept: Song Hong or Yuan Chiang)

$400 What is the Red River? (Accept: Red River of the North)

$500 What is Green Bay?

This category was similar to the one with the "colored" seas (Red, Black, Yellow and White) that had played well a few years earlier, except here the gimmick was the color red. Where Alex had liked this sort of material, it seemed to make George uncomfortable as he was afraid the gimmick wouldn't work.

People of the Month

(This category had been intended for the Tournament of Champions.)

$100 Mike Nichols' former comedy partner, she's also a film director.

$200 She was "The She-Wolf of London" in film before starring on "Lassie" and "Lost in Space" on TV.

$300 Stefanie Powers starred in this role as "The Girl from Uncle."

$400   * Audio Daily Double*
        Heard here, she was born Margaret Battavio & took her stage name
        from the month of her birth:
        (Play "I Will Follow Him.")
$500   This golf pro won $50,000 for a hole in one in Palm Springs in 1961,
        but only $100 for the same hole two years later.

Now see how well you did with these:

People of the Month
$100   Who is Elaine May?
$200   Who is June Lockhart?
$300   Who is April Dancer?
$400   Who is (Little) Peggy March?
$500   Who is Don January?

Once again we'd had similar material in the early years that played
just fine but George simply didn't trust gimmicky categories.

One time Steven wrote a Video Daily Double in which we were
going to show pictures of president Grover Cleveland and Grover from
"Sesame Street" and ask for the name common to both. George actually allowed it into a game but as luck would have it, it was one of
the clues that went unpicked as time ran out. When we put the same
clue in a second game, George axed it. Now here are two categories
that Steven wrote which were fully researched, put into games and
entered into the Chyron computer system only to have George kill
them at the last minute, on tape day:

Marxisms
(Memorable sayings of Groucho, not Karl)
$100   "Say" this & "the duck will come down from the ceiling & give you
        $100."
$200   In "Horse Feathers," Groucho threatened, "I'd horsewhip you—if I had"
        one of these.
$300   "The tusks . . .were imbedded so firmly we couldn't budge them. Of
        course in Alabama . . . "
$400   In "Cocoanuts" Groucho told Margaret Dumont, "they shine like the
        pants of a blue serge suit."
$500   Telling a partner he could dance with her "till the cows come home,"
        he added this second thought.

The Quotable Coolidge

$100   "The business of America is" this.

$200   Asked what a clergyman preaching on sin had said, Coolidge said this.

$300   About the famous sin quote story, Coolidge once said it would be funnier if it were this.

$400   "There is no right to" do this "against the public safety by anybody, anywhere, anytime."

$500   *Daily Double*
        His reply to a woman who said she'd made a bet she could get more than two words out of him.

And the correct responses:

Marxisms

$100   What is "Say the secret word?"

$200   What is a horse?

$300   What is "the Tuscaloosa?"

$400   What were her eyes?

$500   What was "I'd rather dance with the cows and you come home?"

The Quotable Coolidge

$100   What is "business?"

$200   What is "(He said) he was against it?"

$300   What is true?

$400   What is "strike?"

$500   What is "You lose?"

A BIT OF COLOR

Certainly these are not supposed to be your basic, everyday Jeopardy categories. The game with "Marxisms" included categories dealing with Zoology, Transportation, World Literature, History, Africa and Puccini Operas. The game that had Silent Cal's quotes also had Weather, Utah, Education, Literature, World Cities and Recent U. S. History. All we were trying to do was to inject a bit of color and perhaps a bit of humor into shows that were becoming increasingly dry.

On rare occasions, something original and creative did get through. In one instance Steven wrote an entire game board for the "Jeopardy" round in which the name John appeared in *every* clue or response. As usual George was queasy. But Steven and I pointed out the clues were all normal, valid Jeopardy material and managed to convince him the contestants tend to be sufficiently nervous that they play the clues one at a time and don't necessarily catch on to any gimmick we might have going. Rather, we put in the gimmicks to make the show more colorful, interesting and enjoyable *for the viewers.* That time George reluctantly agreed to go along. The "John" board worked out largely as Steven and I had predicted. It played quite well, as the contestants handled the material in the normal manner though they didn't seem to catch on to the gimmick. I think the viewers at home enjoyed it as one by one they did catch on.

BIG WINNINGS

Season six saw the establishment of some new records on Jeopardy. Early in the season Bob Blake, an actuary from Vancouver, British Columbia, won $82,501. In so doing Bob broke Chuck Forrest's five-day record of $72,800 which had stood since our second season. In becoming the first player to break the $75,000 barrier for non-tournament winnings, Bob was required to donate the excess to charity. And so he gave $7,501 to Oxfam of Canada, an international relief organization which aids the impoverished as well as victims of famine and other disasters overseas.

Whereas Chuck Forrest's record had endured for four years, Bob Blake's lasted for just a couple of months as it was soon broken by Frank Spangenberg, a New York City Transit Police officer from Queens. Interests in theology, philosophy and Latin literature all showed as he became the first player to break the $100,000 barrier, amassing $102,597 in five days. His winnings enabled him to buy a house as well as return to school to pursue a theology degree.

As for his excess winnings, Officer Spangenberg donated $27,597 to the Missionaries of Charity, who run a hospice in Manhattan that was in need of repair. It is affiliated with the shelter which Mother Teresa administers in Calcutta. "I've just won too much money on a game show," Frank told the surprised Sisters. "And you're going to get it."

Naturally, we all looked forward to the Tournament of Champions in the Fall of 1990, which featured these two outstanding players. In that competition it was Bob Blake who ultimately emerged on top, winning the hundred grand. Though he's Canadian and game show winnings are not taxable in Canada, Bob still had to pay the IRS because he'd won the money in the U.S.

ANOTHER CHANGE

One change we had late in season six had to do with Final Jeopardy. Over the years we had two or three instances where we had to rule a contestant's Final Jeopardy response wrong only because he neglected to phrase it in the form of a question. Some years earlier we'd put up a large sign in the studio, just offstage and in full view of the players, reminding them to always respond with a question. When that didn't always work Bob Murphy had George see to it that from here on the contestants would always write in "What is," or "Who was," or whatever the appropriate questioning phrase might be, prior to the start of Final Jeopardy. It was done during the commercial break so the viewers never saw it.

Inasmuch as all three contestants are being given the same instructions, no one is being favored over the others. But the viewers have never been informed of the change and so they must think our more recent contestants are better than those in the past in that they always "remember" to write their Final Jeopardy response in the form of a question.

JEOPARDY COLLEGE TOURNAMENT

Season six also saw the introduction of the Jeopardy College Tournament. The Teen Tournament had long been considered the most successful of our three tournaments as it consistently drew the highest ratings. The fact that it aired in February, in the dead of winter when people are more likely to be indoors, didn't hurt. It was therefore decided to hold an annual College Tournament which would air in May and would in many ways resemble the Teen Tournament, which is for high schoolers. In turn, air dates for the Seniors Tournament were pushed back to July when ratings tend to be at their lowest.

As is usually the case in television, the decision to have a College Tournament was made at the last minute. With the shows slated to air in May, taping was set for April. As soon as the go-ahead to hold the tournament was given, which was in March, the contestant department had to scramble to quickly come up with 15 players representing various colleges and universities around the country. Since there wasn't much time, they decided to go to "Spring Break" in Daytona Beach and Palm Springs in the belief students from all over the country would be gathered there, which was certainly true.

For some reason, my instinct told me the type of students who go to Florida and Palm Springs for a week of beer blasts and carousing aren't necessarily going to be the brightest. I therefore had the writers create material for that first College Tournament at about the same level of difficulty as the Teen Tournament. The contestants were told to bring two different sweatshirts with the name of their school prominently displayed, and that became the "uniform" for the College Tournament.

The material proved easy enough for the students to handle in that first College Tournament, while those who made it to the finals did indeed prove to be first-rate Jeopardy players. As was usually the case in our tournaments, there was great camaraderie among the players and a good time seemed to be had by all.

SEDUCTION

Some, however, may have had a better time than others. Word had gotten out that a Jeopardy researcher had seduced and spent a night with one of the college players. George called me in and asked if I heard that a researcher had gotten involved with our college champion. I replied in the negative as that was the first I had heard of it. I was rather shocked as we'd never had anything like that—involving a staffer and a contestant—on Jeopardy before and I was aware there could be legal implications. I was told Columbia lawyers would be interviewing the researcher and would also talk to others on staff if necessary.

About three months earlier George had the following memo distributed to all members of the Jeopardy staff:

It is vital to the continued success of Jeopardy that no doubt exists regarding the integrity of the show and the material presented on it. It is for that reason that you are all required to sign statements pursuant to Sections 508 and 509 of the Federal Communications Act of 1934, stating that you will not engage in conduct which would run counter to the regulations set forth in that section. [In those statements we gave our word we would not in any way pass along information about the games to contestants.]

In addition, I would like to stress that it is important to avoid even the appearance of impropriety. Totally innocent actions might be perceived by others as inappropriate. As an example, it is prudent to avoid contact with ex-contestants, including those who apparently have finished their involvement with the show. As you know, there are times when contestants return to the program because of errors on our part. There is also the possibility that at some time we may elect to bring back former champions for a "Super Tournament."

Casual contact with a recent ex-contestant could be viewed with suspicion and cast doubt on the integrity of the program. Thus, evidence of a relationship, however tenuous, with a returning contestant may necessitate disqualification of the contestant and *dismissal of the employee* [emphasis mine—H.E.].

Therefore, please use your best judgment and discretion in all your conduct. You represent our show to the public. Thank you.

As far as I was concerned, the researcher had opened yet another can of worms. I'd been looking to dismiss her for quite some time and with good reason—lack of productivity. And now she had given us yet another reason. It was clear that under those circumstances the researcher should have been fired. But George was not about to do that nor would he let me.

The rules regarding broadcast standards for game shows do not allow for contestants who are related to, are friends or are just acquaintances of people employed by the producing company or network, where applicable. Everyone who applies to be a contestant must fill out a form on which they are asked to state if they are related to or know anyone in the employ of the show or the company that produces it. One of the things the Columbia attorneys had to find out was whether or not the researcher knew the contestant at the time the shows were taped. Had that been the case the contestant would have been disqualified from any winnings.

The researcher convinced the Columbia lawyers she had only gotten involved after the tapings were over and management was content to let it go at that. The winner of the College Tournament was due to return to participate in the next Tournament of Champions and for a time it was rumored he had been involved in the affair. Fortunately that wasn't the case, as it would have created a very messy situation. Rather, the researcher had gotten involved with one of the losers.

Eventually the researcher eliminated all vestiges of the problem herself by resigning her job at Jeopardy. Inasmuch as we were getting the job done despite her poor productivity, I saw no need to hire a replacement for her on the research staff and none was.

ILLEGAL CONTESTANT WINS $50,000

These matters were hardly the only legal imbroglios involving Jeopardy. Back in 1987 we had a contestant who appeared on the show under the name Barbara Lowe. She appeared rather strange, as she seemed to bounce around behind her lectern. In one instance she did something I'd never seen before or since on Jeopardy. She came right out and challenged Alex's ruling on a response right on the spot when it happened and right in front of everyone.

In their briefing before the shows are taped, contestants are always told to hold any objections to the next commercial break at which point we would deal with them and even reverse a ruling if we were found to be in error. In the case of "Barbara Lowe," the clue had to do with Clarence Darrow's defense of two wealthy college students charged with killing schoolboy Bobby Franks. Her response was, "Who were Leopold and *Leeb?*" Alex ruled her incorrect at which point she immediately shot back, "Leeb is just the German pronunciation of Loeb." Rather than get into an argument with her right in the middle of the show, Alex went ahead and gave it to her. We later got quite a few letters from viewers objecting to her mannerisms and behavior on the show. It was the only time we ever had so many complaints about a single contestant.

"Barbara Lowe" nonetheless managed to win five games and approximately $50,000, and thus qualified for the Tournament of Champions. However, not long after her appearance on our show, we learned through Bob Boden that "Barbara Lowe" was something of a professional game show contestant who had appeared on numerous other programs using a number of aliases.

ABC Compliance and Practices rules, to which Jeopardy was subject, allow for appearances on only two different TV game shows by any one contestant within a five-year period. When people apply to be contestants on Jeopardy or any game show for that matter, they are required to list on their application form the names of all game shows on which they had previously appeared and the dates. Once "Barbara Lowe's" identity was established, it became clear she had not been truthful on her application as she'd previously appeared on many more shows than she had admitted. Under the rules she was therefore disqualified to be a Jeopardy contestant and it was decided to withhold her winnings.

But if you're brazen enough to do what "Barbara Lowe" did, chances are you're brazen enough to do even more. And so "Barbara Lowe" hired an attorney to sue Jeopardy (Merv Griffin Enterprises,

Columbia, et al.) in order to obtain her winnings. At first management was going to contest the matter but they later settled with "Barbara Lowe". Whether management concluded it wasn't worth the legal hassle or didn't want to risk any adverse publicity for the show, I'm not sure. But one thing I do know: At least "Barbara Lowe" didn't participate in the Tournament of Champions. That was where management drew the line.

Prior to working in game shows himself, Jules Minton had been a contestant on a Q & A show called "Bullseye." On that show, a Barry-Enright production, Jules amassed some $50,000 in winnings which ultimately made him the second-highest winner in the history of "Bullseye." The highest all-time winner on that show? You guessed it. Barbara Lowe.

CHAPTER 10

JUDGING ON JEOPARDY!

One of the important qualities Alex Trebek brings to Jeopardy in his capacity as host of the show is the fact that he's well-educated and therefore knows what he's talking about as he reads the clues. That combined with the fact that when he was producer he was in charge of the show got him into the habit of making many of the judgment calls himself. It was only when he wasn't sure of which way to go that he looked over to us and Fred and I would nod "yea" or "nay." In most instances we were able to do that, but there were occasions when we weren't sure either.

Unlike other game shows we generally did not stop the tape in such a case. Alex hated that as it broke his rhythm and so we did it only if we simply had no choice and didn't know which way to call a response without checking further. Most of the time Fred and I would go with our best instincts while the writers and researchers would immediately scramble to further check into the matter and we wouldn't stop the tape until we got to a commercial break. Likewise the contestants were told should they have any objection to a ruling on a response to save it for the next commercial break. At the commercial break the tape was stopped for as long as necessary to satisfactorily resolve the problem. If needed, a writer or researcher would photocopy some sources and bring the copies down and we would show our sources to the contestant who was questioning our judgment. The only other time we would have to stop tape to fully check out a matter to our complete satisfaction was if a player hit a Daily Double. At that point we absolutely had to resolve the issue because in order to be fair to a player who was betting on a D.D., he or she had to know *exactly* how much money both the player and his or her opponents had at the moment.

UNEXPECTED RESPONSES

Every judgment call had to do with unexpected contestant responses. When a player came up with something other than the response we had on our game sheets, he was of course, in most instances, wrong. But it was always our responsibility to be as fair as possible to the players, and sometimes they would come up with alternate responses that also fit the clue. For example in a Rhyme Time category we had a clue that read, "The hens of a great English author." What we were going for was "What are Dickens' chickens?" We'd done our homework on that one and were prepared to accept "Chuck's clucks." The contestant who rang in said, "What are Pepys' (pronounced peeps) cheeps?" Alex looked at us and we nodded yes. It was a bit of a stretch but we gave it to the contestant.

Our judgment was good most of the time, but as long-time viewers of Jeopardy know, we have occasionally had to reverse ourselves. I recall one such instance in a Religion category in which a clue read, "The territory of a church under the jurisdiction of a bishop." What we were going for was, "What is a diocese?" When a player said, "What is a bishopric?" it sounded rather medieval and so we ruled against him. At the next commercial break we checked out dictionaries, found the alternate response was valid, reversed ourselves and credited the player in question. There was another such incident in a Teen Tournament in which we were going for the type of fish that can be served kippered. We were looking for herring but when a contestant said salmon we checked into it and found salmon can be kippered as well.

A KNOW-IT-ALL

What we most dreaded as judges was the occasional situation in which we had a player who knew far more about a specific subject than did we. In our 1988 Seniors Tournament we had one player, Charmion Burns, with considerable expertise in biology, who was at the time working towards her Ph.D. A clue came up in which we asked for the substance that causes maple leaves to turn red in the fall. Our Ph. D. candidate rang in and said, "What is anthocyanin?" At that point a puzzled expression came across our faces as well as Alex's. All we were going for was "What is sugar?" and figured the players would make the connection between maple trees and sugar. My instincts told me anthocyanin is not an alternate name for sugar and so I nodded no. Another player then rang in and said "What is sugar?"

That time my instincts turned out to be wrong. During the commercial break we called several universities and learned that though anthocyanin is indeed not an alternate name or some form of sugar, it is a factor in leaves turning color. It's a class of pigments found in plants. And so, putting fairness above pride, we reversed the ruling.

We had no intention of penalizing a player because we made a mistake. If a contestant had been called wrong when his alternative response also proved to be correct we would give him or her back the amount they'd previously been penalized for the so-called "wrong" response plus the value of the clue to which they were entitled. However if another contestant subsequently rang in with the other correct response (as in the case of "sugar"), the rules of the show allowed for them to remain credited with that correct response as well. However, if we had a situation in which the *second* contestant to ring in responded *incorrectly* and reversed ourselves in favor of the first contestant who rang in, we would give the second player back their loss since they could not have rung in had we called the first player's response correctly at the outset.

CORRECTING THE INCORRECT

Occasionally we inadvertently called someone correct when we should have called them wrong. However, this occurred even more infrequently. In such a case we would come back from commercial and Alex would inform the player he had bad news and we couldn't accept a certain response. We would then have to deduct twice the value of the clue from the contestant's total; first because he didn't earn that clue's winnings, and second because he had to be penalized the value of the clue for a wrong response. Fortunately, those occurrences were quite rare.

One problem that did recur more frequently was that of contestants giving us too much information, with the extraneous information being incorrect. One time we had a clue calling for the correct spelling of the Swiss artist's name that's pronounced "clay." A contestant responded, "What is K-L-E-E *accent acute* over the first 'E.' " Had he stopped with K-L-E-E he would have been fine. Unfortunately the additional information was incorrect as Klee's name takes no accent mark and we had to rule him incorrect. From time to time we've had clues dealing with the famous photographer noted for the pictures he took of the American Civil War. We were of course going for Matthew Brady. "Who was Brady?" by itself would have been acceptable.

One contestant, however, said, "Who was Matthew B. Brady?" and so we had to quickly check out the "B." Fortunately in this instance the "B." was correct. The point here is, if you're going to provide any extra information, be sure it's accurate.

STRICT VS. LENIENT

Judging on Jeopardy is hardly a science but is more like an imprecise art. Generally speaking, there are three ways in which you can judge contestants' responses:

One way is *very strictly.* That's the equivalent of making sure every "t" is crossed and every "i" is dotted. You insist every response be absolutely correct before crediting the player. The lady U.S. Senator from Kansas is Nancy Kassebaum, not Kasse*n*baum. Walt Disney made a movie titled *Lady and the Tramp*; to call it "*The* Lady and the Tramp" is incorrect.

The alternative is to judge *leniently.* When a contestant says the author of *The Prophet* was Khalil Gi*l*bran we understand she meant Khalil Gibran and give it to her because it's obvious she didn't mean Mark Twain.

Finally, you can try to stake out a *middle course* in judging but that's probably the hardest way to go of all because the question invariably arises: where do you draw the line? And if you're going to be consistent, you've got to draw the line somewhere. And if you're not consistent, how can you be fair?

When Alex was producer, his tendency was to judge strictly. On Jeopardy we generally accepted just the last name as a correct response but if there was more than one individual who might fit the clue, Alex would hold out for the first name as well. In a Presidents category, if someone said "Who was Roosevelt?," Alex would say "be more specific," holding out for either Teddy or FDR. If a player asked "Who is Bridges?" in an "Actors and Their Roles" category Alex would want to know if he meant Jeff, Beau or Lloyd.

To some viewers, judging strictly might seem unduly harsh, but it's really not. To others, judging leniently might seem like you're compromising the show and turning it into a piece of cake but that, too, ain't necessarily so. The important thing is *consistency.* Here's why:

Every judgment call affects not only the player whose response is being judged one way or the other but also his opponents. When you're lenient with the player in question you're in effect being hard on his opponents and vice-versa. Jeopardy is, after all, a game of competition in which it helps you at least as much if the call goes against your opponents as when it goes in your favor. (A judgment against an opponent sometimes helps you more than your being credited with a right response because on Jeopardy the value of clues are subtracted for wrong responses, giving the player less money to wager on Daily Doubles and in Final Jeopardy.) So being strict or lenient doesn't matter so much as being consistent and judging all contestants by the same standard as much as possible.

When George Vosburgh took over in our fourth season the result was a change in the standards of judging we'd employed up to that time. Without calling a meeting to address the judging issue, he would simply, from time to time, overrule Alex, Jules and me, at first always coming down on the side of leniency. He sat right behind Jules and me and would call out "give it to him" (or her) and of course we did. When we later asked about this he said a lenient call makes us look like good guys in the eyes of the viewers. I had no problem with being lenient as long as we were consistent.

One day he complained we were getting too soft. And so we went back to a stricter mode of judging and back and forth we'd go. For the Tournament of Champions George would tell us to be strict because lots of money was at stake. One example of a strict ruling in a T of C came in season three (before George took over) and involved Chuck Forrest. One of his responses in a Mythology category had to do with the Greek god of wine and he said "Di-o-ny-si-us" when he should have said "Di-o-ny-sus." Dionysius is also a Greek name but the wine god's name was Dionysus and we ruled him wrong because he added a syllable.

He could have come out better had he remembered the wine god's alternate name was Bacchus and we would have accepted that. Interestingly, when the Tournament was over we met Chuck's mother, who told Jules, "I'm glad you ruled against him—he should have known better."

For the Teen Tournament, on the other hand, we were told to be lenient because it didn't look good to come down hard on the kids. And so the judging went up and down like a yo-yo—strict, lenient, strict, lenient. As in the matter of our degree of difficulty, we'd go through various cycles without ever hitting a happy medium, probably because there was no happy medium—there is no way you can please everyone anyway.

At the very least however, we did need to maintain a level of consistency within each individual game so as to not favor one contestant over his or her opponents and this we genuinely tried to do.

Interestingly, Sony Pictures Entertainment, which owns Jeopardy, has now launched its game show channel on cable on which they have begun to rerun past seasons of the current version of Jeopardy. (I don't believe many of the Art Fleming shows were saved on videotape.) Avid Jeopardy fans who want to study the judging on the show can check out those shows and they will see what I'm talking about.

THE STAFF

To Fred's left at the tapings sat JulieAnn with a P.A., usually Carolyn Shipley, to her left. Both JulieAnn and Carolyn would keep score using pencil and paper, to make sure the electronic scores on the player's lecterns were correct. Again we tried not to stop tape when the scoring machine went awry but would deal with it and make our corrections at the commercial break, unless someone first hit a Daily Double.

People often ask, who are those people you see on stage with Alex and the contestants during that brief interlude just before Final Jeopardy when Johnny usually tells the viewers where to write if they plan to be in the Los Angeles area and would like tickets in order to come and see the show live? The two women you see are usually JulieAnn and Carolyn. They're out there in order to see and record exactly how much each player is wagering for Final Jeopardy. They then figure out what each player's score will be if he gets the final right and if he gets it wrong. That information is then attached to Alex's card that contains the Final Jeopardy clue and response. This enables Alex to tell each player what his final score is immediately after seeing his final response without being dependent on the player's score to first come up on his scoreboard. The tall guy you usually see is co-contestant coordinator Glenn Kagan who's out there to keep the contestants as calm and relaxed as possible, while the man with the headset is stage manager John Lauderdale.

Rocky sat to my right. His job was to keep track of which specific players rang in on each specific clue. From time to time he would remind Alex which player's turn it was to select the next clue. Rocky also noted the contestant's responses and wrote down *exactly* what he or she said. On rare occasions where there was doubt as to what someone said or where one contestant was questioning another's response, George and I would go back to the control booth to hear the audio part of the response in question replayed after which a decision would be reached.

The ABC Compliance and Practices representative sat to Rocky's right. The ABC rep was there to see to it that network and all legal standards were adhered to as regards each show's content and that the game was genuine, the competition unfettered and all players treated fairly. From time to time we'd mention different companies and products in categories such as "Business and Industry" and the network rep would want to be certain no one was paying us anything for some form of subliminal advertising.

SNAFUS

Occasionally we had certain snafus which required changes in the material. Sometimes a player would call for a certain clue which would flash on the board while Alex inadvertently read another clue. Sometimes it would be the other way around with Alex reading the correct one while Doris accidentally brought up the wrong one on the game board. In those instances we'd stop tape and replace both clues—the one revealed on the board and the one Alex read. If the two clues were in different categories the extras would usually suffice. If they were in the same category we'd need two replacements there and since there was only one extra per category, I'd have to run up to get some leftover clues (that had previously been researched) from the writers or they'd run some down to us. For a Potpourri category we sometimes used an extra or leftover clue from another game that was taping that day. And on rare occasions we'd even write and research a clue on the spot using the books we had with us. That once happened to us with a Hollywood Dogs category. Not the kind of category for which a writer was likely to have an extra clue floating around. And so we turned to our in-house Disney maven, Carlo Panno, who came up with "Pongo, Perdita and 99 pups." That's rather cute when you realize the correct response is "Who are the *101 Dalmatians?*"

Fred would then take the changes back to Doris who would enter them in the Chyron. All the while the contestants would be standing on stage with their backs to the game board in the event some additional material was accidentally revealed. The contestants were allowed to turn around after Fred was done and taping would then resume with the contestant whose turn it was calling for the same spot on the board as before. In all such instances the ABC rep would require us to add the disclaimer "portions of this show not affecting its outcome have been edited" to the crawl.

I recall one occasion where Jules thought it would be cute to have "Texas" and "Taxes" next to one another in the same game. Doris found that quite confusing as it was hard to tell exactly which clue the players were calling for. It kept making her nervous and if she was nervous there was a greater likelihood she might expose the wrong clue on the game board. We learned a lesson from that and made it a point from then on to avoid having two categories that sound alike in the same round.

JUDGMENT CALLS

Realizing that any judgment call that helps one contestant automatically hurt his opponents, we tried to be scrupulously fair in judgment, even to the point of reversing ourselves if necessary, despite its attendant embarrassment. Most contestants accepted our decisions in a sportsmanlike manner including those who questioned a call, once we provided backup source material to confirm our rulings.

A few did not and would send us long letters, some resembling college term papers, in an attempt to prove their points. When we were wrong we acknowledged our errors, even to the point where we brought contestants back for another appearance on the show. But a few contestants provided us with some of the most incredible examples of sophistry and farfetched reasoning imaginable in an attempt to have a decision reversed so they could get another shot on the show.

As the main judge, I had to then explain and defend my decisions which required additional research on my part. This ate into my time considerably and I therefore found having to deal with these drawn-out arguments somewhat annoying. Let me cite a couple of examples because with contestants as competitive as they are, dealing with these matters is an integral part of doing a quiz show:

In an "American Revolution" category we had a clue that read as follows: "The Battle of Long Island was the first time the Americans saw action against these soldiers." The first contestant to ring in said "Who are the Prussians?" Alex looked at me and, with my strong background in American history, I immediately nodded "no." Another player quickly rang in with the correct response, "Who were the Hessians?" Had either contestant responded "Who were the Germans?," I would have indicated to Alex to tell the contestant "Be more specific."

This was obviously satisfactory to the viewers, since we got no letters of complaint from them and we always do, it seems, if they suspect even in the slightest that there was an error in the material or that we treated a contestant unfairly. Sometime after we did that show we began receiving a barrage of letters from the contestant I'd ruled against in the above instance, insisting he had been wronged. At first he claimed the German mercenaries whom the King of England had hired to fight the Americans were mostly Prussians but later backed down and merely claimed that "Prussian" was a generic term for all Germans. I asked Ingrid, who has relatives in Germany, how a Bavarian, Swabian or Hessian might feel about being called a Prussian and she said they wouldn't like it at all. I researched the matter further and then had to compose a memo to George pointing out my findings. Here is part of that memo:

The contestant says "Prussian" ought to be accepted in a generic sense for "German" just as we accept*(ed)* "Russian" for "Soviet." His analogy does not follow. Here's why:

Czarist Russia, which was only called "Russia," included not only Russia proper, but also Ukraine, Byelorussia, Georgia, Uzbekistan, etc. It was bigger than the present-day *(sic)* Soviet Union. Since just about all present-day Soviet territory was previously part of (Czarist) Russia, the two terms have become synonymous. The 1984 edition of *World Book* still lists the Soviet Union under "Russia."

Prussia and Germany have never been synonymous. The west German states were never part of Prussia and were never referred to as such. All Prussians are Germans just as all Texans are Americans. But not all Germans are Prussians.

The German mercenaries were contracted for by the rulers of six German states, none of which was Prussia. The majority came from Hesse-Cassel which is why they were called Hessians.

The contestant grants us, "I agree that 'Hessians' is the traditional, simplistic, high school response for this clue." As someone who taught college-level American History, I would challenge him to come up with one published college-level American History text in which the German mercenaries of the American Revolution are called "Prussians." And coming from Austin, home of the University of Texas, he should have access to plenty of them.

I would further ask, of our millions of viewers who are none too quick to point out both our real and supposed errors, inconsistencies and unfairness, did so much as one letter say we handled the "Prussian" response incorrectly (other than the contestant, of course)?

In his letter, the contestant went on to claim "I have since deter-mined that the American Patriots actually saw their first action against the 'Hessians' in the area between Staten Island and Perth Amboy, New Jersey, several weeks before the Battle of Long Island. This would appear to invalidate the clue entirely."

In helping me deal with this claim, our researchers tracked down two books that dealt with the Hessian role in the American Revolu-tion. Both were called *The Hessians*. One was by Rodney Atwood, the other by Edward J. Lowell. The books pointed out that while some Hessians were quartered on Staten Island, they first saw combat in the Battle of Long Island. We could find no reference anywhere to an alleged skirmish having taken place between Staten Island and Perth Amboy. In looking on the map, all I could find between those two places was a strait of water called the Arthur Kill.

Further research showed that Prussia's ruler at the time of the American Revolution, Frederick the Great, was an admirer of George Washington and quite sympathetic to the American cause. But this is just one example of the degree to which some contestants would go in looking for a loose brick.

In a Musical Instruments category, the following clue appeared at the $800 level: "From the Greek 'psallein,' 'to pluck' we get this plucked type of zither that's mentioned in the Bible." The correct re-sponse was, "What is a psaltery?" The word occurs some 26 times in the Old Testament. Psalm 150:3 and First Samuel 10:5 are two ex-amples. When a contestant said "What is a *psalter*?," I gave Alex the "no" nod and he ruled him wrong. The contestant complained claim-ing by definition "psalter" is an alternate form of "psaltery." Here's part of the memo I wrote George in dealing with that issue:

When the contestant answered "What is a psalter?," I said he was wrong because I knew a psalter is a book of psalms, not a musical instrument. The two music dictionaries we have both confirm this. All our encyclo-pedias that have a listing under "psaltery" describe the instrument and none give "psalter" as an alternate name. Had we accepted "psalter" for "psaltery," we would have gotten lots of letters to the effect "You dummies, don't you know a psalter is a *book* of psalms?"

The contestant who claims we should have accepted "psalter" cites *Webster's Third International Dictionary* which says it is an archaic al-ternate of psaltery. My feeling is if that were the *only* definition under "psalter," fine, give it to him. But the fact is the present-day definition means *something else*—a book. (Just like when a contestant said "Bernard" instead of "Barnard" we called him wrong not because of wrong pronunciation but because he'd given us *another* name.)

The *Random House Dictionary*, which the contestant also cites, says the use of "psalter" for "psaltery" went out about the year 900. Since the Bible wasn't translated into English until the Fifteenth Century, I would challenge the contestant to come up with one version of the Bible—any version, and there are lots to choose from—in which the word "psalter" appears, and to meet the requirements of our clue he would definitely have to do that since we said, " this plucked type of zither *that's mentioned in the Bible.*"

We used the King James Version as our basic Bible of record—the one we quoted in our Bible clues—since it is still the most widely used translation in the United States. We were, however, nevertheless sensitive to the fact that our contestants and viewers came from a great many religious backgrounds and were always careful to accept various alternate responses derived from other Bible translations or from differing religious denominations and traditions. For example, among Protestants and Jews "Thou shalt not steal" is the eighth of the Ten Commandments, while in Roman Catholic teaching it is the seventh and we always respected alternate interpretations of Scripture. The First Amendment states "Congress shall make no law respecting an establishment of religion" and we at Jeopardy followed that principle. But unlike some in Hollywood who see religion only as something to either make fun of or totally expunge from American life, we did neither of those. Interesting clues and facts about the Bible and religion have always been an integral part of Jeopardy and have always been treated with respect.

APPEALS

To say that Jeopardy contestants are highly competitive is an understatement. Many apparently dread the thought of losing on Jeopardy and seem to have taken to heart the scolding of loser "Weird Al" Yankovic by Don Pardo on Weird Al's "I Lost on Jeopardy" video: "That's right, Al, you lost. . . . But that's not all. You made yourself look like a jerk in front of millions of people and brought shame and disgrace on your family name for generations to come."

It may not be quite that bad, but many do take it hard and some have cried. If there was one particular clue that cost a player the game, he or she will remember it for the rest of their lives. And so one can see why some players will go to such lengths to have a ruling against them reversed.

On the other hand, we were more than willing to reverse ourselves when we were indeed wrong. In one instance we had a Final Jeopardy which said "This island nation is the most volcanic country in the world."

Our writer and researcher had each come up with a source which stated that that description fit Iceland. One of our contestants said "What is Indonesia" and we ruled her wrong. Following her appearance on the show, she found two books which claimed Indonesia was the most volcanic country. (Remember Krakatoa? Perhaps we should have.) Her sources were no less credible than ours and so we invited her back for another appearance on the show. In retrospect I would say what constitutes "the most volcanic country" is a matter of opinion rather than scientific fact, since it can probably be determined in more than one way—how many volcanoes, how many eruptions, the magnitude of the eruptions, etc. We should have been more wary of the clue to begin with.

Perhaps the most memorable instance of our bringing back a contestant involved Father Tom Smolich, who became known to readers of the October 9, 1989 issue of *People* magazine as "The Jeopardy Priest." Father Smolich, a Jesuit Priest at the Dolores Mission in East Los Angeles, was in need of funding to set up a program to help women get off welfare and into the working world. Some $90,000 was needed to construct a building on church property that could serve as a day-care center for their children. He saw an ad for contestants in the *Los Angeles Times* and decided to try out figuring, "What the heck. It can only be a horrible mistake." He made it onto the show but finished second and therefore out of the money.

That apparently was that—until we got some letters, not from the Father, but from a couple of viewers who pointed out we'd made an error and had wrongly credited one of his opponents for a response that wasn't quite correct. We checked into it, found the letter writers were right and, much to his surprise, invited Father Smolich back for a second appearance on the show. This time his prayers were answered as he ended up winning $39,802 in four days! That was enough for a down payment on the new day-care center.

"A lot of times we get highfalutin' ideas of what miracles are," said Father Smolich. "This was a great thing for me and, more importantly, for our program. I consider it a miracle."

CHAPTER 11

IT'S A BIRD. . .IT'S A PLANE. . . IT'S SUPER JEOPARDY!

For some time we had been hearing stories that Merv Griffin was planning to launch a TV version of Monopoly, the Parker Brothers game which is one of the most popular parlor games of all time. King World, which was by now producing its own original programming, had obtained TV rights to the game and former Jeopardy production executive Dave Williger, among others, had been involved in developing a TV version of the game.

Monopoly was by no means a secret, as the box game had been around for years but no one had been able to come up with a viable TV version. With its houses and hotels and metal tokens moving around the game board, Monopoly as played at home is a three-dimensional game. How to successfully transfer that to the two-dimensional TV screen struck me as a virtually insurmountable challenge. King World was about to take up that challenge when Merv Griffin suddenly threw a monkey wrench into the works.

Merv Griffin Enterprises and King World had a unique agreement stipulating that King World would not distribute any game shows other than those produced by Merv Griffin Enterprises. Insomuch as King World was looking to air its TV version of Monopoly on one of the networks, rather than distribute it via syndication, they felt they would be proceeding within the bounds of their agreement with Griffin. Merv, however, didn't interpret the deal that way and threatened legal action. With "Wheel" and Jeopardy providing half of King World's substantial revenues, the last thing the King brothers needed was a dispute with Merv and so they quickly backed off on the Monopoly issue.

Merv was invited to take over production of TV "Monopoly" with King World as a junior partner, just as in the case of Jeopardy and "Wheel," and regardless of whether the show would air on a network or in syndication. Merv took the King World version of the show and turned it over to his small development department for revision. Since the name belonged to Parker Brothers and the production rights were now Merv's, individuals such as Dave Williger, who had worked on the "Monopoly" project now found themselves totally shut out with no legal recourse. Their work would count for naught.

Burt Wheeler, who had produced "Sale of the Century" from the time George left the show in 1987 until its demise two years later, was named line producer of "Monopoly" and he and Merv were in charge of its continued development. In the course of that development, a number of us from Jeopardy were invited over to act as contestants and to make any suggestions we could think of for improving the show.

As I watched others play the game two obvious weaknesses became apparent. First TV Monopoly lacked a clear, concise, tight format, one that would be easy for a viewer to pick up on and follow, even if he tuned in in the middle of the show. And second, it had no quality about it that drew the viewer in, that enticed him and tempted him to play along with the contestants. Rather, all you were left with was a feeling of watching others play a game that didn't seem particularly interesting anyway. When L.A. *Daily News* columnist Frank Swertlow got an advance look at the show, it struck him as "pathetic." Unfortunately, no one could come up with any concrete suggestions for improving it.

When King World had been trying to launch "Monopoly," ABC was the one network that had expressed some interest. Now Merv Griffin and King World joined forces to try to interest ABC in the new version Merv was developing. ABC seemed noncommittal but did express interest in a kind of super Tournament of Champions for Jeopardy featuring the show's all-time best players. It was quickly dubbed Super Jeopardy and ABC soon indicated it would definitely like to have it to run as a 13-week series, one half hour a week, in the summer. Merv agreed to give it to them provided they take "Monopoly" as well and a deal was made.

Merv continued to develop "Monopoly" practically right up to the first taping and even made some additional changes after the show had been launched. Calling it the biggest and most exciting project he'd ever worked on, he even toyed for a time with employing a midget in top hat and tails dressed up as Uncle Penny Bags. A number of individuals auditioned to host the show before Merv finally settled on Mike Reilly, whose previous game show experience consisted of an appearance as a not-particularly-memorable *contestant* on Jeopardy. Merv seemed to enjoy discovering new talent and had certainly had his successes—Art Fleming, Pat Sajak and Vanna White, to name a few. But every time you try something new in television you take a chance. Sometimes it works. Sometimes it doesn't. Without holding "Monopoly's" format against him, I would say that as a game show emcee Mike Reilly turned out as adequate, at most. He wasn't overly stiff after the first couple of shows but seemed to lack warmth and empathy for the contestants, which is vital for a game show host.

Later that year Merv made an even bigger mistake with former NFL placekicker Rolf Benirschke whom he brought in to replace Pat Sajak on the daytime version of "Wheel," when the latter began his late-night talk show for CBS. Rolf didn't have it at all and daytime "Wheel's" ratings on NBC took such a beating the network cancelled the show. Fortunately for all concerned Pat stayed with syndicated "Wheel" and its ratings continue to top all U.S. syndicated shows for a phenomenal nine years in a row! With Benirschke finally gone, daytime "Wheel" was picked up by CBS with veteran game show emcee Bob Goen as host. But by then daytime "Wheel" was already "goen" and though Bob did fine as host and Vanna was as good as ever, it was too late and the lost daytime audience never came back. After a season on CBS, daytime "Wheel" was cancelled for good.

SUPER JEOPARDY

While Merv's development department was struggling with "Monopoly," it was our task to come up with 13 shows' worth of material for the Super Jeopardy tournament while continuing to do our regular work for the 230 shows that would air that season in syndication. Since ABC was shelling out good money for Super Jeopardy, I was informed we could hire an additional writer to help ease the burden. About that time Michelle Johnson had approached George indicating she'd like to come back to Jeopardy should an opening arise. She knew George pretty well, since her husband, Gary, had worked under George as head writer for "Sale" before becoming producer of "Scrabble."

When George told me Michelle was interested in a writing job I said that was fine with me. I'd always known her to be a hard worker and respected her writing ability as well. And so, for much of 1990, we had a writing staff of six. Michelle was very much the professional who carried her share of the load and more. Her writing is light and lively and the fact she tended to write towards the easy side didn't hurt either as it helped balance out the more difficult material I got from some of the others.

Super Jeopardy also provided enough money for us to enlarge our office space by renting some additional rooms. As a result, from then on each writer and researcher either had a small office of his or her own or shared a larger one with just one other person. Finally we were told that in return for our work on Super Jeopardy those of us who had worked on both that and the regular shows would receive paychecks 50% larger than normal for the 13 weeks that Super Jeopardy aired. For a typical writer earning $700 a week that would mean $350 extra per week.

Super Jeopardy must have been a really good deal for Merv in that he was willing to pay anything extra. Rather his approach was usually that if you were employed by him, he could put you to work on any and all extra projects without paying anything additional. Over the years we worked on episodes and editions of "Mama's Family," ABC's "Nightline," and an ABC Earth Day Special among others, which utilized the Jeopardy set and for which we had to provide written material and/or other services all with no extra compensation.

Along with "Monopoly," Super Jeopardy was going to run in prime time (Saturday nights 8 to 9 Eastern and Pacific time) but unlike "Monopoly" there would be few significant start-up costs, which made it all the more profitable. Merv was especially excited at the thought his game shows were going to be running in *prime time*. As far as he knew, it was the first time the networks would run a game show in prime time since the days of the quiz show scandals and he called us to check if that was indeed the case. I asked Steven and a couple of researchers to look into it and they found there had been a few short-lived game shows in prime time in the sixties but that Super Jeopardy and "Monopoly" would be the first ones since then.

On the down side for me was the fact we'd been planning a New York vacation to coincide with a family event. Unfortunately that was when Super Jeopardy was scheduled to be taped and all we could do was fly out for the weekend and come right back. But that's television and I was used to it. According to Columbia rules I'd been with the company long enough to be entitled to three weeks' annual vacation. I was able to take a week off after Super Jeopardy ended but before we began regular tapings and got one week at the end of the season. But the third week was lost as there wasn't any time that I could spare to take it nor were we allowed to either cash out unused vacation time or carry it over to the next season. It later came out that this Merv Griffin/George Vosburgh rule was contrary to Sony/Columbia policy and people were ultimately repaid for the vacation time that they had lost.

PLANNING FOR THE GAMES

Shortly after we were informed we would be doing Super Jeopardy, Alex came up to the office and sat down with Steven and me in order to decide which contestants we should invite back since the three of us had been with the show from the outset. First prize in the super tournament would be $250,000 with $25,000 for second place and $10,000 to the third place finisher. Since we had, at that point, completed five full seasons on the air, it was decided we would invite a minimum of three players from each season and then round out the group with additional contestants who had been both memorable individuals and outstanding players.

In all, we needed 27 players—three apiece for nine preliminary games. That would yield nine winners for three semi-final games with the three winners of those games going on to compete in a single final game for the big prize. We didn't plan to invite any of the big winners from season six (including Frank Spangenberg, who won over $100,000 and Bob Blake, who had earlier topped Chuck Forrest's five-day regular season record by winning over $80,000) because (1) the last few weeks of that season's shows would still be airing at the same time as Super Jeopardy and (2) that season's contestants hadn't yet appeared in the Tournament of Champions and to first put them on the $250,000 Super Jeopardy would make the regular $100,000 T of C appear anticlimactic. And so 27 invitations were issued. All the former players were thrilled to hear from us and all but one (whose daughter was getting married when we would be taping the shows) were able to make it.

But Merv saw it a little differently than the rest of us. He was upset to learn that players to whom he'd paid out big bucks, like Frank Spangenberg, Bob Blake and his brand-new college champion, Tom Cubbage, hadn't been invited. What were we then to do, as invitations had already been sent out?

Well, Merv can be creative when he wants to be and he quickly decided that for the nine preliminary games of the super tournament *four* contestants, rather than the usual three, should play. The rest of us didn't see why it was essential to have these additional players in Super Jeopardy and felt the untried concept of four players might not work well. But, as the old saying goes, the boss may not always be right but he's always boss. And so nine additional invitations went out, including one to Burns Cameron, the biggest-ever money winner on the old Jeopardy, whom Merv thought it would be a good idea to have as well.

It was now my task and that of the writing and research staffs to come up with the material for the super tournament. Inasmuch as we were going to have the very best players of all combined with the fact there would be four of them in each preliminary game, I felt we could go a little tougher even than the regular Tournament of Champions. But George didn't see it that way and after we completed the games he ordered them eased up. In this regard there was a genuine philosophic difference between us. Not only was George worried that the contestants might not respond correctly to the material, but even if they did he felt tough material tends to be a turn-off to the viewers. I didn't want material that would be missed by the players any more than he did, but where we differed was that I felt players getting tough material right wouldn't turn off the viewers but would *impress* them. One thing I always insisted on was that we avoid the use of esoteric and erudite language, so that no matter how difficult the clue, the average viewer would know what we are talking about, whether or not he himself could come up with the correct response ahead of the contestants. But like Merv, George, too, was the boss and we deferred to his wishes.

Merv, in the meantime, had ordered a few cosmetic changes as well, such as a shiny black floor on stage, instead of the usual bluish-grey carpet we had been using up to that time, and a darkened studio with artificial smoke on stage while the contestants were writing out their Final Jeopardy responses. He also decided to enlarge the value of each clue. First-round clues would be worth 200, 400, 600, 800 and 1000 and Double Jeopardy clues 500, 1000, 1500, 2000 and 2500 but these would not be in dollars but rather would just be points.

In so far as the contestants were playing for set dollar amounts as opposed to whatever they might accumulate in the game, what did it matter? They were able to play the $100,000 Tournament of Champions using the regular dollar amounts and that seemed to work just fine. About all Merv did by enlarging the amounts was create the *illusion* of a tougher, more difficult game. Otherwise they could have used the $10, $20, $30, $40, $50 format of the old Jeopardy and it wouldn't have made a lick of difference.

It turned out many of the contestants, out of habit, inadvertently kept asking for clues worth so many hundred dollars, rather than points. Sometimes they would catch and correct themselves. Other times Alex would correct them. In any case the points only created a little extra, though otherwise harmless, confusion.

The four-contestant format for the preliminary games was not harmless, however. With three outstanding players handling material that wasn't all that difficult you knew there would often be frustration on the part of those whose reflexes at ringing in weren't as fast as others'. With four players there was considerably more frustration. There was an extra player but no extra material to go around and some players seemed completely shut out. I've always felt the point of a Jeopardy game is to show which player knows more about the categories that happened to come up that day, and that overly easy material reduced the game to a contest of who's quicker on the draw—which is what many of the Super Jeopardy games turned out to be. The four-player format also tended to make it difficult for any one player to run any significant streak, even in a category in which he had considerable expertise.

The result was that many of our very best players, including Chuck Forrest, couldn't make it beyond the preliminary round. As for the material itself, it tended to play quite easy throughout all 13 games, with the exception of one or two categories at most. Most games had very few clues that were missed, some just one or two. I feel there's a need for some material to separate the men from the boys and the women from the girls so to speak, and we just didn't have it in Super Jeopardy. The quarter-of-a-million dollars went to Bruce Seymour, who had been a good, though not especially outstanding, player in the past.

Following the final game a luncheon was held at Merv's Beverly Hilton hotel for the players and a few officials of ABC, Columbia, Merv Griffin Enterprises and Jeopardy. As a department head I was invited to attend.

In retrospect, I would not at all be surprised if Jeopardy were to hold another super tournament sometime in the future. But if you missed Super Jeopardy on ABC in June, July and August 1990, chances are you'll never see Jeopardy played with four contestants. And you won't be missing much.

CHAPTER 12

CONTESTANT SEARCH

One of my ongoing responsibilities was to provide the Contestant Department with two complete sets of 50-question tests, plus one for teens, twice each year, in March and September. Though this should not have been a big deal, it had at Jeopardy degenerated into something of an ordeal that took some four days of my time and that of the writers away from our regular work.

In the earlier years of the show, putting together contestant tests was a relatively simple matter. The writers would go through old Jeopardy shows and select certain of the more difficult clues—always from the two lowest horizontal rows of the game board. We would then bring our selections to a meeting with Jules, read them aloud and by consensus select the ones we thought would be best in a test.

To be truly useful, a contestant test must accurately reflect the program and cover as broad a range of categories that are apropos to the show as possible. Since in the course of each Jeopardy game the players are exposed to 13 different categories of knowledge, the idea is to eliminate via the test those individuals whose strengths lie in only one or two specific fields. For example, you may be a whiz when it comes to Shakespeare and the Bible but if you are weak in most other areas it will not be enough to win the game. Besides, there's a good chance those particular categories will not even appear on your particular show.

Our contestant tests originally followed a pattern of 15 academic, 10 lifestyle, 15 pop culture and 10 word play questions which reflected the kind of shows we did in those early days. They were, however, fairly difficult questions. The Contestant Department was ideally looking for people who could at least correctly answer 35 of the 50 questions but there was no passing grade etched in stone. Contestant coordinators Mark Richards and Greg Muntean realized it was only within their capacity to test so many individuals in a given year and they would select the ones they thought best.

FINDING QUALITY CONTESTANTS

Finding good game show contestants is largely a numbers game. At Jeopardy we taped 230 shows per season. Allowing for returning champions and tournaments, this meant we needed about 450 contestants a year. Our three-person contestant department was physically able to test about 15 to 20,000 applicants a year. Hence they needed the top two or three percent of those individuals they were going to see.

They had to find those 450 contestants. They didn't need more and we couldn't do the shows with less. So what difference does a "passing grade" make? None that I could see. What does make a difference is the number of people you test. The more applicants you test, the larger a pool you have to choose from, the higher the caliber of contestant you will find.

So if management was truly concerned with helping the contestant coordinator to find higher caliber players they could increase the manpower of that department enabling them to test a larger number of applicants.

PASSING THE TEST

Susanne Thurber, for her part, considered the concept of a passing grade of 35 to be essential. Though it made no sense to me in considering what was good for the show, I could see why she clung to it. If something went wrong, a rigid passing grade could help shield the Contestant Department if a player did particularly poorly on the show. "Can't blame me. After all he or she did pass the test."

After our group had come up with new tests I would submit them to George. He and Rocky would then take the tests. Their rule of thumb was that one or the other of them would have to get every question correct. Any question that they both missed would have to be replaced with something easier.

Once we had a test on which they could answer every question, it would be proofread and programmed into the Chyron computer system. After a day of taping we would videotape the tests off the regular Jeopardy game board with Alex reading the clues.

When applicants took the test they would be given answer sheets with 50 blank lines. The tape would then be played and they could hear Alex reading the clues while they saw them on the monitor. They would have a few seconds to write in their response before Alex went on to the next clue. Writing in "what is" or "who was" in question format has never been necessary on the contestant test.

In the early years of the show the entire contestant test was in written form and applicants would have 10 minutes to handle 50 clues. That system gave people extra time to think about clues that were more difficult as well as a chance to go back and change their responses if they felt like it. Going to the system of videotaping the clues has made the test much more like the actual show and that was a change for the better.

After Alex taped the tests Susanne would try them out on small groups of applicants. She would administer the two tests, which we referred to as "test 'A'" and "test 'B'" to the same group in order to make sure one was not substantially harder or easier than the other. Since future applicants would only get to take one or the other of the tests, that was only fair. The two tests would be used on an alternating basis so people who had taken the test couldn't tell those about to take it what to expect.

But then Susanne would come back to tell George not enough people had reached the magic number of 35 and the test was therefore too hard. I tried to explain to George that Susanne should have been selecting the best contestants regardless of score, but George insisted on an easier test. It seemed ridiculous to me to have a contestant test significantly easier than the actual show. I pointed out that every other game show in town and every game show of the past we know anything about all had contestant tests substantially *harder* than the actual show. For them, the assumption was that if a contestant could handle a test that was harder than the show, they should do okay on camera, under the hot lights, provided the material was a little easier. What Susanne was proposing was that Jeopardy do just the opposite.

George wasn't buying. He now wanted an easier test and that was all there was to it. I then had to call another meeting with the writers and we had to start all over. Up until then we had been using only old material from the fourth horizontal row of the board ($400 clues from the first round and $800 ones from the second). I had earlier eliminated all clues originally used on the bottom row (the $500 and $1000 ones) as I sensed George would find those too hard. We were now reduced to using clues from the second and third rows of the game board. To a man the writers were all upset about this as it absolutely made no sense to them. It seemed as if we'd be cutting off our nose to spite our face. But this is what the boss wanted and so we gave it to him. After some more trial and error we ultimately had a test

Susanne considered sufficiently easy as it was giving her enough people to choose from with scores over 35.

Since the test must ultimately reflect the show this meant the shows would have to be made easier as well and in the last couple of years they have been getting progressively easier.

CONTESTANT SEARCHES

From time to time the contestant department would go to different cities on contestant searches. But this was done only if the local Jeopardy affiliate agreed to sponsor such a search for a few days. When they occasionally came to a particularly large market such as New York, the response from people wanting to try out for the show would be overwhelming and postcards would have to be drawn to select those who would actually be allowed to take the test. Our New York City transit cop, Frank Spangenberg, for example, didn't have his card selected and he travelled to Scranton, Pennsylvania in order to take the test when a contestant search was held there.

Occasionally the people in the Contestant Department and others on staff would comment that we seemed to get better players from the East. Some seemed to feel the educational standards there were higher. Since the contestant test was readily available in Los Angeles most of the time, many seemed to think we'd pretty much milked the Southern California area for good players.

I therefore had an idea. Atlantic City is within 200 miles of New York, Philadelphia, Wilmington, Baltimore and Washington, DC. Why not hire some contestant coordinators to permanently work out of Merv's Atlantic City Resorts hotel and casino? People from the surrounding markets would be attracted to the hotel to come and take the test, just as others are attracted to the shows and restaurants. Some might stay there overnight and some might even leave a few bucks at the gaming tables. With a permanent contestant testing base in Atlantic City we would test twice as many applicants, giving us twice as many people to choose from, thereby significantly enhancing the caliber of contestant we would ultimately put on the show.

I wrote up this suggestion and submitted it as a memo to George. I would have sent it directly to Merv and Bob Murphy, but George had told us on a number of occasions he didn't want us having any contact with those over him. Merv apparently wasn't interested. He did, however, arrange to have our three-person contestant staff come to Resorts each year and stay for two weeks. In order to test as many people as possible in that two-week period, I was asked to devise two ten-question preliminary tests. People who wanted to try out would first have to take those. Only if they got seven out of ten on one of the preliminary tests would they then be allowed to take the regular test.

Since the Contestant Department was in Atlantic City for just two weeks, only a small percentage of our players came to us as a result of the testing at Resorts. On the whole they proved to be good players and I would hope the availability of testing there will be increased somewhat in the future.

BACK TO THE TEST

What does it take to pass the test and be a successful contestant? Nearly all of our really good players are inveterate readers. Not that they have photographic memories for all information that comes to them, but they do seem to have a knack for remembering *certain* facts. Doug Molitor, who made it to our second Tournament of Champions in 1986, put it this way: "There's no way you can learn all this stuff just for the show. Either you already know it or you don't. My memory for details," he went on to say, "is practically nil. I'm terrible at re-membering names and faces. Yet if I read something—some fact that really has no immediate value to me—it all sticks, somehow."

Danny Green, a high school science teacher who won $27,000 put it more succinctly: "I'm a veritable cesspool of useless information." Useless? Perhaps, except on Jeopardy.

A LITTLE PERSONALITY HELPS A LOT

At every testing session, those people who pass the written test are invited to stay longer and play a mock Jeopardy game after which they're asked to speak about themselves for one minute. Three people at a time play the game just like on the show, except hotel desk bells are used to ring in after the clue has been read. The contestant coordi-nators are looking for two things: the ability to play the game in a competitive situation and that hard-to-define characteristic we call "personality."

By personality I mean one or more qualities that make you stand out from the crowd. Some trait that serves to make you unique and perhaps even memorable in the eyes of the viewers. Regional dialects, unusual experiences, interesting occupations or hobbies all can help. If you've gone skydiving, call it a hobby, even if you've only done it a few times. One game show contestant who was actually a car salesman got considerable mileage from the fact he'd once been a department store Santa Claus. It showed he was jolly and creative and it became a good tag line—"our own Santa Claus . . . ." And so if you're ever trying out, don't be afraid to speak up and brag on yourself but don't ramble on and on.

Another aspect of personality is the ability to hold one's own in front of a group. Someone who gets the jitters playing a mock game or during a brief interview in front of maybe 10 or 12 people will not be perceived as a good candidate to place under the hot lights in front of a studio audience numbering in the hundreds and millions of viewers at home.

Lively but pleasant mannerisms and vocal variety (as opposed to speaking in a monotone) also help. Good looks don't hurt but they're hardly a primary factor in becoming a Jeopardy contestant. We all know every person is unique and special. But to make it on to Jeopardy or any game show, you've got to somehow get your uniqueness across, at least to the contestant coordinators. As one would-be Jeopardy contestant said, "Like most things in life, I figure you have to know more than just how to play the game. You have to know how to play the game it takes to get to play the game."

THE NEXT STEP

If you pass that hurdle and finally get to the real game, you'll have to come to Los Angeles at your own expense. The show tapes on Mondays and Tuesdays and the Contestant Department will try to use the out-of-town players on Monday or early Tuesday at the latest so they won't have to either travel back and forth or stay over a week in the event they win. You'll be asked to bring at least three changes of clothing with you to the studio to be used should you become a returning champion so that the viewers don't get the impression that either many shows are taped per day or that you only have one good outfit to wear on national TV.

Jeopardy tapes three shows in the afternoon, followed by a dinner break after which two more shows are taped. If your presence will be needed for those last two shows, you'll be able to eat with the staff although you'll be kept at a "contestants only" table. That's so no one will be in a position to give you any extra information about the show, particularly the material in the upcoming games. My advice is to eat very little or nothing at all. It's said that when people digest big meals there's a certain flow of blood from the brain to the lower reaches of the body and the mind isn't as sharp as on an empty stomach. Over the years it seems contestants have tended to do a bit worse on average on our after-dinner show, which always airs on Thursdays, than on the other days' shows.

All contestants are required to provide proof of their social security numbers since you'll have to pay Federal income tax on any winnings. In addition the State of California takes five percent whether you're a California resident or not. But look at the bright side. You'll only have to pay if you win and at least it's a cash show so you'll have where to draw the money from. Besides you can at least deduct the cost of your trip to Los Angeles. Taxes can be more of a problem on shows that give away big prizes. You're then required to pay according to the cash value of the prize. As a result some game show contestants actually turn down prizes that they've won—which they're allowed to do.

That's not a problem on Jeopardy. As contestant Sandra Gore said, "I went on Jeopardy because I wanted to win cash. I didn't want to go home with a ceramic dalmatian and parting gifts."

Jeopardy does, however, give parting gifts. You hear announcer Johnny Gilbert rattle them off at the end of the show. Generally seven products are packed into a minute's worth of time. Not only does a company have to really give those products to the contestants but they have to pay for those approximately eight or nine seconds during which Johnny reminds you Paul Mitchell Salon hair care products are never tested on animals.

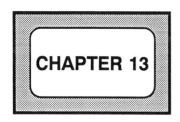

CHAPTER 13

FIFTEEN MINUTES OF FAME

In a free market one of the key determinants of the price of anything is the law of supply and demand. Large supplies and small demand will tend to lower prices while small supplies and great demand tend to raise them. In the market for behind-the-scenes TV employees the laws of supply and demand continually favor employers who are constantly being approached by job seekers. Despite the long hours and low pay in entry level positions, people continue to be drawn to "the business" by its glamourous aspects and the desire to be associated with something famous. This was one of the intangible perks on Jeopardy and one which seemed to mean a great deal to some on staff.

By 1986, the popularity of Jeopardy had been well-established. From that time on there seemed to be a steady stream of calls coming in from representatives of the various media—local and national TV, newspapers, magazines—all eager to do a story on one aspect or another of Jeopardy. Most of the requests from the media were for interviews with Alex, since he's the show's celebrity, the one people see each day and are naturally eager to learn more about. The second-most popular subject of media inquiry, however, was the show's material—who writes it, where does it come from, etc.

Over the years, the writing and research staffs have been written up in *TV Guide, The New York Times,* The *Los Angeles Times Magazine, Sports Illustrated, Games Magazine* and *American Way* (American Airlines' magazine) just to name a few. After the *TV Guide* writer said of Jeopardy, "Some evil genius. . .is in charge of writing the answers; they hover tantalizingly around the fringes of your useful knowledge," Jules went out and bought us individualized name plates for our desks with "Evil Genius" engraved beneath each one's name.

THE TOUGHEST QUESTIONS

One time the five Jeopardy writers were asked to contribute what each thought was his or her toughest question for an article which appeared in the March 1987 issue of *Ladies Home Journal*. I gave them the one about Misha the Bear. Here are what the others contributed under the heading "*Jeopardy!*'s toughest questions":

1. This U.S. president was an ex-hangman who admitted he'd sired an illegitimate son, and didn't marry until he was in the White House.
2. This city is the westernmost national capital in the Western hemisphere.
3. Art Carney and Jacqueline Susann were regulars on his show before he was a regular on Dick Van Dyke's.
4. They are America's only national historic landmark on wheels.

Answers
1. Who was Grover Cleveland?
2. What is Mexico City?
3. Who is Morey Amsterdam?
4. What are the San Francisco cable cars?

MY INTERVIEW

Back when Alex was still producer, syndicated entertainment columnist Frank Sanello, a former contestant who won $12,000 on the show, indicated he wanted to do a story on one Jeopardy writer. Alex arranged for Frank to spend the better part of a day interviewing me and watching what I did. As a result of his column I received a number of letters and calls from people I hadn't seen in years and even decades.

Here's a brief excerpt from that article, which ran in the spring of 1986:

"We're lucky Alex is bright," Eisenberg says. "Most hosts just take what they're given. Alex knows what he's reading on the air."

But today Trebek isn't taking what Harry has given him. Trebek wants Harry to change the word "dynasty" to "family" in a question about the Hapsburgs because Trebek thinks "dynasty" is too obscure a word.

Eisenberg reminds Trebek about the popular nighttime soap of the same name.

Conceding defeat, Trebek motions to a reporter and says, "Now he's gonna write, 'Alex caves in to his writers' " (*sic*).

Eisenberg, a single parent with two small children, taught history at a community college until the teacher he had temporarily replaced returned from sabbatical. He then turned to selling photocopiers, which paid better than his current TV job. Just how much better Eisenberg declines to say, but another "Jeopardy!" employee says writers earn between $500 to $650 a week—not a princely sum by television standards. . . .

Eisenberg says he loves his job. But he hates checking computer printouts to make sure the writers aren't repeating the same categories too often.

It's a thankless—and bizarre—task.

"Just last week I caught five questions on Pakistan," says Eisenberg.

THE MEDIA

In our fourth season (1987–88) we were contacted by people from ABC's popular newsmagazine program "20/20," who indicated they wanted to do a segment on Jeopardy with emphasis on how the material is put together. "20/20" reporter Bob Brown was dispatched to L.A. with a crew and they spent two days in our offices and studio, much of it devoted to interviewing writers and researchers. While they were here it seemed to me that some of our people were practically falling over one another in order to grab their share of the TV "limelight." I tended to back off, as I always saw my role at Jeopardy primarily as one simply trying to earn a living and feed his family. The media "fame" was probably more of a turn-on to my family (especially the children) and friends, whereas I figured the "fame" combined with 75 cents is enough to buy you a cup of coffee. Some of our staff, on the other hand, seemed to practically live for this sort of thing and seemed to derive their entire identity as people from the fact they worked for the well-known, much-acclaimed Jeopardy. These probably make the ideal Jeopardy employees, since they garner so much satisfaction just from being associated with the show, which of course doesn't cost management a thing.

After George had been producer for a while he sent a memo to the entire staff indicating that any media contacts must be cleared through him or Rocky prior to our saying a word to any journalist or reporter. Steven tends to come into the office quite early, usually around 7:00 A.M., and from time to time calls came in from media types on the East Coast where it's of course three hours later. Steven would innocently answer their questions and, as far as I know, never said anything wrong or damaging to the show. But in order to ensure that nothing got out that shouldn't, George went ahead and issued his directive. It struck me as rather strange. We don't deal with Department of Defense classified information, nor do we conduct secret diplomacy on behalf of the State Department. It's only a TV game show. I'd never heard of other TV shows trying to limit media access to their staffs.

THE "HEAD WRITER"

From time to time a reporter would indicate they wished to speak to the "head writer" which, after I'd been named editorial associate producer, meant me. Prior to each of those interviews, George would "brief" me, always reminding me to be sure never to refer to any of my staff as "writers" only "researchers." This used to grate on me to no end. To have to say Jeopardy had no writers, only researchers, struck me as being ordered not only to act the part of a liar but the part of an idiot as well. After all, how could any sane person think a show like Jeopardy didn't have writers?

George's dictum made these interviews, which should have been pleasant, annoying and stressful to me. I didn't want to get in trouble and lose my job and so I went ahead and always referred to the writers as "researchers." In my mind I justified it by reminding myself the writers all did do research from time to time. I did not, however, take my interviewers to be morons, and so I always had to live with the fear some reporter would take a reference I'd made to "researchers" and change it to "writers." For example, a reporter might ask, "How many questions do you write each season?" to which I would respond, "Our researchers come up with over 16,000 answers and questions per season." To protect myself I generally made it a point to have another person present during interviews conducted in person and to tape-record phone interviews.

Occasionally a journalist would ask if our writers were members of the Writers' Guild. My answer to that was that the Guild didn't seem to take much interest in us (note I didn't say "our writers") or in game shows in general. It seemed that, like Merv, some other game show producers were also sidestepping the Guild, which was somewhat unusual in that the TV industry in Hollywood is highly unionized. On the other hand many game show producers continued to be Guild signatories. In my mind I felt the Guild had abandoned us and may well have been "in bed" with management but I wasn't about to *say* that.

SPORTS ILLUSTRATED

One of my more memorable interviews was with Franz Lidz, a writer for *Sports Illustrated*. His was one of the longest, most drawn-out interviews I'd ever given and must have lasted close to three hours. Though he asked about anything and everything, I got the impression he seemed to be probing for any dirt and scandal he could find. I was extremely careful with my words and didn't give him any. In retrospect I could say I was saving it for this book, but I didn't know that at the time.

Rocky and George didn't seem to much care for Franz. When he asked if he could bring in a photographer to take pictures of our offices and the stage, permission was denied. Franz later told me they were using the issue of photographs as leverage in an attempt to obtain editorial control over his article. In other words they would allow a *Sports Illustrated* photographer to come in only if Franz would submit his article for their approval prior to publication. That is something no self-respecting journalist will ordinarily do. George and Rocky probably figured they had Franz over a barrel. After all, as the magazine's name indicates, it is "illustrated." But Franz got the last laugh when he ended up using an artist to illustrate his article. The story, simply titled "What is 'Jeopardy!'?" appeared in the May 1, 1989 issue (for those who want to dig it up at their local libraries). It was quite well written in a cute tongue-in-cheek style. Besides myself, Franz had interviewed a number of other staffers, but only Carol Campbell dared present herself as a "writer."

PLAYBOY

One time it was arranged for me to be interviewed by a writer for *Playboy*. As he was in Chicago and saw no great need to see me in person, we conducted the interview over the phone. *Playboy* is, however, a magazine that emphasizes the visual, and so they considered it necessary to send out a photographer as well as an assistant. George and Rocky approved this as they apparently had more confidence in *Playboy* than in *Sports Illustrated.* Soon strobe lights, reflectors and wires resembling Medusa's hair were strewn all about my office. In all they ended up taking some 150 shots of me in various poses. I gave them just about an entire morning only to eventually learn the editors had decided to kill the piece about me. I guess they concluded I wasn't the type their readership was interested in seeing, my varied poses notwithstanding.

LA TIMES MAGAZINE

An excellent article on us that did make it into print was written by Patricia Ward Biederman and appeared in the *Los Angeles Times Magazine* of January 29, 1989. Its title was "BACKSTAGE AT 'JEOPARDY!' " with a subhead that read "Tune in for the nervous hopefuls, the hard-working researchers, the well-dressed host and the amazing winners on the smart set's favorite game show." In that article writer Steven Dorfman is simply described as a "staffer." Of Kathy Easterling it was said she "comes up" with material. Then there was the following paragraph:

> Questions are pretested, "roundtabled," by a group of at least five staff members. The staff tries to make sure that each question is "pinned," its term for a clue that elicits a single, unambiguous response. Material is also tested for obscurity. Eisenberg doesn't mind hard but he doesn't like esoteric. "If nobody knows an answer except the writer, we throw the question out."

Aaaah! The dreaded "W" word. But I didn't say it. Believe me, I said "researcher." I swear.

CHAPTER 14

I DECIDE TO LEAVE JEOPARDY!

While we were preparing the material for "Super Jeopardy!" in April 1990, Alex up and got married. He had long been considered one of Hollywood's most eligible bachelors and had in the past been romantically linked in the press (and not always accurately) to actresses Susan Sullivan and Stephanie Powers; Shirley Fonda, Rona Barrett and Beverly Sassoon, among others.

Jean Currivan, the lady he married, was a lovely brunette of 26 at the time. He met her the year before at a dinner party where, he told Alan Ebert in an interview for the August 1992 issue of *Good Housekeeping*, he noted she was "both beautiful and bright" but didn't seek any involvement because, "I never dated young girls nor had any desire to. Mainly I saw women my age or older."

That isn't quite accurate. On one occasion Alex brought a beautiful young schoolteacher he was dating to the Jeopardy tapings. Another time, while doing a contestant search in Pittsburgh in conjunction with station KDKA, he met a highly attractive young news reporter who was working there at the time and asked her out. It happened she was married and she turned him down.

Alex went on to tell the reporter he didn't expect to see Jean again but then, "Jean and I just sort of happened without my planning it. When I met Jean months later at another party, it somehow felt right to ask her out and I did."

Alex soon came to see "that despite the 23-year age difference between us, we were very much alike. We share similar values and ethics. But perhaps most important, I quickly learned that Jean is a very giving person. Maturing has taught me that I need that, need a supportive woman. I can build a house. I can host a show. I can be, and am, constantly in charge. But I've recently discovered it's nice to come home and let someone else do the nurturing."

After dating for about a year, they got married April 30, 1990. When asked, in the wedding ceremony, if he would take Jean to be his wife Alex responded, "The answer is . . . yes."

Originally from Huntington, Long Island, Jean has never been in "the business" but had been working in commercial real estate development.

Speaking of married life Alex said, "It feels as if Jean has always been in my life. I like having her around. Although I've not stated this publicly, I have told Jean that I cannot imagine my life without her. She's made the difference between contentment and happiness. I often think, had I not met Jean, I would have become very self-centered, set in my ways. I like me a lot more since I met her."

The following February they had a beautiful dark-haired baby boy, Matthew Alexander Trebek. At 51, Alex had become a biological daddy for the first time. Though the child had come sooner than they planned, Alex was thrilled at having a newborn son.

He built a new house for his new family, along with a nearby guest house for his mother, who had been living with them. "I learned from my first marriage that having more than one mistress of the house is not ideal. Although Jean and my mother are great buddies, it is best that each has a home to call her own," says Alex.

I recalled a time when Alex, Jules and I were together in Alex's dressing room way back in the first season of the show. Both Alex and I were divorced at the time, while Jules had lost his wife in an automobile accident. Alex asked us if we ever hoped to remarry. After indicating we did, we asked him how he felt and he indicated likewise.

One time back in 1987, a contestant correctly responded to a clue having to do with the fact flamingos mate just once a year, to which Alex ad-libbed, "Flamingos and I have a great deal in common." Another time he was talking to a studio audience and perhaps complaining about the degree of solitude in his life told them, "I have the personality of a mollusk."

All that has now changed. From the time he met Jean, Alex seemed happier and his gait seemed lighter (even when he was dead tired from taping "To Tell The Truth," "Classic Concentration" and Jeopardy one day after another). It's not hard to tell when a couple is truly happy with one another and you readily see it with Alex and Jean. And little Matthew Alexander has brought an extra dimension of joy to their lives. Alex is continually as excited about being a father as any man I've ever seen.

Both Jules and I are also now remarried, and some seven years after that brief talk in Alex's dressing room all three of us have been able to find and enjoy the special happiness and fulfillment that only a good marriage can bring. I think our lives have taught us never to take it for granted.

ALEX'S BROTHER

If getting married and having a child didn't provide enough excitement for Alex Trebek in one year, there was still more. The April 16, 1991 issue of the *National Enquirer* had the following headline on its front page:

EXCLUSIVE
'Jeopardy' host's own story
Alex Trebek meets his illegitimate 35-year-old brother for first time

According to the story, Alex, some years back, got the biggest shock of his life when his elderly mother, Lucille, informed him and his sister, Barbara, that they have a half-brother, of whose existence they'd previously had no inkling. The child had been born out of wedlock and was given up by Lucille for adoption back in 1956.

This came as something of a shock to those of us who worked with Alex as well. However, there had been a few instances where tabloid papers had been totally inaccurate in stories about Alex. The next time I saw Alex I asked about it and learned it was indeed true.

Alex and his brother, Michael, finally met for the first time only after a five year search on the part of Alex's 70-year-old mother to find Michael's whereabouts. "It was a wonderful, special, joyous occasion," Alex was quoted as saying "Believe me, it's an odd feeling to meet a 35-year-old brother you never even knew existed!"

Alex had first learned of Michael's existence five years earlier, when his mother told him the story of how Michael was born after Alex's parents had separated. After giving him up for adoption, Lucille lost all knowledge of his whereabouts but was now determined to find him. Alex told his mother he was totally supportive.

After five years, an agency that specializes in finding adopted children located Michael in Belle River, Ontario. The family decided that Barbara should be the first to call him. Michael then called his natural mother and the two spoke to each other for the first time in their lives. Needless to say, it was a highly emotional moment for both. Alex urged his mother to go meet Michael and two weeks later she flew to Canada. Michael met her at the airport. It was a very moving experience for both Michael, who now works as a salesman, and his natural mother as the two hugged and cried. Lucille met Michael's adoptive mother and two grandchildren she'd not previously seen as well.

Then for Thanksgiving (1990) Michael came to California to meet Alex and Barbara. Alex indicated that finally finding Michael brought a special peace and contentment to his mother's life that was lacking before. Since Alex and Michael live so far apart, their paths are not likely to cross often. But he's welcome at my home anytime," says Alex. In reaching out to a long-lost brother in this way Alex showed considerable largeness of heart towards both Michael and their mother. In this act of acceptance and loving kindness he has set an example worthy of emulation.

THE END OF THE SEVENTH SEASON

While Alex and Jean were enjoying their honeymoon, we were preparing material for Super Jeopardy. All the Super Jeopardy shows except the final were taped in late June. Shortly afterwards, Carol Campbell finally tendered her resignation. She either could not or would not (I'm still not sure which) ever write her full quota of 15 categories a week. For me the two-year ongoing war of nerves, in which I was always trying unsuccessfully to get the necessary productivity out of her, was finally over.

Carol indicated she was going to work freelance, and for a time submitted material for "Phone Jeopardy." "Phone Jeopardy" was a combined effort of Merv Griffin Enterprises and Players International, a company that probably was best known for employing Telly Savalas to advertise its discount packages for Las Vegas and Atlantic City. A person would dial a 900 number and pay $1.95 a minute to answer Jeopardy clues that were read by Alex and Johnny Gilbert. The winners received cash prizes with $10,000 and a trip to a Jeopardy taping as the top prize. "Phone Jeopardy" was promoted on a number of Jeopardy programs that aired in the 1990-91 season. There was also a telephone game version of "Wheel" and some other TV game shows had them as well as they looked like easy moneymakers.

CHEST PAINS

As for me, I may have won the war but the fighting had taken its toll. Add to that the pressure of meeting the deadlines combined with the totally thankless and demeaning attitude on the part of management and my body was starting to rebel. Hitherto I'd always been in excellent health and don't recall ever missing a full day's work at Jeopardy due to illness. Besides the digestive problems, which began in 1989, I'd been experiencing occasional chest pains since the spring of 1990. They got progressively worse and I was admitted to the hospital in mid-September on suspicion of having suffered a heart attack. Fortunately, it turned out to be a serious "stress attack" instead.

My body was giving me *warnings* though, and with a wife and three children, including a year-old baby, I concluded I better take the warnings seriously. Debby and I carefully considered our options and after much deliberation we decided to put our house up for sale. We took the extra money I was paid for Super Jeopardy and sunk it into various improvements on the house in order to enhance its appeal in what was starting to become a difficult market in which to sell. In October we listed it with a realtor.

PERSONNEL CHANGES

1990–91 was a good year in terms of the fact there were quite a few new game shows coming on the air. Carlo Panno managed to move up a notch as he got on with one of them, Dick Clark's "Challengers," as Head Researcher. Unfortunately the show lasted just one season.

Finding replacements for Carol and Carlo did not prove difficult. Shortly after "Sale of the Century" had gone off the air in 1989, game show maven Bob Boden had called me to highly recommend one of their writers, Debbie Halpern, should a vacancy arise at Jeopardy. I asked Debbie to submit a writing sample and it looked just fine. George of course knew Debbie from his days as Producer of "Sale" and he was quite willing to go with her as well and so that settled that.

By the time she joined us, Debbie had gotten married and was now Debbie Griffin (no relation to Merv). She brought with her a good professional writing background and proved to be an excellent addition to the staff, in some ways reminding me of Stephanie Spadaccini.

Our new researcher was Billy Holmes, an Easterner originally from Scranton, PA. We'd previously interviewed Bill, who had formerly worked in the concert touring business. I could tell he had the makings of a good researcher and writing potential as well. We'd offered him a job the first time but he'd turned us down indicating he thought it would be too tough to live on the $450 a week, which was all management would pay for beginning researchers.

This was in contrast to "Challengers," which was paying its researchers $550 to $600, as was "Quiz Kids Challenge," a Guber–Peters production belonging to Sony. Both of those were brand new, unproven shows facing considerable start-up costs in contrast to Jeopardy with its astronomical profit level. But if you brought up that comparison to management they'd be quick to remind you that Jeopardy offered much more job security than the new shows and therefore didn't need to pay as much.

When the research vacancy came up, I called Billy to see how he was doing and if he'd had a change of heart. He indicated he was pleased to hear from me and would be glad to join us. Billy turned out to be an outstanding researcher both as regards quality and quantity. He could handle the material in an objective way and could complete his 20- category-a-week quota in two and a half to three days, while catching just about every flaw. (Billy continued to work for Jeopardy after I left the show but could never earn a good living or be recognized for a job well done. When the opportunity presented itself in 1993, he became stage manager for the Los Angeles production of *Sunset Boulevard*. There he was appreciated and paid accordingly. Tragically, however, he developed diverticulitis and passed away at age 35.)

The new additions combined with the old pros gave us what I felt were the best writing and research staffs we'd ever had on Jeopardy and I did not hesitate to tell them so. Except for an occasional complaint about something or other from or about Kathy, my staff problems were mostly a thing of the past. I believe the quality of the staff showed in the material as well. The size of the viewing audience was as high as ever and yet viewers' letters pointed out very few factual flaws in our material that seventh season. I'd always enjoyed doing the work at Jeopardy and having a staff that was for the most part truly professional made me look forward to coming in and dealing with each day's tasks.

THE EMMY

By that time, my third full season as editorial associate producer, George was letting half the games or more go through. As a result the writers and I were able to take a chance and inject slightly more humor and color than might have been the case otherwise, since George tended to quash that sort of material, fearing any joke might not go over with the viewers, and two viewers in particular—Merv and Bob. The material was obviously good, as this was the year we would win our Emmy for writing.

Not that the Emmy came easy. With management opposed to our even being considered for the award it was an uphill struggle all the way. However, by this time (fall of 1990) we were in touch with the Writers' Guild and Guild officials promised us we'd have the right to at least be considered.

With my son Dan now in college I was very much counting on my annual pay raise. It was due in March but we usually didn't get it until May or June. That year however, it was held up until September. Apparently management wasn't comfortable with giving us raises at the same time we were being paid extra for Super Jeopardy. For my part, I was sufficiently upset over the issue that I went into George's office and threatened to resign right then and there. George talked me out of it, pointing out I'd have no source of income at all if I did. That was true and I'd undoubtedly have been in big trouble financially had I left at that point. And so I later thanked George for talking me out of it. On the other hand, taping season was in full swing at that time and *he* would have also been in big trouble had I left and so I don't know if what he did was particularly altruistic.

When the raises finally came through, I received a bigger one than I'd expected—$150 a week, bringing my salary up to $1350 per week. I did think my threatening to leave may have had a bearing on the size of the raise. The idea that you had to first threaten to quit at a time that the show was vulnerable in order to get a good raise didn't especially sit well with me. I was earning considerably less than Gary Lee, who that season served as head writer on "Trump Card." I was however coming close to what Jules had been making when he was pushed out but didn't realize it at the time. I still felt significantly underpaid for what I was doing to contribute to the success of Jeopardy but it would only be later that I would finally learn to what extent. (At that time the Guild *minimum* for a game show writer doing more than just writing questions and answers was $1,427 a week and that didn't include the residuals we were due for reruns and other Guild benefits. Head writers were generally earning even more.) I continued to work away doing all I could to help enrich a company which was not inclined to do right by us.

THE POOR STAFF

My salary was regal, however, compared to many on my staff. I now had a group of writers and researchers that were working hard and working well. I was lavish with praise towards them but could do little else for them. I wrote George a memo pointing out that way back in 1984 we got a salary increase from $450 to $500 after six good months on the job and with the cost of living being what it was six-and-a-half years *later*, couldn't we at least do the same for the researchers, who all acknowledged were working hard? I pointed out that we were working with one fewer researcher than in the past and that Michelle had indicated she'd be leaving at the end of the year (she wanted to return to being a full-time mother) so that there would be one less salary to pay out.

These staffers were trying to make a go of it in a city where it was next to impossible to find an affordable one-bedroom apartment in a decent neighborhood. All they needed was to be hit up for some unexpected expense and they'd be right behind the eight ball. I reminded George what other shows were paying but I might as well have been talking to the wall. George informed me that company policy was to give raises once a year and at no other time. There may have been an exception back in 1984 but there wasn't going to be one now. And so a year went by before the researchers finally got their paltry $50 raise. Merv Griffin seemed to always be in fear of setting off a chain reaction of salary demands. The excuse notwithstanding, I failed to see how it could be right not to pay researchers who were doing a good job more than $450 a week.

THE END

In many ways I was sorry to go. I liked the show and I liked the work. It was fun preparing interesting, entertaining Jeopardy material, to the degree we were allowed to do so. I liked most of the people on staff, was comfortable with them and would miss them.

It was May 1 when I gave notice. Season seven tapings had ended back in March and we were now writing away, preparing material for season eight. Sony informed us they wanted all taping the following season completed by February, for their accounting purposes. That meant the staff would have one fewer month to prepare a full year's worth of material. It has been my experience that once they give notice to leave, many employees completely slack off simply biding their time until they are out the door. Despite everything I still felt a certain sense of loyalty to the show and my co-workers and had no intention of letting them down.

I had told George I would be pleased to do what I could to help acclimate any successor to the job but none was designated. Meanwhile I kept working away. By the end of May I had fully assembled 65 games or 13 weeks worth of shows for season eight. That was about 30 percent of the entire next season's worth of shows. I informed George of that and wrote him a memo indicating I would like to be credited on the crawl of the show for the work I had done.

My last day in the office was May 30. Production Assistant Kimberly Koenen was also leaving the show to go to work for a movie company and we were given a joint going away luncheon. It was the first time anything like that had been done at Jeopardy. George, Rocky and Lisa Finneran didn't attend. Nor did I imagine they would miss me all that much. But everyone else was there. The staffers knew I had tried to do right by them and at that time all of them made it a point to express their appreciation. They were by and large honest, decent people trying to earn an honest living in a time and place where that was becoming increasingly difficult. I sincerely wished them all well.

That afternoon Suzanne and JulieAnn helped me pack up my office. I loaded up my car and drove off the KTLA lot for the last time. My life was no longer in Jeopardy. As I drove home I could not turn on the radio as I was lost in thought. I left Jeopardy just one week short of having spent a full seven calendar years with the show. That is about a tenth of a person's entire life; about a sixth of an average person's working life. But at least I had taken Dave Williger's advice, which he'd given me six years earlier. Unlike Dave, I had not given that company 13 years.

JEOPARDY! IN RETROSPECT

Ironically, it was just three weeks after I left Jeopardy that we won our Emmy for writing. What management did not want to happen had indeed come to pass. Moreover, the non-televised daytime Emmys that year were given out in, of all places, Merv's own Beverly Hilton hotel. Hopefully whatever profits accrued to him from renting out his facility and providing catering for the TV Academy were sufficient consolation for our being recognized as writers. Needless to say, there was no message of congratulations forthcoming to any of the Jeopardy writers from either Merv or Bob Murphy.

A few days later at the televised awards ceremony Jeopardy won its second Emmy for Best Game Show. This time George did acknowledge the writers and researchers in his brief acceptance speech which was seen on national television. So that at least was progress.

The 1991–92 season saw a great many changes at Jeopardy. Back in season seven, when I was still with the show, director Dick Schneider introduced me to Gisela Budeit, a friend of his who works in television in Hamburg, Germany. Gisela was later kind enough to send me a tape of the German version of Jeopardy which is called *Riskant*, in case you're ever over there and want to look it up in the German equivalent of *TV Guide*. (Jeopardy is licensed in a number of foreign countries including England, France and Australia.)

The technology of European television is somewhat different from that in the U.S., so a regular VHS tape from over there will not work with a regular TV and VCR here. But Steven knew of a place where the tape could be copied onto our format and did that. Afterwards we turned over a copy to George and he passed it on to Merv and Bob. The set of *Riskant* was quite modern and glitzy and made ours look 15 years out of date.

When it comes to the set of a show Merv is quite conservative. The first pilot for the current version was still using the old format with printed cards that were pulled up by hand to reveal clues, as had been done on the old Jeopardy. It was only when the King brothers insisted a more modern set was needed, that a second pilot was produced utilizing the 30 electronic TV monitors that made up the game board during the seven years I was with the show. Dick Clark's "Challengers" as well as *Riskant* were using one-piece electronic game boards that very much resemble the electronic picture boards in sports stadiums. Merv finally decided it was time for Jeopardy to take on a more modern look and arrangements were made to install a new game board while moving to a new studio location in Hollywood. In July Jeopardy moved to the Hollywood Center Studios on the old Zoetrope Pictures lot, which they had been considering back in 1986. The lot is owned and managed by the same people who run the KTLA lot where we'd been for the past six years, but the control rooms were much more modern.

The new solid game board gave Jeopardy a more modern look but the color scheme continued to consist almost entirely of just basic red and blue (with too much blue at first). The set still very much lacked the flashy lighting, the bright colors and other exciting effects of *Riskant*.

Prior to my leaving the show there had been much speculation as to who would take my place. I had been grooming Fred for the position from my first year as editorial associate producer. I felt he had good broad general knowledge and a feel for what the show needed as well as good judgment and common sense. He'd been a judge at the tapings for three years, had led the roundtable sessions, had proven himself to be a good writer and had assembled games for me when I was on vacation.

By mid-May it had become clear that whoever they would hire to replace me was coming from the outside. I had offered to work closely with anyone management would designate in order to effect a smooth transition especially because the tight taping schedule necessitated we keep cranking out material. But as the days passed it became clear management had no intention of paying *two* editorial associate producers' salaries, not even for a week.

Speculation in the office then turned to Gary Johnson. Gary had most recently been working as head writer and judge on "Challengers," a material-heavy quiz show that was in many ways similar to Jeopardy. By May, word had gone out that "Challengers" was going to be cancelled, which meant that Gary would probably be available. In addition, Gary had been head writer for a time, under George, at "Sale of the Century" and the two of them were known to get along well. However, in between "Sale" and "Challengers" Gary had been producer of "Scrabble" and was by then pulling down a six-figure salary. "Challengers" may have meant enough to Dick Clark and its creator/producer Ron Greenberg that they were willing to pay that kind of money for the highly experienced and proven Gary Johnson, but there was no way Jeopardy! ever would.

It was only after I left that George finally revealed my successor's identity. He was Terry McDonnell. Terry had been working on "Candid Camera," a show being produced and distributed by King World. Terry was a member of the Writers' Guild and had written for other shows in the past, but never a quiz show utilizing the kind of material we used on Jeopardy. Under those circumstances it fell to Fred and Steven to show Terry the ropes of his new job.

Fred and Steven proved to be sufficiently adequate at what they were doing that Terry was content to let them continue doing so. He didn't have the sense of the degree of difficulty of various clues in a category and left that to each individual writer. By off-loading much of the job onto Steven and Fred he was able to reduce it to an eleven-to-four position, leaving himself time for something he enjoyed doing, writing scripts for the Saturday morning TV cartoon series such as "Ghostbusters" and "Beetlejuice."

In the past Columbia had required each employee to sign a statement promising they would not hold down any outside employment while working at Jeopardy but it was never really enforced. Steven occasionally wrote scripts and submitted story ideas for "Head of the Class." He also wrote for comic magazines, games and puzzles magazines and did other freelance work. JulieAnn would take acting jobs when she could and Steve Tamerius wrote books about Elvis. Others did what they could as well as they were hoping to eventually land something bigger and better than what they had at Jeopardy. And if they were ever called on it, most figured they could point to the fact that Alex was working other shows while hosting Jeopardy.

The first half of the show's eighth season (1991–92) consisted of the 65 games I'd edited and assembled prior to leaving, combined with and mixed among newer shows assembled by Terry. At first Terry was accepting just about anything the writers gave him. Each writer was for a while doing his own thing and the result was those games had a number of off-the-wall categories and lots of word play and other material George calls "squirrelly." The category that most sticks out in my mind from this period was *Henry IV, Part 2*. I've always felt Jeopardy categories should deal with subjects a moderately well-educated American can relate to. *Hamlet* and *Macbeth*, fine, but *Henry IV, Part 2*?

This free-for-all period for the writers lasted for a short while until word came down from on high. George then put Terry under the same "lots of meat and potatoes" restrictions under which I'd always operated—no more than one show biz and one word play category per game and lots of history, geography, literature and science. There was then so much of those categories you would sometimes see two geography, two literature or two history categories in one game, perhaps The Civil War in the first round with World History in Double Jeopardy.

As previously mentioned, Terry left the matter of degree of difficulty to each writer. Heretofore I'd worked hard to keep $800 and $1000 clues sufficiently more difficult than $100 or $200 ones. In other words, what I was trying to do was to put the easier categories in the first round and the tougher ones in Double Jeopardy. In addition, I tried as much as possible to make sure all the categories in each round were approximately equal in difficulty. But my efforts in that regard never meant much to George and it therefore wasn't necessary for Terry to have to worry about it. As a result you now had very easy categories sitting next to much tougher ones on the same game board with contestants having no way of knowing which category might be easy or hard until after having selected it.

In watching the shows, I personally found it annoying to see one contestant pick up an easy $1000 for one clue, while another had to struggle with a much tougher clue for the same money. Overall, however, the shows in season eight tended to be considerably easier than in the past. As such, they tended to reflect the much easier contestant tests that were now being used. But one result of the easier material was that there were more runaways—shows in which the outcome has been determined prior to Final Jeopardy because one player has more than twice as much money as either of his opponents. That's because easy material will heavily favor the player with the best reflexes on the signalling button.

Season eight was rather uneventful at Jeopardy. They began putting Daily Double clues in small boxes on the upper right hand corner of the TV screen, which made them harder to read than the other clues, but that is only a minor flaw. The ratings were however starting to slip. Where the show previously had a solid lock on second place among all syndicated shows, it was now fluctuating between second and fourth place. Though the drop wasn't too serious, it was significant. It reflected, I believe, the fact that the shows were becoming increasingly dry. There is a lack of vitality, of sparkle, of creativity. The show needs more brand new categories, more lively categories, more fun categories. To maintain Jeopardy's integrity these should, of course, be balanced with more weighty categories. But at this point in time the show has gone way too far in the direction of dry, serious material. There should be lots of Audio and Video Daily Doubles. In the past Alex swallowed helium, displayed various objects and we even had a live dog once (when JulieAnn brought on her Bagels). The show needs surprises like that as much as the writers' creativity and technical conditions will allow. In the early years of the show we were encouraged to make it interesting. Jeopardy has now fallen into a rut of using similar, humdrum material day after day with few exceptions. Surprising, original and unexpected categories and clues, on the other hand, are a good example of what's interesting. The only reason the drop in ratings hasn't been any worse is that for quiz show fans, Jeopardy currently remains the only game in town.

One attempt to liven things up a bit came early in season nine which finally saw Jeopardy's first Celebrity Tournament, featuring a number of well-known celebrities who were playing for charity. Alex had first brought up that idea back when he was still producer and Merv finally came around. Unfortunately the show could only come up with one week's worth of celebrity players. The standard, two-week tournament format, consisting of quarter-finals, semi-finals and a two-day final to determine the overall champ, could not be used. Instead the player with the highest score of the week was declared the winner.

One would have hoped, and even expected, that a Celebrity Tournament would mean the inclusion of more humor and lighthearted fare among the game material. But that was not the case in 1992, though George did allow a few more pop culture and show biz categories than usual. As for a bit more fun and frivolity in the Celebrity Tournament, maybe in the future.

Over the years King World has marketed Jeopardy quite aggressively and usually in tandem with the top-rated "Wheel of Fortune." As a result the two shows are almost always on the same station in each market and usually air back to back. King World now reports that Jeopardy has now been sold in many markets through 1999. This guarantees the current version of the show a 15-year run compared to the 11 year (1964–74) original life of the old Jeopardy. The show will most likely last much longer than that.

The life of a network TV show is unpredictable. A network can cancel a show at anytime for any reason, or for no reason for that matter, and that's it. Time for the last wrap party. Jeopardy's future is much more predictable because syndicated shows are sold separately in every market. Jeopardy goes into about 200 different TV markets and if one station cancels, you still have 199 stations left, as well as the possibility of latching on with a competing station in the same city in which you had the cancellation. Nor will a few cancellations necessarily mean the end of the show by any means. Though it's on in some 200 markets now, a show like Jeopardy could be profitable even if it were on in less than 50 markets. Due to the very low production costs of game shows compared to other forms of TV programming, Jeopardy could lose three-quarters of all its markets and still be quite profitable. Not that I expect that to happen any time soon. On the contrary, considering its current standing in the ratings it is most likely that Jeopardy will still be in production in the 21st century. Then the writers can write a clue to see if the contestants can correctly come up with the first day of the 22nd century.

Sony, in conjunction with Mark Goodson Productions, has now launched its cable TV "Game Show Channel." On this channel, Sony plans to rerun thousands of game show episodes it has on tape including many of "Wheel", Jeopardy and Chuck Barris' "The Gong Show." (Oy, get the hook. . . .)

The seven years of Jeopardy described in this book can be recognized in many ways. As older shows are shown, you will see Alex's hair much darker. You'll see a time when he didn't need glasses and you'll see the various incidents as well as trends on the show explained for the first time in this book. The years covered in this book will also stand out by the unique set with the 30 television monitors and the credits of the show which fail to acknowledge the existence of Jeopardy writers (unless they are edited for rerun).

When I view these shows my feelings will be bittersweet. Since time heals all wounds, the memories will be more sweet than bitter. Memories of a contribution to a show which has become very much ingrained in our American culture. Memories of camaraderie with good people who were trying to do a decent job and who, each in his own way, were trying to contribute a little something to brighten the atmosphere in which we worked. Memories of sharing the triumphs and tragedies and personal milestones in the lives of co-workers who came to be your friends. Memories of people you meet in the studio audience who become your lifelong friends as well. Memories of bright, competitive contestants and hard-fought games for which we were trying to be as scrupulously fair in judgment as is humanly possible. Memories of Alex dealing with the show from an attitude of maturity and personal responsibility when he was producer. Moments of lighthearted banter in the dressing room. Scrambling to the judges' table as director Dick Schneider, a professional's professional, called for "places, please." And always that impeccable introduction by consummate gentleman Announcer Johnny Gilbert featuring the exultant cry, "*THIS* IS JEOPARDY!"

CHAPTER 15

JEOPARDY! ON JEOPARDY!

"JEOPARDY!" FACTS

- Since its syndication debut, "JEOPARDY!" has been the recipient of 15 Daytime Emmy Awards out of a total of 38 nominations.

- Merv Griffin created "JEOPARDY!" in 1964 in the dining room of his apartment. Griffin also composed the show's "think" theme music.

- Almost 5,000 people have appeared as contestants on "JEOPARDY!" since its inception, an average of 440 per year, and the show has awarded more than $38 million in cash and prizes to date. "JEOPARDY!" awards an average of $3.5 million in cash and prizes per year.

- The biggest "JEOPARDY!" money winner is Frank Spangenberg, an officer with the New York Police Department. Officer Spangenberg's winnings to date total $144,397. The recipient of the largest five-day total the show has ever awarded, Frank also played in "SUPER JEOPARDY!" and won "JEOPARDY!'s" Tenth Anniversary championship.

- "JEOPARDY!" is the #1 quiz show in America. It has ranked first among all quiz shows in the Nielsen ratings for 560 weeks (NTI: 6/25/95) and has reigned as the #2 show in syndication for 39 consecutive sweeps periods (NSI: May, 1995).

- When the "JEOPARDY!" staff learned that notables such as Billy Crystal, Madonna and Frank Sinatra were "JEOPARDY!" fans, "CELEBRITY JEOPARDY!" was created. Star contestants who

have played in the celebrity competition include General Norman
Schwarzkopf, Kareem Abdul-Jammab, Jason Alexander, Larry
King, Tony Randall, Markie Post, Marilu Henner, Kathy Mattea,
Michael Sabatino, Kelsey Grammer, Luke Perry, Dean Cain, An-
drew Shue, Pat Sajak, Regis Philbin, Sinbad, Cheech Marin, Leslie
Nielsen, Jerry Orbach, Carol Burnett, Emma Samms and Terri Garr
-- to name a few.

• Who researches and writes the "JEOPARDY!" categories and questions? The quiz show's production staff includes five full-time researchers and five writers whose job is to create and assemble
categories and questions for the show. Executive Producer Merv
Griffin and host Alex Trebek often suggest categories as well.

• The unique answer-question format of "JEOPARDY!" has become
a popular tool with educators around the country. Teachers recommend that their students watch the show, and often create their
own version of "JEOPARDY!" to encourage student participation
in the classroom. In the May 1994 issue of Dartmouth magazine,
a powerful testimony to "JEOPARDY!'s" ability to teach while it
entertains was made by Assistant Professor of Government Thomas M. Nichols who said "JEOPARDY!" is the SAT of television
gavme shows."

ALEX TREBEK

Handsome, well-educated an urbane, Alex Trebek represents the best
of all possible choices to host "JEOPARDY!", the most fun, cerebral
quiz show on television.
    Indeed, after a decade with the incredibly popular program,
Trebek's unique charm and straightforward approach to the show fits
"JEOPARDY!'s" fast-paced, intellectual format. The show and its host
are now so firmly entrenched in the minds of viewers that it is virtually impossible to think of one without the other.
    A native of Ontario, Canada, Trebek graduated from the Univer-
sity of Ottawa with degrees in philosophy before moving toward a
career in broadcast news. Joining the Canadian Broadcasting Company
in Ottawa as an announcer and newsman, he covered national news,
as well as special events for both CBC's radio and television divi-
sions. As a harbinger of things to come, he also hosted a popular television game show for high school students. His introduction to U.S.

audiences came when he auditioned for, and landed, the host position on the successful game show, "Wizard of Odds." Many others followed.

And then came "JEOPARDY!" Trebek readily acknowledges that he had no idea when he joined the show in 1984 that it would become the long-running hit that it is. "But," Trebek asserts, "I did feel it was the right show for me because it rewards people for their knowledge, an old-time value I heartily endorese."

Today, Trebek maintains an innate respect for both the intellectual integrity of "JEOPARDY!," as well as its participants. "The show challenges viewers to examine their knowledge from the general to the arcane," he states. "In terms of our contestants, I am constantly amazed with their breadth of knowledge."

Trebek attributes the show's continuing popularity to several factors: "First, it's the kind of show people never have to apologize for watching. It's also a show that test people -- deep inside, we all want to find out how much we know. Then, people enjoy acquiring information in an entertaining manner, which "JEOPARDY!" provides."

Trebek travels annually with the show's contestant scouting team to audition prospective participants serving on military bases throughout the world. These trips are coordinated with the USO, an organization for which Trebek serves on the World Board of Governors.

Equally active in a wide variety of charitable and educational organizations, he is often on the road to the far corners of the earth for World Vision, an international organization whose purpose is to raise money for the needy children of Third World nations, many of whom he sponsors. Trebek also serves as a board member of the National Geographic Society Education Foundation and hosts the annual National Geography Bee. Additionally, Trebek is on the board of the National Advisory Council for the Literacy Volunteers of America.

A chef who thrives on culinary artistry when entertaining at home, Trebek also owns a winery in Paso Robles, California, and a home in Studio City, where he lives with his wife Jean, and their young children, Matthew and Emily.

MERV GRIFFIN

Over the years, Merv Griffin has been described in a variety of ways: television critics have called him "the total performer", newspaper writers and editors have described him as an "entrepreneurial powerhouse"; celebrities, world leaders and Presidents call him "friend and confidant." He is regarded as the man that for a quarter century brought a virtual "who's who" of the world into America's living rooms as host of the Emmy Award-winning "The Merv Griffin Show." He is known for creating the two most popular game shows in television syndication history, "WHEEL OF FORTUNE" and "JEOPARDY!," watched by hundreds of millions of people all over the world. In the business community he is identified ast he Chairman and visionary of The Griffin Group. Any way you describe him, Merv Griffin, the genial host, entertainer and businessman, continues to be one of this country's most popular personalities.

Born in the San Francisco suburb of San Mateo, Merv "came up through the ranks" in the classic sense, entering talent contests, writing songs, singing on local radio station KFRC in San Francisco and later touring with "Freddy Martin and His Orchestra."

Merv became increasingly popular with nightclub audiences and his fame soared among the general public when he struck gold in 1950 with"I've Got a Lovely Bunch of Coconuts," reaching the number-one spot on the Hit Parade and selling three million copies. He continued to record hits, including "Wilhemina" and "Never Been Kissed," until Doris Day saw his nightclub performance and was so impressed, she arranged a screen test for Merv at Warner Bros. Studios. While under contract at Warner's, Merv appeared in a number of hit movies including, "So This is Love" with Kathryn Grayson, "The Boy from Oklahoma" with Will Rogers, Jr. and Lon Chaney, Jr., and "By the Light of the Silvery Moon" co-starring Doris Day and Gordon MacRae. During this time, he also became a regular on the Las Vegas nightclub circuit.

Television then discovered Merv. As a regular performer on "The Arthur Murray Show," "The Jack Paar Show" and others, he was offered the opportunity to host his own television show in 1958 called "Play Your Hunch." The success of this show led to another Merv-hosted program which he produced in 1963 called "Word for Word." It was during this period that Merv conceived the idea for what was to become one of the most successful game shows in television history -- "JEOPARDY!," which was first aired in 1964.

However, it was in 1962 that Merv's career would take its most dramatic turn. He became a regular guest host of Jack Paar's "The Tonight Show" and the "Merv-phenomenon" swept the late night audience, scoring some of the highest ratings the show had ever seen. As a result, that year NBC gave him his own hour-long talk show program and "The Merv Griffin Show" was born. Over the years, Merv would pioneer a talk show format that has become the prototype for every successful talk show aired since. Merv's comfortable but probing interviewing style often prompted candid, revealing responses from people of all walks of life. Peter Ustinov once commented that he enjoyed appearing on "The Merv Griffin Show" because "I find out what I think about things."

In the high profile arena of game shows, Merv was scoring big as well. "JEOPARDY!" became a tremendous success and remains the second-highest-rated game show in television syndication. Other successes included "One in a Million" and "Joe Garagiola's Memory Game" both airing on ABC and NBC's "Let's Play Post Office" and "Reach for the Stars." And, of course, there is television's most phenomenal hit ever, "WHEEL OF FORTUNE," which continues to be the longest-running game show to hold the number-one spot in television syndication history. Based on this success, in 1986 Merv sold his production company, Merv Griffin Enterprises, to Coca-Cola's Columbia Pictures Television unit for $250 million and continuing share in the profits of the shows. At that time, the transaction represented the largest acquisition of an entertainment company owned by a single individual. Subsequently, Sony Pictures Entertainment purchased Columbia and as a result, Merv Griffin Enterprises. Merv has continued as executive producer of both "WHEEL OF FORTUNE" and "JEOPARDY!"

Through Merv Griffin Entertainment, the entertainment division of The Griffin Group, Merv continues to develop and produce game shows and other forms of television programming. In addition to a number of other specials, Merv is currently preparing his fifth annual "Merv Griffin's New Year's Eve Special" for syndication. Looking toward the new information superhighway, Merv is now creating new products for multimedia and interactive television based on a variety of subjects, including game and talk show formats.

Early in his career, Merv decided that it would be almost as much fun owning radio stations as it was performing on them Over the years he has acquired a number of stations, and under his guidance, many have become market leaders. To better take advantage of recent changes in station ownership rules, Merv merged his seven wholly owned radio stations with those of Liberty Broadcasting Group to form a 17-station radio group. The combined entity is now one of the largest broadcasting groups in the country with stations in major cities throughout the East Coast. In addition to his ownership position in the group, Merv is actively involved in creating and producing radio programming that is syndicated by Liberty.

Combine these activities with the release of a new home video series based on Merv's interviews with many of the most well-known personalities of our time, developing location-based entertainment concepts for his various properties and creating fresh ideas for a line of greeting cards distributed by his publishing company, and it is clear that Merv continues to be on the cutting edge of new entertainment opportunities.

From his years of touring and literally "living out of hotels," came Merv's passion for the hospitality business. He as often said that being in the hotel business is just like being in the entertainment business: "Bring the people in, entertain them and give them a reason to come back." Merv's agressive hotel acquisition strategy began in 1987 whith the purchase of The Beverly Hilton Hotel in Beverly Hills. His active involvement in the management and promotion of the property, together with his extensive and imaginative renovation of the hotel, has made The Beverly Hilton the venue of choice for virtually all of the town's most high profile events, such as The Golden Globe Awards, The Soap Opera DIgest Awards, The American Film Institute's Lifetime Achievement Awards, The Scopus Awards, a variety of George Schlatter's Specials, and The Carousel Ball.

Through Mer Griffin Hotels, the hospitality division of The Griffin Group, Merv has more recently added to his hotel portfolio the Doubletree Hotel Albuquerque, the Deerfield Beach/Boca Raton Hilton and the Scottsdale Hilton Resort and Villas.

Blazing new trails in yet another area, Merv set his sights on gaming in Atlantic City. In 1988, he purchased Resorts International and set about turning the company around. Today, Merv Griffin's Resorts Casino Hotel is one of the healthiest and busiest casinos on the much famed Atlantic City Boardwalk. Merv's marketing savvy and Hollywood flair has turned Resorts into an exciting destination through innovative promotions such as the "Griffin Games," an exciting series of gaming tournaments. Additionally, Resorts reamins one of the few Boardwalk casinos to showcase top headliner talent. Add to this his role as creator and executive producer of Resorts' live cabaret and musical shows, and Merv stands out as one of the most active and prolific owner/operators in Atlantic City.

Always tracking new trends, Merv foresaw that gaming would expand outside Nevada and New Jersey, in the form of riverboat gaming. He would later identify what has become one of the most successful gaming locations in the country, Lake Charles, LA. Merv partnered with long time associates in Players International, Inc., te develop this and other riverboat gaming opportunities and, in 1992, became the company's largest shareholder. Merv and his team are directly involved in the marketing of the Lake Charles casino, as well as Players' other casino in Metropolis, IL and a 500-room destination resort and casino under construction in Mesquite, NV. The arrival of

"Players Riverboat Casino at Merv Griffin's Landing" in Metropolis created 800 new jobs in an otherwise despressed area of the country and the mayor credited Merv and the Players team with "bringing the city back to life again."

Merv's love of horses (he owns 40 of them and is active in the thoroughbred racing circuit) led to the purchase of a closed-circuit broadcasting, surveillance and photo finish company offering services to race tracks, Off Track Betting and other pari-mutual locations. Hos passion for fine food and wine led him to develop a private vineyard in Carmel Valley, CA, where he oversees the bottling of wines distributed under his "Mont Merveilleux" label.

Through it all, Merv still finds time to create puzzles for "WHEEL OF FORTUNE," oversee development of a 157 acre tract of land he owns in Beverly Hills and host a variety of charity events, including the annual "Christmas Tree Lane" benefitting "City Hearts, Kids Say YEs to the Arts."

Recently honored with the prestigious 1994 Broadcasting & Cable "Hall of Fame" Award, Merv stood with other honorees including Diane Sawyer and Dan Rather. Winner of 15 Emmy Awards, Merv was presented an Outstanding Game/Audience Participation Show Emmy for 1994-1995 as executive producer of "JEOPARDY!" Merv has also been the recipient of the coveted Scopus Award from the American Friends of Hebrew University, has been honored by the American Ireland Fund and is Chairman of The La Quinta Arts Foundation which promotes the work of local artisans and craftsmen through its annual art show in Palm Springs, CA.

• • •

JEOPARDY! — Still the Most Popular and Intellectually Challenging Quiz Show on Earth!

Think fast. Be knowledgeable in a wide variety of subjects. Smile at host Alex Trebek. And don't forget to respond in the form of a question! The basic rules for being a contestant on "JEOPARDY!" are still the same. But, believe it or not, this mind-stimulating quiz show is preparing an even more dynamic lineup for its 12th syndicated season.

This year, "JEOPARDY!" (along with "WHEEL OF FORTUNE") becomes the first regularly scheduled television program to sponsor the Atlanta Olympic Summer Games. Producer George Vosburgh says he's proud that his show is an Official Sponsor of the Games. " 'JEOP-

ARDY!' will feature an Olympic-themed viewer contest in which trips to Atlanta and tickets to Olympic events will be awarded," he notes. "We'll also be producing a special international competition featuring contestants from foreign countries which currently air a version of 'JEOPARDY!'"

Alex Trebek, the show's congenial and sophisticated host, is also excited about the Olympic Games connection. "'JEOPARDY!'s unprecedented association with the Summer Games is another first in the history of television," says Alex. "It's an honor to be able to help support (the U.S. Team), the Games, and the Olympic Movement. I believe that our loyal viewers will also embrace this connection."

In support of Atlanta Centennial Olympic Properties (ACOP), "JEOPARDY!" will offer collectible Olympic Games merchandise available exclusively during a special promotional period. All profits realized from the sale of this merchandise will be donated to help support American Olympic athletes and the Games. International Sports and Entertainment Strategies (ISES), a sports marketing and sports television firm, coordinated the development of the Olympics Games merchandising promotion for "JEOPARDY!"

For the 1995-96 season, "JEOPARDY" will continue its famous theme "Everyone Gets Into 'JEOPARDY!'" The ever-popular Celebrity "JEOPARDY!" will be back in November with fifteen renowned stars competing for their favorite charities, and "JEOPARDY!'s" Olympic sponsorship, look for the first-ever "JEOPARDY!" Olympic Games Tournament, featuring English-speaking champs from various countries, to air July 15th thru 18th.

And yes, there's more. Fans can also find an exciting new "JEOPARDY!" Web site on the information superhighway. "JEOPARDY!" has launched a popular "rest stop" on Sony Pictures Entertainment's (SPE's) World Wide Web site. By accessing this site, fans can learn behind-the-scenes information about the Emmy Award-winning show, and discover what life is like when you're into "JEOPARDY!" -- literally! To access SPE's Web site, simply enter in: http://www.sony.com.

Because of the show's ever-increasing popularity among viewers of varying age groups, fans continually ask the questions, "How can I become a contestant, and where can I audition?" The answer: Each year, Alex Trebek and the show's contestant team host searches throughout America and foreign countries to attract a broad range of contestants. To qualify, applicants are required to take a difficult written examination comprised of 50 general knowledge answers. Those who pass go on to the next stage which is a high-pressure simulated game. A select few of those who succeed move on the play the televised "JEOPARDY!" game.

Producer George Vosburgh, who marks his ninth year with "JEOPARDY!," attributes the show's success and tremendous popularity to the fact that it provides a challenging contest for viewers. "People enjoy testing their knowledge at home and shouting out the questions when Alex poses the answers. Young and old alike enjoy Alex's witty remarks and feel that the show helps them learn something about the world we live in. It's an entertaining way of exercising your brain cells and opening your mind to the wonderful universe of information that surrounds us."

Ratings statistics alone attest to "JEOPARDY!'s" phenomenal popularity: it has ranked as the #1 quiz show in the Nielsen ratings for 560 weeks (NTI: 6/25/95) and has reigned as the #2 show in syndication for 39 consecutive sweeps periods (NSI: May, 1995). Additionally, "JEOPARDY!" has amassed 15 prestigious Daytime Emmy Awards since its 1984 syndication debut, including the 1995 "Outstanding Game Show" award. It is also broadcast in 44 foreign territories and to servicement and women all over the world through the AFRTS (Armed Forces Radio and Television Services). Presently, Belgium, the Czech Republic, Germany, Hungary, Norway, Russia, Sweden, Turkey and the United Kingdom produce an original version of "JEOPARDY!" in their own languages.

Commenting on the enduring success of the multi-Emmy Award-winning show, Michael King, President and Chief Executive Officer of King World, stated, " 'JEOPARDY!' " continues to set new standards of excellence for the entire television industry, so we are delighted, but not surprised at the enthusiastic way viewers have supported the show season after season. This is a program that has a powerful, loyal following, and King World is truly proud of its phenomenal success."

"JEOPARDY!" is produced by Columbia TriStar Television, a Sony Pictures Entertainment Company, and is distributed worldwide by King World Productions, Inc.

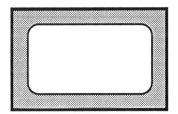

AFTERWORD

Books that purport to give the reader a "behind the scenes" look at a specific TV show are not all that uncommon. But most do so with a "rah, rah, isn't the show great" approach and appear to be the product of whatever public relations firm the show is employing to represent it.

Oscar Levant once said of Hollywood, "Strip away the phony tinsel (and) you can find the real tinsel underneath." Well underneath the real tinsel are real people with real hopes and dreams, real achievements and disappointments, real families; husbands, wives, parents, children and the real struggles to find their way in a complex world that we all face.

I wrote this book to take the reader behind the tinsel and into the unadorned world of those who work to earn a living on this most popular quiz show in American TV history. I wanted the reader to see that television is far more than the simple two-dimensional world interspersed with commercials that we see on the little screen. Even a question-and-answer game show which seems to enjoy the simplest of all TV formats is a complex operation that requires the talent, dedication and hard work of those behind-the-scenes individuals who are otherwise nothing more than names that quickly roll by on the show's credits.

Amazingly Jeopardy is the *only* question and answer program that has been able to survive in the competitive world of national television these past eleven years. As such it enjoys a cult following numbering in the millions. People like the Atlanta realtor who will delay "closing" a house until she's watched Jeopardy or the hundreds of school teachers across the U.S. who have crafted quizzes, course outlines and exams in the manner of the Jeopardy game board. Jeopardy fans tend to be intelligent people who enjoy coming up with the correct response ahead of the contestants. Intelligent people are often curious people and I hope this book has addressed and answered many of those curiosities.

Many people wonder what it is like to actually work on a TV show. Young people contemplating career choices have a wealth of books from which to choose in order to learn something about what it's like to be a doctor, lawyer, accountant, architect, computer programmer, pilot or auto mechanic. Books describing what it's like to work in television are less common, partly because many still do not see it as a traditional career choice. Rather, the lore of the entertainment industry still seems to hold that working in "the business" is supposed to happen largely by accident. You're somehow supposed to "be discovered" or in some other way "get a break." For some that is still true although the majority in television nowadays are there by deliberate design.

Still the lore continues to hold, because to a certain extent it's still true, even for those deliberately planning a TV career. Television is still a career in which you can't make it all happen by yourself. You still need that "break." You can qualify for medical school, study hard, complete an internship and residency and become licensed by the state to practice medicine. If you have the ability to repair broken down cars and make them run well you have a marketable skill and are sure to find work somewhere. If you can repair computers, your skills are so much in demand employers may be looking for you.

But television is like none of the aforementioned occupations. There are no measurable skills. Neither writers, producers or even directors are licensed by the state to "practice" in the TV industry. It's all supposed to be a matter of talent and talent is a very subjective commodity. What seems like talent to one person can be mediocrity or even worse in the eyes of another. There's no one winning formula to develop and improve talent and there's no means by which to measure it. A lawyer may rarely lose a case. A baseball player may bat .300. But in television there's nothing that can prove anything.

I would like to think my talent, ability and hard work made a difference in helping Jeopardy achieve the high ratings the show enjoyed while I was there. But can I prove it? A management that has less regard for my talent than do I might say I had very little to do with it. They might say none of us on staff had much to do with it and that it was largely a matter of timing. The show had a good following in the past and came back on the air at the height of the trivia craze of the mid-Eighties and therefore was bound to succeed. It was all in the timing.

*   *   *

For someone who's worked in television, I don't tend to watch a great deal of it as much of it strikes me as inane nonsense. The comedies don't seem especially funny and the dramas don't seem very realistic but they all too often seem quite interested in pandering to the baser instincts within human nature and in that sense I believe television has seriously declined since the Fifties and Sixties. I do, however, make it a point to watch the news.

Fred Graham, who used to be with CBS, was the best legal reporter in the history of TV news. That didn't prevent CBS from dropping him in 1987. You can get the story from his perspective in his book *Happy Talk*. Graham largely attributes what happened to him to his relationship or lack of one with Dan Rather. That's how it is in television. Personal relationships mean a lot. No one will ever convince me George Vosburgh is a better Jeopardy producer than Alex was but he definitely has a different relationship with Merv and in television that's what counts.

But as we can see from our national divorce statistics, relationships do change and that, in large measure accounts for the instability that characterizes many a career in television. Alex may be a great game show host but he was unemployed for a year before getting the job at Jeopardy. That's television, especially national television out of Hollywood and New York.

Some local stations pride themselves on stability in the area of personnel while others are a veritable revolving door. Even in Hollywood and New York, there are those who can make a lifetime career working for one station or network, though it's much less common than in local markets. That many people in "the industry" can be characterized as *insecure* would be an understatement. It's not difficult to conclude that the tightfisted greed that characterizes so many in the industry may be a direct result of the feelings of insecurity of their earlier years that have never left them.

To succeed in television takes a lot more than being bitten by the show biz bug and becoming star-struck. One must persevere, persevere, persevere. As a writer I'm used to living with rejection. As a salesman I also encountered rejection but the difference was that I was always free to go find another publisher or another sales prospect after someone turned me down. In television the number of prospects is quite limited while the competition for the jobs seems infinite. As a result, your chances of success are always going to depend in large measure on the whims of others. For me that was the hardest aspect of working in television.

Individuals' personalities and priorities are different. I happen to come from the old school and see my role primarily as that of a provider for my family. In order for me to succeed at that I have to be able to *take charge* of my life in such a way that I can set goals and *know* that I am making progress towards achieving them. Life in Hollywood is too dicey. The contestant who hits "bankrupt" on the "Wheel of Fortune" isn't necessarily a poorer player than his opponents; he may, in fact, be better.

I'm not a gambler. Some people try to count cards in a game of blackjack because that way the odds are with them. But it's ridiculous to play seriously if the odds are against you. It's good to take risks but the risks should be calculated ones. Hollywood is always a longshot. While I have no desire to necessarily be in control of the lives of others, I do need to feel I have some control over my own. I found it interesting that the majority of people on staff at Jeopardy were single and I'm convinced that's characteristic of the industry as a whole. When you're single your priorities are different and you may be better equipped mentally to endure the roller coaster ride. This may also help explain why Hollywood marriages are less likely to succeed than those of the general population.

Having thus far provided a discouraging picture for those contemplating a behind-the-scenes career in television, let me now offer some words of encouragement. The TV industry in the United States is currently undergoing a very rapid and highly significant evolution. It wasn't long ago that the big three TV networks, ABC, CBS and NBC, accounted for an 80% or more audience share in most markets. Today their market share is hovering at about 50% and still declining. This has been due primarily to the advent and growth of cable TV.

Cable is still in its infancy and will continue to grow for years to come. Today a typical cable service may offer 30 or 40 channels but some are already experimenting with as many as 150. Some people are even predicting the average cable viewer will eventually have around 300 stations from which to choose.

While the over-the-air networks try to offer a little of everything, most cable channels' formats are much more specialized, much like radio. Cable stations today specialize in country and rock music, news, sports, comedy, nostalgia, children's programming, history, travel, cartoons, even law and the courts. There is a game show channel as well now, and we can look for numerous other formats in the not too distant future. For the networks it used to be that a 20% audience share was mediocre or worse. For a cable channel competing with a hundred or more others, a 2% audience share will be terrific.

With the industry moving in that direction, it is doubtful we will ever again see game shows, or any shows for that matter, as financially profitable as "Wheel of Fortune" and Jeopardy. But what we will see is considerable competition among the increasingly numerous specialty channels, each striving for its place in the ratings sun. For those contemplating a career in television it will mean greater opportunity than ever before.

When there will be 150 or more channels competing for viewer attention, that competition will be intense. For many cable networks getting decent ratings will be a matter of sheer survival. There will therefore be considerable demand for hardworking talented individuals—people who can produce and thrive in such an atmosphere of intense competition. Inasmuch as the ratings of individual cable channels will be much lower than what the networks have been used to, programs on cable may not be able to pay the kind of salaries that shows which drew audiences of 15 or 20 million could afford. But there can be no doubt that under more competitive conditions employers will be more appreciative of those who are, when all is said and done, buttering their bread. And they will do what they can to show it.

Many have accused the networks of fearing creativity and innovation (except when it represents some new low point in pandering to the prurient instincts of the audience). In tomorrow's diverse and competitive market there will be opportunities for producers, writers, directors, technicians and others as never before. New ideas will be eagerly sought, especially if they can be brought to fruition within the more limited budgets on which cable channels must operate. When Ted Turner first proposed an all-news cable channel many thought it could never work. Some mockingly called CNN the Chicken Noodle Network. Today it is profitable and having a significant impact not only in the U.S. but around the world.

The same vision, perspicacity and drive that has made CNN a success will yet be seen in the birth of other cable channels and yet-to-be-tried formats. Just as CNN has raised the quality of television news to a more in-depth and more objective level so other cable channels are and will continue to raise the quality of TV programming to heights heretofore unseen.

Many people who enjoy reading and feel a need to be informed have lamented the demise of many major daily newspapers to the point where a city with more than one daily has become the exception rather than the rule. But, like reading, television, too, is a form of communication and for better or worse more and more people are electing to have much if not most of the communicative stimuli that is reaching them come via the TV screen.

The continued growth and diversification of television is nearly certain. What is not at all certain is whether the growth will be primarily in the direction of *quality* programming. In most countries, even many democracies, television programming is and has always been a function of the government. In those countries government officials and bureaucratic functionaries decide what shows the people can watch.

In America TV programming is a wide-open field, limited only by FCC definitions of good taste versus indecency (which are becoming looser all the time). Ultimately the American people will get the kind of programming they want. Many ask why Hollywood and the TV industry produce so much low-class sleaze. It is a valid question and one that should be asked and considered.

The United States is not a police state. In the early days of the motion picture industry Hollywood was willing to take on the responsibility to police itself as with the Hays code. Back then the industry showed the strength of character to practice self-discipline. But as greed became more important than virtue, producers embarked on a game of leapfrog, one leaping over the next to see whose production could give us more and more of what had previously been avoided. Producers claimed what they were now giving us was "realism." Yet if it were truly realism, we'd all have been either committing rape or being raped, then get shot a few times before finally being killed, all before age 25!

Once Hollywood was ruled by the moguls, the bosses who some say ran the major studios like medieval fiefdoms. Nevertheless there was such a thing as individual responsibility and accountability. When a studio's logo went on a film or TV production, everyone knew just who the boss was and if something wasn't right there was someone to hold accountable.

Today's entertainment industry is run largely by faceless MBAs, lawyers and corporate accountants for whom the bottom line is the one at the bottom of their ledgers. If low-grade shows and movies are going to be profitable, then low-grade shows and movies are going to be produced.

So the ultimate question is not only why does the industry produce low quality entertainment but, and equally important, why does the American public buy it?

Nowadays there is a great deal of talk about "family values." Much of that talk emanates from the mouths of politicians. But the politicians are bringing it up only because they have indications that the American people consider family values important.

Now definitions of family values may vary somewhat but most everyone would agree that love and concern of the individual family members for one another is central. Television in the 1990s features a great deal of sex but much less love. "Putting one over" on somebody, often in a cruel or violent way, is commonly played up while deeds of loving kindness, compassion, altruism and forgiveness are rarely emphasized.

In a physical sense, it's been said we are what we eat. In a mental and spiritual sense it can be said we are what we think. As Americans grow increasingly health conscious, many of us are ever more careful about what we put in our bodies, avoiding too much cholesterol, sodium, caffeine, alcohol, nicotine, etc. If we are truly concerned about family values then it is surely time we became more careful about what we put into our minds and into the minds of our children.

If we should ever reach the point in America where sleaze television and movies cease to be produced not because of government censorship but because *they are no longer profitable*, it will surely be the greatest time yet in this country's history. Americans are free to smoke yet most of us resist the habit because we know it isn't good for us and we live longer as a result. Wouldn't it be great if we could resist the glorification of the violent and the crass and be happier people as a result of that?

To say we're for family values and then freely choose for our entertainment TV and films that portray just the opposite is nothing more than hypocrisy. To the degree that honest, industrious, successful, happy, well-adjusted, God-fearing people are the result of good family life, then we all want that result. But if we want the result and the effect, we must also want and freely choose the *cause*.

We are what we think as well as what we eat. There's no doubt about it. What we watch on TV does affect how and what we think about. It affects us as individuals and ultimately society as a whole. Thus, in choosing what we watch on TV, we in no small measure choose what kind of people we want to be and what kind of society we will ultimately have. That choice is up to each one of us.